<STRONG> IDEAS SERIES

Edited by David Weinberger

The Ideas Series explores the latest ideas about how technology is affecting culture, business, science, and everyday life. Written for general readers by leading technology thinkers and makers, books in this series advance provocative hypotheses about the meaning of new technologies for contemporary society.

The Ideas Series is published with the generous support of the MIT Libraries.

THE DIGITAL CLOSET

HOW THE INTERNET BECAME STRAIGHT

ALEXANDER MONEA
FOREWORD BY VIOLET BLUE

The MIT Press
Cambridge, Massachusetts
London, England

The MIT Press would like to thank the anonymous peer reviewers who provided comments on drafts of this book. The generous work of academic experts is essential for establishing the authority and quality of our publications. We acknowledge with gratitude the contributions of these otherwise uncredited readers.

This book was set in Bembo Book MT Pro by the MIT Press. Printed and bound in the United States of America.

Library of Congress Cataloging-in-Publication Data

Names: Monea, Alexander, author.
Title: The digital closet : how the internet became straight / Alexander
    Monea ; foreword by Violet Blue.
Description: Cambridge, Massachusetts : The MIT Press, [2022] | Series:
    Strong ideas series | Includes bibliographical references and index.
Identifiers: LCCN 2021019772 | ISBN 9780262046770 (hardcover)
Subjects: LCSH: Internet—Social aspects. | Homophobia. | Sexism.
Classification: LCC HM851 .M6593 2022 | DDC 302.23/1—dc23
LC record available at https://lccn.loc.gov/2021019772

10 9 8 7 6 5 4 3 2 1

This book is dedicated to my mother, who made me go to college against my will, and my father, who gave me my work ethic.

CONTENTS

FOREWORD: THE PROFITEERS OF REPRESSION

VIOLET BLUE

In May 2017 *The Guardian* published a leaked copy of Facebook's internal rulebook on content moderation. Called *The Facebook Files,* the exposé revealed Facebook's exceptionalism for harmful content. As long as its users didn't run afoul of a slim set of edge-case rules, the company maintained a mainstream, protected platform for racist speech and hate groups. While Facebook ruthlessly policed what was posted and messaged about sexual content and artistic nudity, anyone characterizing immigrants as rapists or robbers got a free pass (as long as they weren't technically "equating" them with rapists or robbers).

The Facebook Files also shined a bright light on the company's disturbing Holocaust-denial protections. Namely, that the company enshrined in its policies a safe space for communities and Groups perpetuating and promoting deeply harmful Holocaust denial falsehoods. When media outlets came asking questions, Facebook doubled down. The company's go-to response was that it disallowed Holocaust denial content only in countries where it was illegal, like Germany. This policy remains.

Facebook launched Groups in 2010. I often wonder what eleven years of fostering, growing, and protecting Holocaust denial has done to generations of kids around the world who have grown up using the platform.

A millennium ago, back in 2003, I formed an online group for women to discuss pornography on a now-defunct and mostly forgotten footnote of a website called Tribe.net. The premise of that group was that some women liked porn, some did not, others were curious, and some were offended by it: I wanted a place where we could talk about all of these things as explicitly (or not) as we felt. We called it the "Smart Girls' Porn Club" and it was trans-inclusive.

It was a successful and popular group. The discussions would range week to week from "I think [this thing in porn] is gross" and "am I weird for liking [this one thing]" to exploring the topic of degradation, porn, and feminism; swapping tips on how to find videos to watch with a partner; and discussing why (at the time) it seemed that so few women made pornography. The group inspired a book, which landed in O: The Oprah Winfrey Magazine and put me on Oprah's show talking about women, porn, and inclusive female sexuality.

The free and open internet had made this unique situation possible in a way that had never happened before. Porn's distribution had changed from specifically male spaces to the internet, where observing and exploring it was much safer. For the first time, women were able to privately look at porn online without gatekeepers or spies, without judgment or threat, and decide what we were seeing and feeling for ourselves. What's more, we could talk to other women from all over the world about it: my group had women of all colors, genders, orientations, and backgrounds. But the real history-making part of it, in my eyes, was that the discussion group contained sex workers, porn performers, LGBTQIA+ and straight women alike, as well as women who made pornography.

Before that point in time, there had been no way for regular people to find out if popular media narratives in film, TV, and news media about the experiences of sex workers and porn performers was truth or fiction. Now, anyone could ask if what we were told about sex for work or entertainment was true.

Some of us who personally knew sex workers and performers were well aware that the stereotypes were incorrect, harmful, misogynist, anti-queer, and racist. But suddenly anyone could ask performers how they got involved in porn, if a sex act was painful, or how being a married porn star worked, exactly. Or ask sex workers if they were being forced to do it or what it meant for them to "come out" to family or friends. This naturally blossomed into sharing sex education resources and discussions of sexual health and discovery, as well as ofboundaries and informed consent.

As the women in my forum found out, the truths were equally fascinating (as sex often is) and as boring (and filled with practicalities) as any job can be. What we discovered is still true: they were as diverse as society.

I was excited that, for once, people were starting to speak for themselves about sex for pleasure or work in open, explicit, and honest ways. The conversation was no longer the sole provenance of those with agendas focused on control of our bodies—moral policing that restricted the "right" expressions of sexuality as reproductive-only, and then only within the confines of heterosexual marriage. The same morality that excluded and demonized LGBTQIA+ and BIPOC people by sexualizing them.

The internet back then felt like a weird, wonderful, creative, and exciting place for new discoveries, filled with art, provocative writing, and connection.

Before Google's 1998 launch, the internet's most popular website and social hub was Nerve.com (1997). A rival of Salon.com (1995), Nerve was primarily an online magazine with high-quality articles and erotic artists. Nerve's personals were brimming and its forums were a 24-7 hub of activity; it launched one of the first blogging services and quickly became wildly popular. The company had an offline sex book-publishing arm producing terrific books by writers and photographers. For many years, Nerve was the most fun, exciting, sex-positive place to be and hang out online, bursting with creative communities, optimism, and hope that a vital future was being explored.

"For many, Nerve represented a new era in which we could finally, freely talk about sex, gender, orientation, sex culture—and exchange ideas," I wrote for *Engadget* in 2019. "Thanks to Nerve's 'literate smut' tagline and ethos, private acts of creation could make tortured people feel valid and whole. People don't make sites like Nerve anymore. No one can."

The internet back then was not a place where Nazis, incels, Holocaust-deniers, or "alt-right" terror-mongers were emboldened, tolerated, and given a platform to organize attacks as if they were any other Facebook community resource. They were certainly online, but they had not been handed power, mainstream platforms, or credibility. You might ask, so what happened? This book, *The Digital Closet*, holds the answers.

Our adult video discussion group flourished for two years with hundreds of members. Much like Tumblr before its infamous and badly bungled "porn purge," Tribe had become a popular, busy social site where everyone shared interests from archery and politics to erotic art and queer mental health, and beyond.

In 2005 Tribe.net banned sexual content under the banner of protecting children from obscenity. Everything deemed sexual—from LGBTQIA+ communities to discussion groups like mine, and more—was removed or hidden through automation, and lost forever: automation created by the same demographic that would create and test facial-scanning automation on 5,000 people yet result in an AI that can't "see" Black faces; a demographic that would've put a stop to this obvious problem if they had only considered Black faces as things that belong to *people*.

Turns out, things about "porn" are also things that are about censorship, sexual and mental health, business trends, discovering and setting boundaries, sex work, politics, gender, online attacks, art, news and history, LGBTQIA+ people, and women. Things that center our humanity.

In well-documented public arguments I repeatedly explained to Tribe. net's representatives that in a court case for obscenity, the accused is held to whatever the local community's standards are for obscenity, as determined by a jury. Pardon me for generalizing, but it was not lost on anyone that the people setting and enforcing Tribe's policy were all people representing a demographic of conservative Caucasian men, and not a community of its users' peers.

I attempted a women's porn discussion group again in 2008 on Facebook. We named it "Our Porn, Ourselves" in a reference to *Our Bodies, Ourselves*, a revolutionary, self-empowering book that provided clear, accurate, explicit, and nonjudgmental information about female sexual health. A book that had changed all our lives (and certainly even saved a few) with its explicit illustrated diagrams and frank talk about sexual pleasure and its crucial role in sexual health. Once again, women of all orientations and identities from around the world joined our gender-inclusive erotic video discussion group.

Anti-porn groups on Facebook openly organized to get our group removed. Facebook, already cultivating a safe haven for hate speech, readily complied. It was clear to all, including reporters who covered the group's targeting and removal, that *some* kind of sexual speech was allowed on Facebook—but only the "right" kind.

As a reporter with bylines in *Financial Times*, CNN, *Forbes*, CBS News, *Engadget*, O magazine, and many other outlets, I documented the exact repeat of this anti-sex, anti-woman, and anti-gay discrimination online over the course of fifteen years. Anti-sex censorship continued to silence and disappear communities sexualized by right-wing conservatives, often to disastrous, and sometimes deadly, effects that were sadly not difficult to document, both from myself, and others, with journalistic rigor. You will find that work extensively referenced throughout *The Digital Closet*.

The result is that women, LGBTQIA+ people, and sexualized BIPOC demographics exist online in a culture of fear. Not just from online trolls, but also from right-wing conservative groups and digital platforms who mutually benefit from assumed power that facilitates controlling, silencing, and oppressing at-risk populations via sexual repression.

Anyone falling outside evangelical fictions about sexuality—or runs the risk of being perceived as sexualized—has learned to live in a digital twilight of fear. We would come out of the closet to find community on one platform, we would try to use online business tools for payment processing that should be legally available to us, or we'd emerge from isolation seeking pleasure-focused (nonreproductive) sex information, and we would be forced off platforms and back into closets. Repeatedly.

As you'll read in *The Digital Closet*, the levers rendering us invisible and silent once again sexualized and infantilized us, put us on secret lists, and banned us (sometimes by name). Healthy adult content became systematically banned on platforms that has allowed far-right extremist content to remain and flourish. This is no coincidence, as the values of anti-sex misogyny and far-right extremism are not just in line with each other: they are one and the same.

If you think the above statements are an exaggeration, read this book. It contains all the documentation you will ever require for proof.

Obscenity is determined by community standards. So when Tribe erased "obscenity" in 2005, Google's 2013 AdWords sex purge removed breast cancer topics, Facebook banned sex workers and "sexual slang" in 2018, and eBay purged all content perceived to be sexual or LGBTQIA+ while carving out exemptions for *Playboy* and *Penthouse* in May 2021—it is all under the banner of removing obscenity to "keep our community safe" (as Facebook states in its policies), which begged one question to be answered: *Whose* community, exactly?

The Digital Closet unpacks and answers the question of "whose community" is being kept safe when so-called community-safety policies regarding human sexuality are imposed onto online communities.

There is a moral gravity here. Our experience of the internet, and therefore our ability to work, play, grow, heal, and love, has been warped by structures of power only accountable to themselves. *The Digital Closet* documents in painstaking detail the hideous agenda behind anti-sex censorship online. This agenda conflates adult women with children, sex work with rape, and LGBTQIA+ and BIPOC people with sex objects. In these pages we see that the people behind both algorithms and FOSTA don't care about the consent and safety of women or LGBTQIA+ and BIPOC people. What we learn proves that the intent of sex censorship is to subvert the consent and safety of the very people they police and to place them in harm's way.

The agenda of online sex censorship becomes particularly sadistic when applied to sex workers, adult performers, and queer youth. How can the arbiters of sexual speech care about their own slogans of "saving women" or "protecting children" when they so brazenly silence, ignore, and eliminate access to public spaces for the very people they claim to save? How are people handed unquestioned authority about a subject when they so obviously refuse to engage with the people they claim to be "saving"?

These arbiters have been handed exactly that: unquestioned authority. In *The Digital Closet* we see that this authority, and the standards of censoring sensible sex-positive discussions about situations from basic to explicit, is built on an unaccountable, performative assumption of power.

This assumption of getting away with anything because of assumed authority surely registers with everyone after a lifetime of police violence on Black citizens. The authority is handed to conservative techies, evangelicals cosplaying as protectors of children and saviors of adult women, peddlers of pseudoscientific "cures" for "sex addiction" and masturbation, and policers of LGBTQIA+ and BIPOC sexuality. With this authority, a bloodthirsty mob is able to drive LGBTQIA+ people back into the closet and sex workers back onto dangerous corners. It illuminates the logic behind anti-abortion laws that terrorize and traumatize women who miscarry; behind the literal whitewashing of trans- and kink-inclusive queer history about Stonewall and the AIDS crisis; behind Pennsylvania Republicans' refusal to repeal a state law that makes books, pictures, and videos about gay topics a crime *in May 2021*.

As *The Digital Closet* makes painfully clear, the motives of sexual censorship and denial of basic services based on sexual discrimination should no longer be above suspicion. In fact, it should have never been above suspicion. Especially now that the full horror of the app and platform sector's surveillance state unravels before our eyes.

It's here in these pages that we dig deeper in stats and data to make the connections between anti-sex conservatives and their extremist alt-right brothers. *The Digital Closet* calls on us to understand how the silencing of sexual speech online is foundational in weaponizing and furthering the agenda of far-right extremism and its handmaidens: systemic racism, systemic misogyny, and the erasure of queer culture.

This book is also a stark reminder that the internet was made for communication.

It's hard to imagine what it would have been like to survive the pandemic's first year without our ability to stay connected to each other via the internet. Remotely staying in school and maintaining jobs, or finding new work when laid off. Enjoying an overwhelming sense of shared experience from a COVID-19 meme, or amplifying links for those in crisis. Yearning to create a better tomorrow and expanding ourselves through online research about the environment, social justice, and vaccine equity. Via video we reassured frightened family members, helped loved ones through hardships, found bright spots with friends in a dark and isolating time, and sometimes bore the unbearable: saying goodbye for the last time via iPad.

Yet for all its connectiveness the internet has fractured us. Put more accurately, the internet's stewards have nearly shattered us. For all its fiefdoms offering community and the equalizing opportunities of open communication, the platforms most everyone regards as "the internet" are steered and architected by those who have utterly failed to understand that communication is centered not on bytes and bits, nor on blind profit, but on humanity.

All of humanity. Not just the parts of it most profitable to advertisers, appeasing to misogynistic evangelicals, or palatable to far-right, conservative tech executives.

—San Francisco, June 2021

I don't know why. They "trust me. . . ." Dumb fucks.
—Mark Zuckerberg, Facebook CEO[1]

We do not use social media and other internet platforms because we "trust" them, or at least nobody in my social circle seems to be such a "dumb fuck" in the words of Facebook founder and CEO Mark Zuckerberg. We use such platforms *despite* a lack of trust because they are no longer opt-in systems. The structure of the contemporary economy and governance increasingly demands digital participation.[2] We are generally aware that the cost of this participation is our privacy. We submit to ceding our privacy upon realization that participation is not optional and escaping the scope of digital surveillance is near impossible, even if participation were truly optional.[3] But what if the costs are greater than a total loss of privacy? It is hard to imagine that the asking price for access to internet platforms could be higher, but it is. I will be making the case throughout this book that the cost of admission also includes the continued marginalization of LGBTQIA+ communities and the amplification of misogyny and heteronormativity as they become automatically reproduced across the internet. This has both symbolic and material impacts on society. Decades of scholarship have demonstrated that representation in the media matters, that public visibility helps determine our collective assessment of who matters, which issues are important, and what our obligations are as a society.[4] It also has material impacts on members of the LGBTQIA+ community, like lack of access to health information, online community, online revenue streams, and the precarity of having to seek out things like dates, community, and customers offline.

The rhetoric of Silicon Valley is filled with imagined inevitabilities.[5] This is perhaps nowhere truer than in the rise of online content moderation.

Billions upon billions of pieces of content are being uploaded to internet platforms every year. How could any individual, human or corporate, ever hope to keep up? Human nature can be brutish, hypersexualized, and vile. How can we hope to stem the deluge of offensive content reflective of these "facts"? In typical TED Talk fashion, we are asked to believe that there is only one solution, but the silver lining is it's a panacea: automated content moderation. By leveraging advanced machine learning and artificial intelligence (AI) techniques, the web can learn to police itself (and algorithmically organized humans can pick up any slack). In so doing, machines will be able to parse what we'll term *sexual speech*, a broad term meant to encapsulate all potentially "adult" content from discourse about sex, to sex education, to pornography, and other online sex work. However, a machine learning algorithm is only as good as its input data and training parameters. Unfortunately, when it comes to moderating sexual speech, the data is hopelessly flawed, and the parameters designed by Silicon Valley coders are not much better. They all contain heteronormative biases so severe it would be comical if it were not so damned tragic.

Our collective social discourse in the United States, particularly that which occurs online, contains rampant anti-LGBTQIA+ biases. Contrary to many popular narratives, these biases have increased in recent years. The Gay and Lesbian Alliance Against Defamation's annual Accelerating Acceptance report conducted by the Harris Poll reports radical declines in LGBTQIA+ acceptance in the United States since 2016. The percentage of non-LGBTQIA+ 18- to 34-year-olds classified as allies—those who report being "very" or "somewhat" comfortable with LGBTQIA+ individuals in all situations— dropped precipitously in the Trump era. Whereas 63 percent of the US population were classified as allies in 2016, that number dropped to 45 percent by 2018, and the total of male allies dropped from 62 percent to only 35 percent.[6] Many of the most powerful internet platforms are based in the United States and are deeply impacted by these biases. The prejudices of a particularly vocal subsection of the population infect the training data, code, and coders behind automated content moderation to deleterious effect. The resulting algorithms end up over scrutinizing, policing, and suppressing LGBTQIA+ discourse, including community forums, resources, outreach initiatives, activism, sex education, women's bodies, sex workers, and pornography. People targeted for algorithmic censorship have little recourse. While large, vertically integrated corporations like mainstream heteroporn production companies—the types of San Fernando Valley companies that produce aggressively hetero-sexual, frequently misogynistic, and now almost exclusively gonzo or point of view (POV) porn—may escape censorship, but niche content producers of sexual speech ranging from LGBTQIA+ advocacy to feminist and queer pornography are rarely so lucky.

The result of this new regime of automated content moderation is what I call the *digital closet*. This term is meant to signify the ways in which LGBTQIA+ individuals may be allowed to enter the digital public sphere but only so long as they bracket and obscure their sexual identities. Their very being is so pornographied by automated content filters that they are largely barred from sexual expression online. To participate in our digital world, as is increasingly necessary today, requires a silence that is alienating and damaging. Any exit from the digital closet will be met with swift punish-ment. LGBTQIA+ people will find their content flagged and censored, their account banned or de-prioritized and thus rendered invisible, will lose any streams of online revenue, and will find this system weaponized against them by alt-right[7] trolls looking to trigger all the aforementioned punishments. To add insult to injury, all of this will occur while tube sites like Pornhub operate walled gardens of heteronormative sexual expression, unhindered by the new platform economy. It seems as if a treaty has been made between the people in a moral panic over the proliferation of pornography and the internet platforms at the expense of the LGBTQIA+ community. *Porn* will be given a corner of the internet where it will flourish, as long as it's not *that* kind of porn.

PANDORA'S BOX OF PORN

[T]he arc of internet sex censorship is long, and it bends as far away from justice (and reason) as possible. Corporations controlling the internet had been steadily (and sneakily, hypocritically) moving in this direction all along, at great expense to women, LGBT people, artists, educators, writers, and marginalized communities—and to the delight of bigots and conservatives everywhere.[8]

A common narrative over the past two decades has been that the internet opened a Pandora's box of porn. The argument goes something like this: the proliferation of internet connectivity and digital video cameras has created a situation in which not only are conservatives lacking sufficient manpower, financial resources, and political capital to combat pornography but also the very possibility of doing so has become technologically infeasible. Practicality demands that conservatives abandon their embattlements, allow pornography to sweep the nation, and focus on other, more achievable goals. Donna Rice Hughes, president and CEO of Enough Is Enough, a leading anti-pornography nonprofit organization, has said, "When you have a nonprofit like mine, donors want to see progress. And to be honest, we haven't seen any."[9] Tony Perkins, president of the Family Research Council, has said, "I mean, even before the internet, the government didn't do a good job of policing [porn]. So how do you get the genie back in the bottle?"[10] The religious right, in particular, is seen to have backslid on the issue of pornography. Jerry Falwell Sr. helped crystallize the Moral Majority by crusading against pornographers, stirred to action by an interview President Jimmy Carter gave in *Playboy* magazine. His son, Jerry Falwell Jr., called former President Donald Trump "God's man," despite his extramarital affairs with a Playmate and a hard-core adult film actress, and in one photo with Trump, Falwell Jr. can be seen posing with Trump in front of a framed issue of *Playboy* with Trump on the cover.[11]

For some liberals, libertarians, and leftists—an odd coalition that tends to align about as frequently as the planets, often in relation to free speech issues—this deluge of pornography represents not only a battle won but also the introduction of a digital pornotopia. This latter perspective is best exemplified by an internet meme called *Rule 34*, which states, "If it exists, there is porn of it." While the origins of this meme are difficult to track, most attribute its initial popularity to a 2005 web comic by Peter Morley-Souter that was drawn after he stumbled upon *Calvin and Hobbes* erotica online.[12] It has since been popularized on 4chan message boards and Reddit threads, specifically showcasing literotica, fan fiction, slash fiction, and hentai, all low-cost and easily anonymized media for the grassroots production of any and all imaginable pornography. The fulfillment of Rule 34 is made certain by *Rule 35*, which goes, "If no porn is found at the moment, it will be made." The sum of these two rules doesn't just equal the signifier for a sex position, it also creates a self-fulfilling libertine prophecy of an internet that can satisfy any erotic desire, no matter how niche or deviant.

It is easy to see how both sides of the aisle have arrived at this conclusion about the inevitability of pornography's ubiquity. While industry numbers are hard to come by or accurately assess due to the large number of privately owned porn companies, a 2015 estimate valued the global porn industry at $97 billion, with $10–$12 billion of that coming from the United States alone.[13] Porhhub, the largest online porn disseminator releases detailed annual statistics on its users that best exemplify the seeming ubiquity of pornography. In 2018, Pornhub had 33.5 billion visits and is currently averaging more than 100 million visits per day. It served up 30.3 billion searches (about a thousand per second) and transferred 4,403 petabytes of data (about 147 gigabytes per second). Every minute over 200,000 videos were viewed, fifty-five of which were Kim Kardashian's sex tape, the most popular Pornhub video of all time. The site had 4.79 million new videos totaling over a million hours of new content uploaded in 2018 alone, an average of twelve videos and two hours of content uploaded per minute. More people voted on their favorite videos in 2018 than voted in the 2016 US presidential election.[14] For reference, Pornhub, which is just one of a number of porn tubes owned and operated by MindGeek, alone ranks as the twenty-eighth most popular internet site globally. For comparison, Netflix holds the twenty-fifth spot.[15]

While it is important to acknowledge the unprecedented scale of pornography's dissemination on the internet, it is also important to keep in mind that these changes in scale are endemic to digital media and communications technologies, particularly internet-based platforms. For the first time in history, we can literally saturate every waking moment of our lives with media content, and we increasingly choose to do so.[16] As we'll see throughout this book, isolating the explosion of pornographic content from its technological milieu can lead to mistaken conclusions not only about what porn people are consuming but also, more importantly, *why* they are consuming it. It also provides a more acceptable outlet for unchecked dystopian technophobia by bracketing its application to a historically stigmatized domain. In doing so, conservative ideology can more easily frame our cultural discourse on sexuality by situating the proliferation of pornography as a unique and distinct crisis that needs to be combated via ideological warfare (i.e., "the war on porn"). These sorts of tactics recur across the historical record of cultural contestations over sexual speech. They often lead to détentes where conservatives reconcile themselves to the existence of pornography, provided it doesn't deviate too far from an imagined majority's sexual mores. It will be my argument that allowing these discourses to proceed unchecked most often leads to the reification of heteronormativity.

Highlighting the technological infrastructures within which these changes to the production and consumption of pornography occur affords us two key insights. First, the political economy of contemporary pornography is deeply entangled with the political economy of the internet writ large. Pornography is operating under the same platform paradigms as other sectors of the digital economy, leading to similar problems with homogenized content in filter bubbles or echo chambers, and it is subject to similar critiques in terms of labor practices (extraction of free labor, vampirism of the tube economy, and so on), environmentalism (carbon emissions from data-intensive video storage and streaming, and so on), and penetration of everyday life (gamification of user interfaces, personalization, and so on). Just like other sectors of the digital economy, porn is subject to an attention economy amid what Mark Andrejevic has called *infoglut*—the glut of information online.[17] Just because porn *exists* does not mean it is *seen*, and the capacity to locate and access pornography beyond the first page or two of results on anything from Google to Pornhub requires a specific kind of literacy that we might call a *pornoliteracy*. While it may be true that queer and niche pornography is readily available to those who know how to find it, we cannot take for granted either that (1) this means there is not a broad movement toward heteronormativity online that brackets and sequesters LGBTQIA+ sexual speech or (2) that everyone, especially young people, have the requisite pornoliteracy to know how to find it. The problems of contemporary pornography only become clear within this larger context of the attention economy, infloglut, and echo chambers online.

Second, a focus on the connection between pornography and its technological infrastructures allows us to identify a history to this conjuncture that is too often dehistoricized in popular discourse. This dehistoricization is doubly motivated. First, it is part of the crisis logic that is wielded rhetorically to garner clicks in the contemporary attention economy. Second, it allows conservatives to engage in scare tactics under the cover of this crisis logic. The "crisis" of pornography is nothing new and, in fact, repeats each time a new media or communication technology debuts in public. History is littered with episodic crises where pornography proliferates via new media and communications technologies, triggering conservative attempts to contain it.

Many histories of pornography examine its intersection with the printing press and printmaking techniques, such as lithography. Take, for example, the story of Marcantonio Raimondi, a printmaker and engraver employed by Raphael at the center of libertine culture in Renaissance Rome, who published a volume of male-female pornographic art titled *I Modi* by Giulio Romano, Rafael's most talented assistant and the only Italian artist mentioned by Shakespeare. Pope Clement VII imprisoned Raimondi—Romano fled before being captured—yet was unable to stop the spread of copies across all of Europe.[18] A similarly famous instance occurred two centuries later when John Cleland published *Fanny Hill* in 1748. Despite Cleland's decision to cease publication of the erotic novel after his imprisonment on corruption charges, the book was pirated and replicated widely across the Western Hemisphere.[19]

Pornography is always closely tied to media and communication technologies, and we can find similar crises emerging with the introduction of the daguerreotype, resin glue, and cheaper printing techniques (e.g., pulp fiction literotica, and romance novels); Polaroid cameras; VCRs; camcorders; cable TV; premium telephone services; Minitel; computers; and the internet.[20] The previous war on pornography was centered on the introduction of VCRs, camcorders, and cable TV, which collectively lowered production costs and, more importantly, allowed audiovisual pornography to be disseminated directly into the home. Conservatives would cling to this latter change in particular and introduce the trope of children's unwanted exposure to pornography as their last charge in that war on pornography. In the standard narratives, their political will gave out in the wake of a series of defeated regulations at the hands of the Supreme Court and the radical alterations to the political economy of pornography introduced by the internet. As we will see, the idea that the anti-pornography movement ever gave up or ceased making progress is false and more likely due to a lack of attention to the issue in mainstream media between the September 11 terrorist attacks and the 2008 recession.

Usually, these episodic crises end when pornographers become horizontally and vertically integrated enough to form large industrial corporations that can leverage a near-monopoly market share to systematically avoid regulation or shape it to their advantage. Heteronormative pornographers are usually best positioned to survive these clashes with censors. Affluent white heterosexual men are predominantly the ones positioned to be able to take on the expense and risk of adopting new technologies early on.[21] As such, heteronormative porn often comes first because it appeals to the broadest market of early adopters. Its creators amass capital early on and position themselves at the center of the political economy. It is only in the middle of these cycles when media technologies are accessible and affordable but not yet overly regulated that more niche pornography can flourish. Wars on porn often crush niche pornography first due to its lack of access to capital. These first victories often exhaust the political capital of anti-porn crusaders and appease at least conservatives by achieving a heteronormalization of pornography.

In short, the Pandora's box narrative of pornography is overly reductive. It is a mask used by conservatives to stress the uniqueness and distinctiveness of a new coupling of pornography and technology such that it can be articulated as a crisis, all in aid of mobilizing political capital. It also hides the way in which political economies of pornography eventually stabilize, favoring large industrial corporations that frequently homogenize content in a heteronormative fashion to appeal to the wealthy white early adopters with disposable income to spend on pornography. If we want to get a clearer picture of just what is going on, we need to examine the cultural contexts, technological infrastructures, and political economies within which successive pornographies emerge. It is only by doing so that we can historicize both the dystopic crisis narrative and utopic pornotopia narrative that dominate our thinking about pornography.

Further, as I will show throughout the book, the porn industry's deepest, darkest secret isn't that porn is exploitative, socially corrosive, or a catalyst for misogynistic violence—though these can all be true. It's that porn is *boring*. In fact, the entire logic of the industry is built around combating this fact. The industry's worst nightmare is that we might all come to this realization when cycling through the thousand or more professional gonzo POV anal videos and amateur incest role-play videos uploaded to porn tube sites every day. Porn is boring because it's caught in a heteronormative filter bubble. The entire infrastructure is articulated such that porn producers must navigate between the Scylla of boring porn that reifies the same heteronormative tropes such that it can be tagged with the appropriate keywords and rendered locatable via index and recommendation algorithm and the Charybdis of abnormal porn whose very innovation renders it invisible within this heteronormative filter bubble.

COLLATERAL DAMAGE IN THE WAR ON PORN

There is a much larger problem that the war on porn introduces than its heteronormalization of pornography, and lest the reader think that they've gotten themselves into an entire book on hard-core pornography, they can rest assured that the bulk of the book, in fact, is focused on this spillover effect where any and all sexual speech gets overly censored. Every war on porn produces this collateral damage, by which I mean that regulation is more often than not applied overbroadly and ends up censoring large amounts of nonpornographic content, particularly sex education materials, LGBTQIA+ activism, and LGBTQIA+ community-building discourse. This overbroad censorship is especially prevalent once the rhetoric of children's unwanted exposure is used to drum up support for anti-porn regulation. Once this rhetorical trope is leveraged, it easily becomes possible for people to perceive the unwanted censorship of some nonpornographic material as immensely preferable to even a single piece of pornography slipping through and being seen by children.

In the Comstock era at the turn of the twentieth century, for instance, this overbroad application of obscenity regulations led to the censorship of art, literature, and sex education materials, such as those circulated by suffragettes like Elizabeth Cady Stanton, which provided information about reproductive health and birth control methods. In the middle of the twentieth century, the Supreme Court's efforts to channel "community standards" in regulating obscenity led to their censorship of LGBTQIA+ magazines, despite letting *Playboy* build a global pornographic empire. This same problem recurs today, except it is occurring at web scale, and the regulations are being produced secretly by internet platforms and adjudicated by opaque algorithms and inaccessible offshore temporary content moderation laborers who often render their decisions in a matter of seconds. Every post, picture, and link on the internet is now subject to this invisible censorship mechanism.

While this book will be primarily focused on the impacts that the overzealous censorship of sexual speech online has on LGBTQIA+ communities, decades of feminist scholarship tells us that heteronormativity's deep connections with patriarchy and misogyny mean that it is a detriment to straight people as well and one that is borne inordinately by women of color.[22] This line of argument is taken up most forcefully by Jane Ward in her recent book *The Tragedy of Heterosexuality*, where she argues that heterosexuality is "erotically uninspired or coercive, given shape by the most predictable and punishing gender roles, emotionally scripted by decades of inane media and self-help projects, and outright illogical as a set of intimate relations anchored in a complaint-ridden swirl of desire and misogyny."[23] Ward argues that feminism and queer theory ought to look outward and examine more closely the tragedy of heterosexuality, evidenced by a long history of what she terms the "heterosexual repair industry." The contradictions and tensions in heterosexuality, which will be further examined below, have produced over a hundred years of industries—including eugenics, psychiatry, sexology, porno magazines, homosocial spaces (from fraternal clubs to video game squads), self-help books and seminars, hygiene products (soaping, douching, bleaching), the beauty industry, the fitness industry, seduction and relationship coaches, and so on—meant to "fix" straight people and deliver the promises of heterosexual, monogamous, marital bliss. In Ward's eyes, heterosexuals suffer from boredom, complaint, lack of imagination, the straight gaze and objectification, bad sex, and an obsession with genitals, all of which might be alleviated by queering straightness and introducing feminism to dissipate the rampant misogyny.[24]

In short, *everyone* suffers from the heteronormativity of the internet, a point that I will try to gesture toward throughout the book without losing the more precise focus on LGBTQIA+ communities. I think that this focus on a well-recognized category of marginalized identity that is already connected to broader activist networks is strategically useful, as it stands a better chance of leading to the mobilization of resistance against the internet's heteronormativity. Further, the legal recognition of sexuality (e.g., Title IX) as a protected identity class makes this a tactically strong point from which to attack content moderation online. Lastly, the case studies in the book most clearly highlight a trend toward anti-LGBTQIA+ prejudice in the operations of algorithms and content moderation online, despite the wider implications this has for cisgender heterosexual audiences.

All of these considerations are essential because there has been no large-scale study to this point on the impact of heteronormative content moderation online. Only a few pioneering journalists have kept any sort of record of the myriad people and pieces of their nonpornographic content that have been censored. I will rely on them heavily throughout the book to demonstrate that pornography is not all that is at stake here. The internet itself is being policed by overbroad, heteronormative algorithms that are routinely censoring art, literature, and LGBTQIA+ content across the world. Most of the book will be dedicated to making this process more transparent, showing how everything from internet discourse writ large, to the coders at internet platforms, to the code itself, to the offshore content moderators have, intentionally or not, become party to globalizing this uniquely American, white, middle-class form of heteronormativity.

The first chapter will look at the current landscape of political activists focusing on censoring pornography, including, perhaps unexpectedly, the alt-right. I show how evangelical conservatives, anti-porn feminists, and the alt-right have become unlikely bedfellows in the war on pornography and demonstrate how their arguments against pornography are extremely heteronormative—and often misogynistic. This chapter's focus on the alt-right has the added benefit of contextualizing some of the discourse going on among the largely male, frequently libertarian-leaning coders responsible for producing the algorithms that police the internet.

The second chapter looks at the coders, code, and moderators that make web-scale censorship possible and demonstrates how each level of the apparatus, from coders to code to reviewers, works to reify heteronormativity. I analyze research into the culture and political leanings of the average Silicon Valley coder and contextualize it through a close reading of James Damore's infamous Google memo. I examine the image recognition algorithms that are used to automate content filters at web scale and demonstrate how heteronormativity is literally embedded at the foundation of their code, in their very data structures. And finally, I examine the work of offshore content moderators who are given heteronormative guidebooks, taught to deprioritize assessments of obscenity and focus instead on political speech, and given only a matter of seconds to decide whether content violates community standards surrounding sexual speech.

The third chapter focuses on the collateral damage from the ongoing war on porn. I look in detail at the censorship of LGBTQIA+ community resources, sex education materials, art, literature, and other forms of speech that flirt with the sexual or erotic but would rarely be categorized as pornography by today's standards in the United States. This chapter also examines the passage of the Stop Enabling Sex Traffickers Act (FOSTA-SESTA) by the US Congress in 2017, a purposefully overbroad regulation of internet communications that has radically accelerated censorship efforts and has already had detrimental impacts for the LGBTQIA+ community.

The fourth chapter returns to the opening issue of pornography and examines its current political economy within the context of internet infrastructures. I show how the architecture of the web produces two different avenues for the heteronormalization of pornography: first, I show how Google SafeSearch structures web traffic even when it is turned off, channeling traffic to mainstream heteroporn and offering unique opportunities to large-scale pornographers to capture the majority of web traffic through confined search terms that are easy to optimize for; second, I show how the structure of porn platforms, such as tube sites (e.g., Pornhub, xHamster), reinforce heteronormativity through their data structures, particularly the keywords by which the site can be navigated, which tend to structure even amateur content uploaded to the site. The end result is that Pandora's box of porn ends up being more of a Sisyphean eternal return of the same boring old heteroporn.

Before moving on, however, it is worth getting clear about what exactly I mean by the word *heteronormativity* and the limitations of the book for fully addressing the ways that sexuality intersects with other logics of marginalization like race, class, ability, and nationality. Readers who feel like they have a strong handle on heteronormativity are welcome to jump right to the first chapter, but I think the term warrants deeper consideration. As I'll show, it is a nebulous concept, intentionally ambiguous, shot through with contradictions, and one that masquerades as a (scientifically legitimated) universal set of norms and morals despite actually being historically contextual. To pin it down, one has to analyze its essential links to a diverse set of concepts, including queerness, LGBTQIA+ sex acts, the closet, gender roles, reproductive sex, and the family, to name a few. The form of heteronormativity that is getting embedded into the very infrastructure of the internet is one that was developed by predominantly white, middle-class, ostensibly heterosexual Americans over the past 150 years or so. As such, the analysis that follows focuses specifically on the American iteration of heteronormativity.

WHAT EVEN IS HETERONORMATIVITY?

Heteronormativity has never been a stable construct in the United States. In fact, we might productively understand it as a purposefully vague concept that uses its constantly shifting meanings to avoid ever being pinned down and rendered falsifiable. One of the most important components of heteronormativity is, thus, its capacity to engage in code switching. What I mean by this is that heteronormativity as a concept contains a number of ambiguities, sometimes even contradictions, that provide it with the flexibility to evade analysis and critique, particularly in nonspecialized public discourse like popular arguments, be they at the dinner table or in the comments section of an article posted online.

Take, for example, what I would argue is the foundational ambiguity of heteronormativity: Is sexuality the result of a procreative instinct or a libidinous drive toward pleasure? As Jonathan Kay has demonstrated at length in his book *The Invention of Heterosexuality*, the term *heterosexuality* has a history, and its emergence was tethered to navigating this particular ambiguity.[25] Prior to the 1890s, in the United States, sex was most frequently understood as an instinct to reproduce the species. The sexual ethic was primarily based on procreation. Masturbation, sodomy, and bestiality were banned not so much because they were less natural sexual desires but because they were nonprocreative. In fact, no sexual desire was considered pure or normal, as procreation was a religious and civic obligation for the colonists, not an outlet for seeking pleasure. As Katz writes, "In these colonies, erotic desire for members of a same sex was not constructed as deviant because erotic desire for a different sex was not construed as a norm. Even within marriage, no other-sex erotic object was completely legitimate, in and of itself."[26] Onanism, the spilling of seed outside of a fertile womb, was always-already deviant and had few gradations. Legal retributions, up to and including execution, were possible for sodomy, bestiality, and masturbation.[27] Thus, in this articulation, sexual desire is always a sin, an urge that needs to be controlled even within the confines of marriage and directed solely toward procreation.

At the turn of the twentieth century, this sexual ethic began to metamorphose as psychologists began analyzing human sexuality in greater detail. These psychologists began to understand sexuality as an innate—and thus *natural*—drive that was oriented as much or more toward achieving pleasure as toward procreation. The earliest known use of the term "heterosexual" was actually in reference to this form of sexual deviance—desiring male-female sex for its own sake. As psychologists continued to examine it, its connection to the procreative function came to be silent, left implicit to the concept, and the previously deviant impetus toward different-sex erotic pleasure came to be emphasized and thus normalized. In a Faustian bargain, sexuality was liberated from its mooring to procreation but in exchange was tethered instead to a biologically essentialist drive toward male-female couplings.[28]

In tandem with this development of a biologically essentialized libido, the Victorians were exploring romantic love as a similar mechanism for reconceptualizing sexuality. While publicly reticent to speak on sexual matters, the Victorians privately explored different-sex erotics and their connections to romantic love.[29] This was echoed in America, where, as John D'Emilio and Estelle B. Freedman have shown, "Throughout much of the nineteenth century, the meaning of sexuality for white middle-class Americans balanced uncomfortably between reproductive moorings of the past and the romantic and erotic leanings of the present, between female control and male license, between private passion and public reticence."[30] This too became part of the Faustian bargain, as romantic love became an increasingly acceptable legitimator for different-sex erotic desire, provided its ultimate goal was monogamous marriage. We can see how deeply this prong of heteronormativity remains in contemporary ideas of polyamory, which is gaining increasing social acceptability by couching its ideas about nonmonogamous relationships within the language of romantic love, in contrast to "hookup culture." While I certainly do not mean to condescend to people working at a social frontier and experimenting with new social scripts for erotic and amorous relationships, I do think there is something telling about the focus on the latter term and the role that it plays in legitimating the movement.

Lastly, it is worth noting that this new version of heterosexuality that ambulated between procreative, libidinal/erotic, and amorous legitimations contained deep class antagonisms from its inception. It only emerged once the bourgeoisie felt secure in its social standing and sure that its new heterosexual discourse had the capacity to strongly distinguish itself from "the eroticism of the rich" and "the sensuality of the poor, the colored, and the foreign."[31] By internalizing the control of sexual desire within the confines of medical and psychological acceptability—in short, by maintaining heterosexual desire in private sex acts tending toward monogamous marriage—the middle class assured itself of its moral superiority, and it leveraged this superiority to establish external controls over the sexual practices of the working class and racialized others. It also established a safety valve for sexual desire, as libidinous middle-class men were frequently permitted transgressions with working-class and/or racialized women, another contradictory gender-based double standard that shoots through heteronormativity as a concept.[32] As Katz writes, "The invention of heterosexuality publicly named, scientifically normalized, and ethically justified the middle-class practice of different-sex pleasure."[33] And it is worth keeping in mind that this justified pursuit of pleasure was in practice often limited to the middle class, even in the more permissive free love periods of the mid-twentieth century, as it required a socialization and style of living restricted to those with privilege. White working-class communities maintained more pronounced gender roles and earlier childbearing, and Black communities often maintained close kinship networks and faced economic instability. These factors limited the freedom for sexual experimentation that was enjoyed by the white middle class. Heteronormativity thus constitutes the attempt to universalize a white, middle-class sexual morality and is subsequently always permeated by class and racial tensions.

The largest category of difference that heteronormativity inflects is gender. It does so first through its deep entanglement with cisnormativity. Here anatomical sex is conflated with gender, and this slippage is leveraged to provide biological essentialism to gender roles. This is a tactic that the alt-right uses repeatedly, as we'll see in chapter 1, and one that gets embedded in platform algorithms and internet architecture, as we'll see in chapter 2. In fact, this cisnormative entanglement is so strong in many of the materials that I examine in the book that I repeatedly found it slipping into my own writing. Using the appropriate language while also accurately representing and analyzing cisnormative rhetoric, data categories, and company policies was a challenge I'm afraid I've inevitably failed at despite my best efforts and will rely on others to help correct. As we'll see in these cases, cisnormativity is often a bastion for heteronormativity. As Kristen Schilt and Laurel Westbrook have demonstrated, "doing gender in a way that does not reflect biological sex can be perceived as a threat to heterosexuality."[34]

Second, heteronormativity's obsession with gender at times makes it difficult to differentiate between gender and sexuality. This is because heteronormativity is definitionally tethered to the nuclear family and the gender roles it dictates. The family is a powerful and persistent force in American life because it is not simply a structure imposed from above or ideologically inculcated in an unwilling or unwitting population. Investing in the concept of marriage is a highly rational choice for the majority of the population because of the massive material and ideological privileges it grants to its adherents, ranging from fiscal benefits (e.g., cohabitation or tax incentives), to promises of emotional security and care later in life, to the offer of a privileged site for rearing children. The family also offers a sense of "naturalness," including a set of social scripts that work as formulas for—and almost algorithms for automating—complex social interactions, such as dating, socializing, and procreating. The family is thus difficult to critique because it offers, though often fails to deliver, widely held social ideals like intimacy, commitment, nurturance, and collectivity.[35]

That said, it is a myth that marriage is a naturally occurring dynamic in society. First and foremost, like heterosexuality, the family is not a singular concept but instead varies widely in its definition and form across space and time. As Michael Anderson notes,

> The one unambiguous fact which has emerged in the last twenty years is that there can be no simple history of *the* Western family since the sixteenth century because there is not, nor ever has there been, a single family system. The West has always been characterized by a diversity of family forms, by diversity of family functions and by diversity in attitudes to family relationships not only over time but at any one point in time. There is, except at the most trivial level, no Western family type.[36]

What does seem common across this history is that the family is never actually defined by networks of kinship so much as it is determined politically and economically by the needs of the state and capital to reproduce the population and reinforce patriarchal authority.[37]

Jacques Donzelot has traced such a shift from governance issued from families to government *through the family*, demonstrating a shift from the patriarchy of the head of the family to a patriarchy of the state.[38] In this new structure, the dynamic articulation of the structure of the family is constantly modulated by the state to serve the interests of capital. The family is both the privileged social site and a "prisoner" of the state, being used to police sexuality, reproduction, education, the inculcation of ideology, and the general formation of good citizens. A huge portion of the family's function within the capitalist state is to reinforce gender norms, most notably because they offer a means through which unpaid care and domestic labor can be morally assigned to a portion of the population—namely women. Despite feminist victories in the twentieth century that, at least partially, granted women financial and sexual independence, this function is only amplified by the neoliberal turn.

The evacuation of state welfare responsibilities in the latter half of the twentieth century only amplified the need to extract unpaid care and domestic labor from the population. In short, as Barret and McIntosh note, "[I]f marriage is the basis of the family, then this supposedly individual and freely chosen form has a state instrument at its heart."[39] The family thus serves as a key site for the perpetuation of heteronormative ideology as administered by the state.

The reproduction of the working class has also historically involved a policing of sexuality. Friedrich Engels pointed out as early as the nineteenth century that it was no coincidence that monogamous marriage and prostitution became cultural staples in the same moment.[40] What we can take from this is that the internal structure of marriage shapes the kind of sexuality that can exist outside of marriage, and, as Barrett and McIntosh explain, marital monogamy is not the answer to the problem of sexuality but the cause of "deviant" or "abnormal" sexual behavior.[41] Much like proponents of Ptolemy's geocentric model of the solar system through the ages, proponents of marital, monogamous heterosexuality continually fail to realize that the starting point to their sexual schema is flawed. Instead, they continually create exceptions and carve-outs to explain the model's failure to map onto human desire. The majority of these exceptions and carve-outs were historically for male, heterosexual desire, such as the acceptance of male promiscuity and the maintenance of precarious female bodies through which they could sate their desires in excess of the opportunities offered through marriage. Though the twentieth century also saw some partial concessions to female, heterosexual desire, allowing for premarital sex but only within the confines of amorous relationships with the apparent promise of long-term monogamous viability. These concessions to female sexuality were always contradictorily coupled with a misogynistic backlash though; women who took advantage of them were labeled "sluts," unfit for male commitment and thus the financial and ideological benefits of monogamous marriage, and, paradoxically, women who abstained were labeled "prudes" or "bitches," not deserving the time or energy required to build the foundation for a monogamous marriage.

LGBTQIA+ sex acts have historically occurred at the limits of these exceptions and carve-outs, stretching the Ptolemaic model of heterosexuality to its limits, demonstrating its internal contradictions, and, thus, frequently triggering violent and reactionary policing from the state and its privileged mechanism of sexual power, the family. In a sort of détente, the state is willing to tolerate these acts so long as they remain silent or

invisible and in so doing alleviate the threat of exposing the contradictions of heteronormativity. "The closet" can be understood as the mechanism through which a space—a silent or invisible space, and thus a partial
or nonspace—is produced at the myriad sites of these contradictions in
heteronormativity that can capture, contain, alleviate, and thus nullify the
threat of deviance and aberration. As Eve Sedgwick writes, "'Closeted-
ness' itself is a performance initiated as such by the speech act of a silence—
not a particular silence, but a silence that accrues particularity by fits and
starts, in relation to the discourse that surrounds and differentially constitutes it."[42] Sedgwick has persuasively demonstrated how these silent and
invisible spaces are just as essential to the structure of heteronormativity
as are its more vocal and visible portions. Their silence and invisibility
are foundational to the structure of heteronormativity. Similarly, the
increasing silence and invisibility of LGBTQIA+ sexual expression online
is emblematic of a digital closet and is foundational to a heteronormative
internet.

We can see this more concretely when it comes to the problem that
LGBTQIA+ communities face when trying to publicly organize movements
based around acts that state power relegates to the closet. As Michael Warner
and Lauren Berlant have shown, confining sexuality to the private sphere of
the bedroom, and LGBTQIA+ sex acts to the closet, is always at odds with
civil rights activism.[43] This is because LGBTQIA+ individuals don't have the
luxury of confining their sex acts to the bedroom. Instead, they must don
the identity that comes with those sex acts, even when they are out in public.
Here it is impossible to confine sex to the bedroom, to keep it silent and invisible, because LGBTQIA+ sex acts form the keystone to cultures, communities, and identities that definitionally exceed the confines of the closet. Nancy
Fraser has similarly argued that when sex acts are the organizing principles
of entire identity formations, then barring them from the public sphere and
treating them as purely matters of private concern effectively brackets sexual
politics from democratic mechanisms and procedures.[44]

Gayle Rubin has forcefully argued that sex is by default considered to
be a "dangerous, destructive, negative force."[45] The United States reverses
its famous juridical dictum when it comes to sex: all erotic behavior is considered sinful until proven innocent. For Rubin, this is a remnant of Christian religiosity that makes sex more meaningful ethically, culturally, and
politically than it needs to be. As we have seen, at the turn of the twentieth

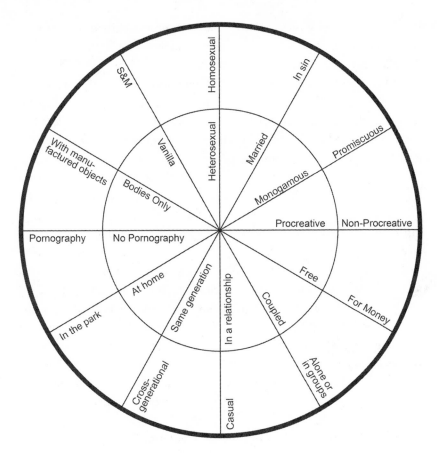

Figure 0.1
Gayle Rubin's Charmed Circle and the Outer Limits. *Source:* Gayle Rubin, "Thinking Sex: Notes for a Radical Theory of the Politics of Sexuality," in *Pleasure and Danger: Exploring Female Sexuality*, ed. Carole S. Vance (New York: Routledge, 1984), 281.

century, the proof of innocence shifted from a Christian imperative toward procreation to a scientific and medical imperative toward healthy outlets for the libido. This paradoxical shift brought with it an increase in the number of categories used to describe sexual misconduct, which Rubin visualizes through her diagram of the charmed circle and the outer limits (see figure 0.1). The charmed circle consists of several descriptors of sex acts that have frequently been understood as "good," "normal," "natural," and "blessed." The outer limit consists of descriptors of sex acts that have frequently been understood as "bad," "abnormal," "unnatural," and "damned."

Rubin's concept of the charmed circle is certainly dated and could benefit from several additions, such as one's gender identity conforming to versus differing from anatomical sex on state identification documents. That said, it can help us wrap our heads around the slippery concept of "queerness" and the paradoxical nature of heteronormativity. The paradox of heterosexuality is that it has conflicting definitions. On the one hand, heterosexual sex acts seem to be definitionally dominated by the anatomical sex of the people engaging in them—gay and lesbian sex acts are categorically different from straight sex acts, regardless of how kinky those straight sex acts are. On the other hand, one can deviate from heteronormativity even in anatomically male/female sex acts in several ways, like, for instance, using sex toys, engaging in BDSM, having cross-generational love affairs, or having group sex. For an example of this paradox in action, take, for instance, the fetish called *vore*, which most often involves the simulation of men being eaten by women (or a female playing the role of an imaginary being). Vore has a small but dedicated group of pornographers producing content readily available if one knows the appropriate keyword to search with. The oddness of heteronormativity is that it positions vore as being only different in degree from heterosexuality, whereas missionary sex acts between people in a long-term monogamous relationship who happen to have the same genitalia are positioned as being different in kind. Yet somehow at the very same time, it can condemn vore as an aberration.

The utility of the concept of queerness, at least for the purposes of this book, then is that it functions as an umbrella term for capturing all of the types of sex acts that are positioned as deviations from heteronormativity without equating the degree or the stakes of their deviation. It is important to note here that the idea that homosexuality differs in kind from heterosexuality, while vore differs only in degree, in combination with the publicly identifiable performative dimensions of LGBTQIA+ identities, leads to different stakes for gay, lesbian, or trans people, for instance, than for vore fetishists. In essence, they face different degrees, and maybe different kinds, of marginalization, and the former have all too real bodily, psychological, familial, and financial risks associated with their identities that the latter might not. Queerness is thus a slippery concept because it is articulated in response to an irresolvable paradox at the heart of heteronormativity. It at the same time must capture all forms of deviation while preserving their unique differences and stakes.

It is impossible to neatly tie up the proliferating contradictions contained within heteronormativity or the dynamic forms it takes across space and time. I hope that this short overview of some of the forms it has taken and contradictions it has contained might be indicative, if not wholly representative of, the current functions and stakes of heteronormativity in American society. I also hope to have demonstrated the essential connections between the concept of heteronormativity and its attendant phenomena, like reproduction and the family, gender roles, LGBTQIA+ sex acts and the closet, and queerness. As we will see throughout the following chapters, the emergence of porn filters is deeply tethered to the perpetuation of heteronormativity and has dire stakes for the future of LGBTQIA+ communities and sexual expression. With this necessarily partial and hopelessly imperfect articulation, I would now like to turn to one last matter of concern, which is the role that feminism and intersectionality will play in shaping this book, as well as its limitations for fully addressing all of their attendant concerns.

SEX-CRITICAL FEMINISM AND INTERSECTIONALITY

Locating one's work within feminist scholarship on pornography is difficult, as feminists have had a sustained and multifaceted conversation on pornography for the past fifty years. Chief among these difficulties is navigating between a sex-negative carceral feminism and a sex-positive postfeminism, both of which fail to address the material conditions of sex work or provide adequate social justice frameworks for sex workers. The sex-negative, carceral, and/or anti-pornography varieties of feminism draw on what Melissa Gira Grant describes as "the prostitute imaginary."[46] This imaginary is one in which the sex worker is articulated as "other," full of sexual excess, loss of social standing, and the possibility of contagion. The sex worker is both a structurally necessary outlet for desire and a dangerous temptation. In their book *Revolting Prostitutes*, Juno Mac and Molly Smith explain the prostitute imaginary through the historical social understanding of the vagina:

Ugly, stretched, odorous, unclean, potentially infected, desirable, mysterious, tantalising—the patriarchy's ambivalence towards vaginas is well established and has a lot in common with attitudes around sex work. On the one hand, the lure of the vagina is a threat; it's seen as a place where a penis might risk encountering the traces of another man or a full set of gnashing teeth. At the same time, it's viewed as an inherently submissive body part that must be "broken in" to bring about sexual maturity. The idea of the vagina as fundamentally compromised or pitiful is helped along in part by a longstanding feminist perception of the penetrative sexual act as indicative of subjugation.[47]

As Mac and Smith note, this conceptualization is interlinked with heteronormative anxieties about trans people and gay men. It connects to heteronormative anxieties over the status of trans people's genitals, their ability to "pass," and, subsequently, their capacity to "trick" cisgendered heteronormative people into having sex with them. As Leo Bersani notes, it also connects to heteronormative anxieties over gay men, who might "turn" heterosexual men gay and threaten contagion through HIV.[48]

This formulation of feminism often uses humiliating and misogynist language to describe sex workers in an attempt to differentiate "decent," "respectable," "independent" women from "sluts," "whores," and "holes."[49] As Jo Doezema explains, "What [these] feminists most want of sex workers is that they close their holes—shut their mouths, cross their legs—to prevent the taking in and spilling out of substances and words they find noxious."[50] As we'll see in the following chapter, in the worst instances, this dehumanization of sex workers leads to carceral feminism, which allies itself with Christian conservative anti-pornography crusaders in its focus on criminal justice reform to address the ills of sex work and pornography. This is often framed in the lens of "penal welfare" or "therapeutic policing," whereby police intervention is considered necessary to dislodge sex workers from their environments, leverage the criminal justice system to push them into rehabilitative services, and make deviant lifestyles so uncomfortable that people will accept state interventions.[51] Carceral feminism joins Christian conservatism in leveraging a focus on human trafficking—particularly of children—to rhetorically legitimate its sex-negative, anti-pornography, carceral position.

The predominant alternative to this approach is often formulated along the lines of what many feminist scholars have described as "postfeminism," which works to transcend feminism, positioning it as a mission accomplished and envisioning a subsequent world in which women are empowered to act as men's equals.[52] As Sarah Banet-Weiser notes, postfeminism understands this empowerment to act as men's equals in problematic ways, stressing things like "leaning in," being a "girl boss," and embracing and expressing female sexual desires, all of which often get channeled through structural patriarchy and end up looking a lot less like what feminists had envisioned empowerment to look like.[53] Their corollary in the sex work community is those that stress the value of sex work, describing it as enjoyable, rewarding, freely chosen by empowered and autonomous actors. In doing so, they attempt to make sex work look less like work and more like the type of sex that is more common and socially acceptable.[54] This presents inherent problems though, as it tends to equate the desire of the worker and the client, eliding the commercial interaction in such a way that can downplay the sex worker's needs as, well, a *worker*.

What all these forms of feminism have in common is that they tend to reinforce rather than destroy structural patriarchy, translating feminist demands into a palatable and defanged heteropatriarchal discourse. Further, by envisioning empowerment through this patriarchal lens and achieving partial empowerment for *some*, they end up losing sight of allies left behind—most frequently Black and Indigenous people of color (BIPOC), the LGBTQIA+ community, the disabled, the working class, and those from the Third World or Global South. As Mac and Smith note, "Sex positive sex work politics are useful for the [postfeminists] who advocate them *and* for carceral feminists who push for criminalization. These groups *share an interest* in glossing over the material conditions of sex workers' workplaces."[55]

In this book, I hope to avoid identifying with either pole of this unfortunate dichotomy, though the range of sources I draw on, voices that I incorporate, and issues that I touch on may make this commitment difficult to track throughout the book. I'd like then to set out a few parameters for the project that might help keep things clear and that I will try to remain consistent on and refer back to throughout the book. When it comes to sex work, I identify with anti-prostitution and sex-critical feminists in their commitment to ameliorating the material conditions that leave people no option other than sex work *and* that make sex work bad work (lack of access to health care; inability to benefit from labor laws and regulations; exposure to violence, danger, and trauma; social stigmatization; and marginalization, and so on). Highlighting an anti-prostitution framework is complicated by the digital nature of much of my investigation, as much less of the feminist discourse and empirical evidence deals with the peculiarities of sex work online. My aim in regard to online sex work is to make some of the material and structural components that undergird it transparent so that sex workers and their allies might better critique internet platforms and organize and advocate for change.

The primary focus of the book, however, is not on sex work but instead on the broader infrastructure of the internet—from misogynist and heteronormative discourses to the coding labor, algorithms, and content moderation policies that govern what is visible and invisible online to the impact that this infrastructure has on *both* sex workers *and* the broader LGBTQIA+ community online. Much of the book focuses on advocating that internet service providers (ISPs) and social media platforms stop censoring LGBTQIA+ speech online that few would consider pornographic. However, in places—particularly chapter 4—that do look at pornography, I try to strike a balance between the seemingly contradictory advocacy for more porn *and* less porn. This position is rooted in the assumption that porn is not going anywhere; it is here to stay. As such, I'm advocating for more *varieties* of pornography, rather than more total content, so that the porn that exists and is readily available to people might be more diverse, representative, and imaginative, allowing people more freedom to explore their erotic desires. On the other hand, I'm advocating for *fewer* people to face the negative ramifications of the mainstream heteroporn industry and online sex work, whether this is achieved by democratizing the ownership, profits, and production of porn *or* by providing a social welfare and social justice framework robust enough that online sex work is truly optional. This broader focus on LGBTQIA+ censorship online tends to highlight the former of these commitments, often tempting me to celebrate attempts to democratize and diversify pornography online. That said, I remain equally committed to the latter position and hope to highlight the material conditions of online sex work as well and some of the steps we might take to make it more just, equitable, and optional.

The overbroad censorship of sexual speech online has amplified consequences for people that face intersectional forms of marginalization—in the United States, the most predominant of these is race. In this book, race primarily makes an appearance through intersectional analyses of who bears the weight of overzealous censorship most heavily. In the many, many posts about and reports of sexual speech being censored online that I came across, race was rarely mentioned as a factor and was difficult to disentangle in the case studies I performed. While I did find evidence of racial bias in some of the datasets I looked at, I had trouble making a direct and empirical connection to the censorship of sexual speech—and LGBTQIA+ content in particular—that I was tracing for the book.[56] Instead, I mostly found race at the margins in my account, as an intersectional factor that, along with class, nationality, ability, and transgender identity, caused certain people to be inordinately impacted by LGBTQIA+ censorship online. This censorship is not a weight born equally across the LGBTQIA+ community and is connected to a much longer history of policing the sexuality of working-class, racialized, and otherwise marginalized populations, as I've shown above.

While I will try to gesture toward these intersectional concerns throughout the book, the extent of the new ground that needs to be covered and the intent to make a convincing argument that heteronormativity is getting embedded in the infrastructure of the internet will inevitably at points occlude these intersectional concerns and prevent me from doing them full justice. As such, it is my hope that I can refer readers to scholars who highlight these other perspectives in their work and that readers might look at their work alongside this book and find ways to correct and expand my analyses. Scholars like Charlton D. McIlwain and André Brock have shown that BIPOC communities, and African Americans in particular, have been early and influential adopters of internet and computer technologies.[57] Their work stands in contrast to dominant narratives about the "digital divide," the lack of technological literacy in BIPOC communities, and assumptions that the internet is a predominantly white space. Scholars like Janet Abbate, Mar Hicks, and Nathan Ensmenger have produced similar work in regard to gender.[58] I've found little similar scholarship problematizing these narratives when it comes to class and nationality but imagine similar work could be done productively on these topics.

Scholars like Joy Buolamwini, Timnit Gebru, Ruha Benjamin, and Safiya Noble have worked to show how the logic of racialization is at the center of many algorithms, datasets, interfaces, and platforms that make up the internet and our everyday computational environment. Buolamwini and Gebru have most notably demonstrated empirically that racial and gender bias are deeply embedded in many of our most prominent facial recognition algorithms.[59] Ruha Benjamin coined the term "the new Jim Code" to describe the ways in which computer and internet technologies are producing a new form of scientific racism, reflecting and reproducing existing inequities under the veneer of seemingly more objective and progressive technological apparatuses—specifically machine learning and predictive analytics.[60] Safiya Noble has coined the term "technological redlining" to similarly describe the ways in which algorithms "reinforce oppressive social relationships and enact new modes of racial profiling."[61] She demonstrates how Google Search engages in technological redlining, shaping the experience and representation of race online in ways that reinforce the oppression of Black people. Scholars like Elizabeth Ellcessor have made similar arguments about disability, demonstrating the ways in which internet technologies reinforce the ableist architecture of everyday life by not adequately addressing accessibility concerns and connected this to disabled representation online.[62] Again, to my knowledge, there is less robust scholarly discourse on similar issues vis-à-vis class and nationality online. Throughout this book, I will make similar arguments about the ways in which gender norms and heteronormativity are reinforced by algorithms and datasets online. By reading my work alongside these, and many other, important contributions from critical race scholars, my hope is that we might lay the foundation for a more fully intersectional analysis of normativity, marginalization, and power as it operates in our digitally networked world.

UNLIKELY BEDFELLOWS

THE MORAL MAJORITY AND ANTI-PORN FEMINISTS

The Moral Majority, largely organized by American Southern Baptist pastor and televangelist Jerry Falwell Sr. and composed mostly of evangelical Christians, emerged in the 1970s to combat the spread of pornography in the United States. The movement had little to fear with Richard Nixon holding the presidency. Nixon dedicated himself to maintaining the federal government's efforts to "control and eliminate smut from our national life."[1] However, the election of populist Democrat Jimmy Carter to the presidency provided a new opening for the movement to leverage anti-pornography sentiment to gain national attention. The Moral Majority was catapulted onto the national stage in 1976 when Carter gave an interview in *Playboy* magazine, acknowledging that he had "lusted in his heart," an attempt to humanize himself and acknowledge that despite his dedication to Christianity, he, too, struggled with sin.[2] For many, this was a convenient line of attack against a populist Democratic president, but others were horror-struck in earnest. As one reporter wrote, "For faith leaders, it was an easily exploitable issue; for Falwell, it was a crusade."[3] Further, mobilizing these communities against pornography was the proving grounds for the rhetoric of "family values," the same rhetoric that would later be used to mobilize conservative Christians in opposition to feminism, gay rights, and abortion access.[4]

By the 1980s, the Moral Majority had leveraged popular anti-pornography sentiment to build a powerful movement, as demonstrated by their impact on Ronald Reagan's presidency. Reagan's reelection campaign of 1984 saw anti-pornography rhetoric added to the Republican Party platform for the first time, and shortly thereafter, he appointed Edwin Meese, his extremely conservative attorney general, to spearhead a new presidential commission on pornography. The nearly 2,000-page Meese Report was inflammatory, unilaterally condemning "smut" as a threat to American culture and morality.[5] Reagan quickly leveraged the report to institute a new "obscenity strike force" meant to crack down on the proliferation of pornography made possible by VCRs, camcorders, and cable television. For the following five years, the federal government was able to leverage the community standards of small, conservative areas of the country to prosecute pornographers distributing mail-order tapes, films, and magazines, slowing the growth of the pornography industry.

While none of this is particularly surprising to anyone glancingly familiar with the history of conservative Christian politics in the United States, what *is* surprising is the unlikely bedfellows that the Moral Majority found in their war on porn: anti-porn feminists. None are more emblematic of this strand of feminism than Catharine MacKinnon and Andrea Dworkin. In 1987, MacKinnon defined pornography as

> the graphic sexually explicit subordination of women through pictures or words that also includes women dehumanized as sexual objects, things, or commodities; enjoying pain or humiliation or rape; being tied up, cut up, mutilated, bruised, or physically hurt; in postures of sexual submission or servility or display; reduced to body parts, penetrated by objects or animals, or presented in scenarios of degradation, injury, torture; shown as filthy or inferior; bleeding, bruised, or hurt in a context that makes these conditions sexual.[6]

For MacKinnon, this definition naturally led to the feminist insight that all pornography is a form of rape that reinforces gender inequality and status quo sexual politics, most notably normalizing and encouraging violence and discrimination against women.[7] Andrea Dworkin largely shared this perspective and worked with MacKinnon to push anti-porn feminist activism to new heights in her attempts to get the Antipornography Civil Rights Ordinance (ACRO) passed. The ACRO would've legally treated pornography as a violation of women's civil rights and allowed them to sue for damages in courts of law in the United States.[8] Dworkin also testified against pornography before the Meese Commission and went so far as to pen a book on the potential alliance to be struck between anti-porn feminists and right-wing women.[9]

As many critics were quick to point out, this strand of anti-porn feminism failed to substantially distinguish itself from the conservative anti-porn positions it was allying itself with.[10] In fact, anti-porn feminism opened a rift that has continued to fracture any attempts to produce a unified feminist front since the 1980s.[11] Anti-porn feminism also precludes feminism from cleanly allying itself with LGBTQIA+ studies and activism because it places heteronormativity at the foundation of feminist critique. As Gayle Rubin has argued, the ideology of anti-porn feminism contains an implied, if not explicit, condemnation of sadomasochism. It argues that sadomasochism is the bedrock of all pornography, and through this association, tethers BDSM practices to the objectification, exploitation, and rape of women.[12] Further, as Jay Daniel Thompson has shown at length, anti-porn feminism to this day continues to silently position heterosexuality as the archetype of all pornography, denying the very possibility of LGBTQIA+ pornographies and instead interpreting them as mere variations on the heteroporn genre. Thompson argues that without an explicit analysis of heterosexuality in our critiques of pornography, we will never get an accurate critique. Instead, we will simply reproduce heteronormative anti-porn assumptions.[13]

While I wouldn't go so far as to dismiss MacKinnon and Dworkin's work, which certainly was responding to legitimate and important feminist concerns about the material impacts of sex work, objectification, misogyny, and rape culture, I do think it's important to keep in mind how the turn to the criminal justice system and the alliance with other anti-pornography crusaders frequently undermined their attempts to achieve their more laudable goals of improving the material lives of women.

Popular anxiety around sex, sexuality, and pornography produces unlikely bedfellows—in this instance, between anti-porn feminists and arch-conservatives. Whatever their differences, these anti-porn allies tend to share a common commitment, whether they openly espouse it or are not quite conscious of it, to the reinforcement of heteronormativity. This chapter will work to trace the emergence of a new set of unlikely bedfellows in the war on pornography: the alt-right and pseudoscientific conservative Christian nonprofit organizations. We will see in great detail how the popular "Pandora's box of porn" narrative has concealed a large amount of anti-porn activism and organizing. By tracing the new set of cultural and political forces that have formed a strategic coalition to battle the scourge of pornography today, we will see just how central this issue is to contemporary American politics and culture. The first section of the chapter will examine the *manosphere*, a portion of the internet in which men's rights activists articulate new forms of masculinity, and particularly look at the digital footprints of the pickup artist Roosh V, the NoFap movement, Proud Boys, and incels. The second section will turn to Morality in Media—also known as the National Council on Sex Exploitation (NCOSE)—as emblematic of a revitalized Christian conservative anti-porn movement in the United States that leverages pseudoscience and nonprofit think tank strategies to advance its cause.

It is worth noting that I struggled with deciding how much of this discourse to include in the book for fear of perpetuating it or representing it as being the common and openly held beliefs of the majority of Americans. The discourse is certainly not omnipresent or potent enough to warrant such conclusions. In the end, I decided to include this information because, while these may be fringe extremist movements on the internet, they also are constituted by men who have the time and technical savvy to hold an oversized influence online.[14] These groups are the breeding ground of many internet trolls, and their message boards have been used to organize systematic campaigns to target sex workers and adult entertainers, as we'll see in chapter 4, with a particularly detrimental effect on LGBTQIA+ sexual speech online. They exert direct power over internet discourse through campaigns of harassment and exploit internet platforms' community guidelines, terms of service agreements, and community flagging features to censor feminist and LGBTQIA+ content. They also exert indirect power over internet discourse because their extremist ideas are often translated into a less toxic version by intermediaries who help them achieve greater public visibility. As we'll see in chapter 2, many men in Silicon Valley from low-level coders to executives profess a similar ideology. While it is important to understand the manosphere and the targeted ways in which it exerts power over sexual speech online, my hope is that readers will be able to take their claims to universality and cultural and political agency with a grain of salt. They are not and should not be taken as representative of what most Americans think, feel, say, or do.

ENTER THE MANOSPHERE

In an interview for *New York Magazine*, Sarah Diefendorf, a sociologist and Scholars Strategy Network postdoctoral fellow at the University of Utah, has argued that the manosphere can be understood as sharing some basic beliefs and ideological commitments, including gender essentialism, biologically determined gender roles, an objectification of and sense of ownership over women's bodies, and an urgent feeling that they are "losing power or control."[15] Sarah Banet-Weiser similarly argues that the manosphere has emerged in relation to a crisis in masculinity and a felt sense of loss of power to feminists. She describes the manosphere as ranging "from the more moderate, such as support for father's rights and custody rights, doubts over the prevalence of domestic violence, and reflexive support of the military, to the more extreme, such as normalizing rape and sexual violence, manipulating and controlling women into sex, and making death threats against a vast number of people (mostly women) who disagree with these views."[16] While misogyny and heteronormativity are nothing new, they have been catalyzed by social media and internet forums like 4chan and Reddit.[17]

These online communities are diverse, individually fragmented across different forums and media, with participants crossing boundaries between them frequently, and their discourse is often loaded with irony and proliferating neologisms. It can thus be difficult to pin down what exactly different groups of men's rights activists actually believe. That said, recent research has demonstrated that these communities are growing, that members tend to migrate from less extreme peripheral groups toward more hateful, toxic, and potentially violent groups, and that by our best approximation, participants' online expression becomes more toxic and hateful as they make this migration.[18] The manosphere has helped to manifest what Jack Bratich has called a "cultural will-to-humiliation," which operates as a form of power to reinforce white patriarchy and heteronormativity.[19] Shame and humiliation are essential to the power of the manosphere.[20] The manosphere's internet trolls wield shame and humiliation to destroy relationships, ruin careers, and force their targets for harassment to leave online social spaces. Their vitriol is borne primarily by women and disproportionately by women of color.[21]

While there have been several recent academic studies that work to make sense of the heterogeneous discourse of the manosphere, they largely stick to examining it in terms of misogyny and thus analyze it in terms of gender.[22] The analysis in this chapter looks to build on that discourse by examining the manosphere in terms of heteronormativity, including the complicated ways in which gender and sexuality are articulated together in digital misogynist discourse. The manosphere is also an interesting conjuncture to explore because men's rights activists frequently have deep concerns over the role that pornography is playing in contemporary American life. The manosphere thus frequently joins the traditional alliance between anti-porn feminists and Christian conservatives, itself alive and well in the work of Gail Dines, for instance.[23] Who would've thought those two groups would get into bed with men's rights activists?

While these digital misogynists have many permutations on the web, there are four groups in particular that spend a lot of time thinking and writing about pornography: pickup artists and similar theorists of neomasculinity, the #NoFap community, Proud Boys, and incels. Each of these communities structures their opposition to pornography slightly differently and diverges widely on other aspects of politics and culture, yet each share a common commitment to preserving traditional gender roles—to the point of making pseudoscientific arguments about their biological innateness—and reinforcing heteronormativity. As Banet-Weiser has argued, while the various permutations of the manosphere—incels, Proud Boys, Men Going Their Own Way (MGTOW), pickup artists, #NoFap—analyzed in this chapter may present as distinct and disconnected, they operate as a network, a shared *system* of misogynist ideology, each helping to authorize and support the other.[24] Further, while the communities participating in each of these discourses are small, they wield an inordinate amount of power on the internet because of their organizing tactics, exploitation of internet infrastructure and platform community guidelines and terms and conditions, and the amount of time, money, and technical expertise they have to dedicate to their movements.

ROOSH V, PICKUP ARTISTRY, AND NEOMASCULINITY

Take, for example, Daryush Valizadeh, better known as Roosh V, a self-proclaimed pickup artist who writes about his sexual exploits, pickup artistry, masculinity, and other issues related to the "manosphere," and who has been described by the Southern Poverty Law Center as a "male supremacist."[25] While it is difficult to establish just how popular Roosh's writings are, it is safe to assume he has a wide readership. His website *Return of Kings* published 5,800 articles before shuttering in 2018.[26] His books currently on Amazon hover within the top one hundred to top one thousand for most of the categories they are ranked in.[27] He planned, and later canceled, a global day of meetings in one hundred cities in forty countries that elicited angry petitions with hundreds of thousands of signatures and responses from mayors, legislators, and police chiefs.[28] He was even doxed by Anonymous, a prominent online hacker collective that released his address, phone number, and a picture of his house in Washington, DC, where he supposedly lives with his mother.[29]

A quick Google search reveals both mountains of forum posts that support and extend Roosh's thinking and a tidal wave of criticism, mostly directed at his bragging about sex acts that seem to have been nonconsensual and his arguments in favor of legalizing rape, both of which he has walked back and claimed were instances of sarcasm.[30] This claim of sarcasm, satire, or other forms of humor is a standard tactic that internet trolls, and the alt-right in particular, use to simultaneously voice extremist thoughts and distance themselves from responsibility for having voiced them.[31] In short, Roosh is a popular and provocative writer on contemporary masculinity whose work also happens to spend a lot of time connecting the standard tenets of alt-right ideology to heteronormativity. As such, he is worth examining in detail to get a better sense of the contemporary cultural context within which content moderation has emerged, particularly the visceral and heteronormatively inflected disgust that drives much of its draconian suppression of not just pornography but all sexual speech.

In 2015, Roosh wrote a post on his website introducing the term *neomasculinity* to describe the "developing ideology" that has been pieced together across his media platform (including Return of Kings and RVF, the Roosh V Forum).[32] In an article for Return of Kings exploring the origins of neomasculinity, one of the site's most popular contributors Quintus Curtius situated neomasculinity as a return to and continuation of Reagan-era conservative politics based on optimism, pragmatism, and faith in traditional institutions.[33] He writes, "Neomasculinity employs new methods to achieve old aims. [. . .] Neomasculinity is deeply conservative."[34] For Roosh, neomasculinity meant pursuing or believing in at least half of the items on the following list:

- *Game [i.e., pickup artistry]*
- *Traditional sex roles*
- Self-improvement
- *Understanding the true nature of women*
- *Patriarchy*
- Weightlifting/fitness
- Individual responsibility
- Equal legal rights, free speech, due process
- *Testosterone*
- Entrepreneurship
- Hard work ethic
- Red pill truths

- *Sexual marketplace value*
- *Male-only spaces*
- *Hedonistic moderation*
- *Nuclear family*
- *Binary sex model*
- Natural health and hygiene (baking soda, apple cider vinegar, etc)
- Male virtue
- *Anti-socialism*
- Technological skepticism
- *Feminine beauty ideals*
- Deeper life meaning and/or spirituality
- Lifestyle optimization[35]

I've italicized the items here that speak particularly strongly to hetero-normativity to demonstrate that, in aligning with at least half of the list, nearly all neomasculinists will subscribe to some components of heteronormativity as I have set out in the introduction, if not to heteronormativity writ large. Below I analyze how Roosh positions some of the items on this list as they reveal the overlapping and contradictory ideological tenets of the alt-right, which perpetuates heteronormativity online and helps to produce the digital closet.

For Roosh, game or pickup artistry is an essential component of contem-porary masculinity. For a host of undertheorized reasons, Roosh argues that the majority of men's "natural" selves will leave them involuntarily celibate, or at best, only able to have sex with women of lower socioeconomic status and attractiveness. It is worth noting that Roosh understands women's attrac-tiveness to be an objective trait determined by body measurements and facial symmetry, whereas men's attractiveness is more subjective and correlated to personality traits and status symbols. Obviously, objectification is alive and well here, reified by pseudoscientific arguments. To return to the point at hand, this imbalance is the result of a liberal sexual economy, which Roosh addresses under the term "sexual marketplace value." This sexual economy not only mirrors the free-market capitalist economy, but it is also deeply influenced by it. Women's ability to achieve financial independence has led to them "leisurely shopping around for the most high status male [they] can obtain."[36] Roosh claims that women now dominate the workplace through political correctness—policing human resources departments and control the domestic sphere by leveraging false rape and domestic violence charges or threats thereof. In short, women are increasingly empowered and use this empowerment to dominate men and almost exclusively sleep with more attractive and wealthy men, knowing that they can always settle down into a monogamous marriage in their thirties after they are well past their "peak beauty and fertility."[37]

The result for low-status men, often referred to as *betas* in alt-right dis-course, is that they have less access to sex, which Roosh describes as part of "their basic survival needs."[38] In many ways, Roosh longs for bygone eras where Christian morality would leverage the threat of shame and ostraciza-tion to pressure women into marrying "the first good man they bed, one they often met through family or church."[39] He writes, "This ensured society stability and sexual equality in that most able-bodied men would be able to procure a wife."[40] Ideally, Roosh wants a woman to be "punished for her mistakes."[41] Here we can clearly see the deep entanglement of neomasculinity with heteronormativity. Roosh alternates between the reproductive and carnal drives as the bedrock for sexuality, bracketing sex almost exclusively to male-female couplings. He tries to map heterosexual monogamous familism onto a broader pseudoscientific argument about the maintenance of society or the species, a move that is obviously false.[42] By this logic, though, humans would actually be behaving more "naturally" if only the "alphas" were allowed to impregnate all the world's females, as is the case in many other animal species' mating patterns. In short, the human species and human society doesn't need betas to have sex to "survive." The real aim is to revive power structures that preserve beta males' unrestrained access to women's bodies for heterosexual intercourse. Roosh acknowledges this explicitly: "Patriarchal systems must [. . .] be regained as the primary organizing structure of modern societies."[43]

Roosh's position is based on both a cisnormative and a heteronormative presumption of traditional gender roles. He argues that gender equality is nothing but "a myth that has no scientific basis."[44] Instead, men and women are binary categories that have "likely existed since the beginning of the human species."[45] For Roosh, men have essential traits like dominance, independence, rationality, and analytical thinking, whereas women have essential traits like submissiveness, dependence, emotional nature, faster intuition, and cooperative sharing. It is worth noting that Roosh here demonstrates the biological determinist or essentialist point of view that ignores a host of evidence on the role of epigenesis and sociocultural factors on gender and sexuality. This manifests, as we've seen above, in the slippage between the terms "species" and "society" in Roosh's writing, a useful conflation that allows Roosh to alternate between biological determinist and social constructionist claims whenever it suits his arguments. For example, Roosh also argues, "A woman's nature is therefore not static, and takes the shape of the container of her environment. The true nature of men, on the other hand, is in turn reactionary to signals women put out that declare their sexual preferences in males."[46] Thus women are at one point genetically submissive, dependent, emotional, intuitive, and cooperative and at another subject to hedonistic sex drives that lead them to adapt their behavioral traits to any given social context to maximize pleasure.

Further, as is common in the discourse, women are once again positioned as the second sex, the marked subjects, as men's sexual decision-making is purely reactionary and natural. Yet, in the same article, Roosh argues for the essential role that testosterone plays in masculinity. He writes, "Being a man is not a social construct—it's primarily biological construct [*sic*] that is heavily dependent on healthy body and brain functioning that results from appropriate testosterone levels."[47] Men are somehow both reactionary and stable, as they apparently do not take on the shape of the container they fill. Again, the entire theory is grounded upon a heteronormative model of binary sex differences. Roosh acknowledges this explicitly, noting that sex is determined at birth by genetics and is necessarily tethered to the manifestation of masculine and feminine behavioral characteristics. This is a vast oversimplification. While anatomical sex differences are often dimorphic, they are determined not simply by "genes" but by *five* factors: (1) the presence or absence of a Y chromosome, (2) type of gonads, (3) sex hormones, (4) internal reproductive anatomy, and (5) external genitalia.[48] While in the majority of people all five of these factors align according to the dimorphic sex model, an estimated 1.7 percent of people are born *intersex*, with one or more of these factors not only inverted but possibly somewhere on a spectrum between the dimorphic poles.[49] Thus, even the markers of anatomical sex can be blurry, let alone the performative aspects of gender.[50] Roosh acknowledges this dismissively, writing, "There are also exceptions with hermaphrodites, deformed humans who are born with genitalia from both sexes."[51] Here Roosh is profoundly cisnormative, intentionally denigrating, and out of step with scientific discourse, which no longer uses the term "hermaphrodite" in favor of "disorders of sex development," itself a denigrating term to intersex people.[52]

As is to be expected, Roosh quickly jumps from anatomical sex to gender, importing the same binary model and essentialism that he mistakenly extracted from the "scientific evidence." He works this out in a passage that is worth quoting at length:

> Any attempt to manually seek out a gender or identity outside of the binary sex model is artificial, non-biological, and deviant. Such a practice is not conducive to family formation or sanity on a societal level. A society can be definitively labeled ill if it enables its citizens to artificially invent gender identities and pick them at will as if shopping for fruit in a supermarket. Even worse is outright facilitating mentally ill individuals to change their sex, which leads to an increase in suicide and drug use without alleviating the underlying mental disorder. . . .[53]

The binary sex model has flaws in that it will not perfectly suit those who possess personality and behavioral traits from the opposite sex, meaning that institutions and spaces for homosexuals or transsexuals won't be constructed, but at the same time it is inappropriate to encourage or enable a person to jump out of their genetically determined sex by opening the door on dozens of different gender identities and orientations that definitively harm the individual.

In a patriarchal society with traditional sex roles, only a tiny minority will have trouble with their assigned sex at birth. They should not be allowed to disrupt the lifestyle and healthy traditions of those who soundly fit into the natural binary model.

There are a number of issues worth picking out from this passage. First, Roosh conflates anatomical sex and gender strategically so that he might use the pseudoscientific evidence he has gathered on the dimorphism of anatomical sex to argue for essentialized, binary, heteronormative gender roles. As we'll see, this is a common argumentative thread across alt-right, neo-Christian conservative, and Silicon Valley tech discourses. Second, as is to be expected, Roosh connects these essentialized gender roles to familism, and through familism to the health of "society." Again, here he conflates society with species, as the health of society is a subjective determination based on value judgments, while the health of the species is closer to an objectively determinable aspect based on reproduction, among other determinants. Third, he forges a false will of the majority by essentializing heterosexuality, and thus the reason he has to hold the ground of biological essentialism becomes clear. If people, including their gender identities and sexualities, take the shape of the container they fill, then the proliferation of gender identities and sexualities he so ardently fears might break his constructed majority as more people deviate from traditional binarized gender norms and heterosexuality, the latter of which was intentionally defined ambiguously to make space to accommodate enough deviance to forge a majority.

Lastly, he tries to combine the language of psychiatric disorders with a misuse of social scientific evidence as if it were biologically determined to falsely reverse the causality of transgender, nonbinary, and gender-nonconforming people's suffering and vulnerability. What I mean by this is that he looks at trends in data on drug use, suicide, and life satisfaction among transgender populations to argue that trans people use drugs, commit suicide, or are generally unhappy *because* they are trans. This is a biologically determinist reading of social phenomena, which any 101 course would teach students is an improper way to treat social scientific data. Instead, our best evidence shows that trans people use drugs, commit suicide, and are unhappy most often because they are one of the most precarious populations on earth, subject to state-sponsored and freelance violence on a daily basis, and constantly struggling to navigate and find acceptance performing their gender identity in a profoundly cisnormative world.[54] Then, in a double faux pas, he extrapolates from his bad interpretation of the social scientific data to other forms of gender nonconformance and queer sexualities, arguing that they too "definitively harm the individual."[55]

In short, Roosh's whole philosophy leverages badly interpreted social scientific and neurological data to essentialize not only the dimorphism of anatomical sex but also binary gender identities, traditional gender roles, familism, heterosexuality, and, in the end, patriarchy, all so that betas can get laid. Any deviance from these essentialized norms is treated as an aberration, dangerous to the individual, society, and the species. Roosh admits that deviation happens at different levels of this schema from intersex to genderqueer to homosexuality but thinks these people ought to conform to the "majority" rather than be "accommodated" in society. In essence, he wants LGBTQIA+ people to stay in the closet, both in real life and digitally. All of this is packed with a bizarre combination of desiring that women be available for heterosexual intercourse while castigating them for ever consenting to it pre- (or worse, extra-) maritally.[56] Here we find yet again the tired dichotomy of the "frigid bitch" and the "whore," the perpetual dichotomy of feminine sexuality as imagined by cisgender, heterosexual men. Yet this time it comes from the oddest possible spokesman. But if Donald Trump can ride to the presidency on the back of evangelical voters, then who is to tell a self-professed pickup artist that he cannot preach sexual moderation in his manuals for how to play the game?

Since 2018, Roosh's online publishing platforms have been on the decline, Amazon has removed several of his books from their self-publishing platform, YouTube has sanctioned him, and PayPal and Discus have terminated their partnerships with him.[57] While his influence may be waning and his Return of Kings site may be on indefinite hiatus, one can see the deep influence his platform has had on the manosphere in the sheer number of references to this platform in the NoFap, Proud Boy, and incel discourses. Further, as we will see in chapter 2, this paradoxical discourse that combines pickup artistry with more traditional heteronormative values is deeply influential in Silicon Valley. Silicon Valley is a world populated by self-identified nerds, a number of whom found themselves wealthy enough nearly overnight to have all the sex they missed out on in their youth. It is no wonder then that this odd combination of "beta" angst over spurned sexual overtures with "alpha" entitlement to women's bodies has become so pervasive online.

NOFAP

The NoFap community originated on Reddit and has largely been organized through the r/NoFap subreddit started by Alexander Rhodes in 2011. The r/NoFap subreddit currently has 449,000 subscribers.[58] The community is centrally organized around abstaining from pornography, masturbation, and/or orgasm (PMO) for set periods of time and takes its name from an onomatopoeic synonym for masturbation—*fap*—that originated in a Japanese comic strip in 1999.[59] If you follow the forum, you will see between the banal and the misogynist posts a stream of (largely male) participants reporting the effects of abstaining from PMO as being akin to the awakening of "superpowers." Posts regularly report effects like increases in concentration, energy, physical activity, confidence, and success with women. While there is certainly nothing *un*healthy about abstaining from PMO for periods of time, the discourse on the NoFap forums is problematic in a number of senses: (1) it tends to oversimplify scientific evidence, (2) it tends to overhype the effects and correlate them too strongly to increased testosterone levels, (3) it reifies a fundamentally moral argument against PMO, and (4) by combining an emphasis on testosterone with an emphasis on this moral tradition of self-control, NoFap reifies heteronormativity.

Clinical psychologist and author of *The Myth of Sex Addiction* David Ley has written of the NoFap movement, "I'm not in opposition to them, but I do think their ideas are simplistic, naïve and promote a sad, reductionistic and distorted view of male sexuality and masculinity."[60] This is a common sentiment in the discourse of experts on psychology and human behavior when addressing the NoFap movement. The proponents of NoFap often ground their claims on bad interpretations of science or pseudoscience. Since 1972, the American Medical Association has considered masturbation to be normal human behavior.[61] Since then, research has shown that masturbation is correlated to a number of health benefits, such as a release of sexual tension, reduced stress, better sleep, improved self-esteem and body image, relief of menstrual cramps and muscle tension, strengthening of muscle tone in the pelvic and anal areas, and it can help treat sexual problems.[62] While for some people masturbation can compensate for a lack of partnered sex or sexual satisfaction, and thus potentially inhibit the formation of relationships, it is also frequently a component of an active and pleasurable sex life.[63] The science is in on masturbation, and it indicates that there are no significant health risks.

There is certainly a rise in diagnoses of psychogenic erectile dysfunction (ED) among men under forty—which many researchers examine as instances of potential pornography-induced erectile dysfunction (PIED) in which the arousal mechanisms of the (male) body are short-circuited by the novelty and extremity of pornography. That said, there are many factors beyond the novelty thesis that may contribute to this rise. One important factor to be considered is the inadvertent sexual conditioning through pornography leading to unrealistic sexual expectations.[64] Another factor is simply better diagnostic tools and an increased willingness of men to speak to their doctors about ED. However, the first peer-reviewed academic study on PIED found that viewing pornography correlates to greater sexual responsiveness rather than ED but also that there likely is no such thing as a biological addiction to pornography.[65] In other words, the science is still out on PIED. We need much more research on the social conditioning factor, which would benefit from critical analyses of pornography content as well. What does seem clear is that whatever impact pornography is having on sexual health, it is not biological. Another study has shown that there is no change in the neuro-endocrine response to orgasm after abstaining from PMO—thus indicating that many of the felt changes reported by members of the NoFap movement are psychological rather than biological in nature. However, this study did show that male abstinence can lead to elevated testosterone levels, and this is the data that members of the NoFap movement most frequently cling to.[66]

While the NoFap community is purportedly gender-neutral, much of its discourse is caught up in the reification of hegemonic masculinity, and this is the most likely explanation for the fixation on testosterone levels. Social psychologists Kris Taylor and Sue Jackson have studied the NoFap community and argue that its members "employ idealized discourses of innate masculinity and the need for 'real sex' to justify their resistance to pornography use and masturbation."[67] In this discourse, men are positioned as biologically inclined to seek pleasure from women, which in turn reifies traditional gender roles and sexual expectations.

A frequent reference in this community is the work of Gary Wilson, an anti-porn activist and author of *Your Brain on Porn*.[68] Wilson argues that males are biologically wired to seek novelty during sexual selection—each female offers a novel genetic opportunity, and men are genetically programmed to seek them out, have sex with them, and impregnate them. For Wilson, online pornography simulates this experience of bringing an infinite stream of new females into view, thus desensitizing males to the novelty of females and subsequently to the desire to realize the genetic opportunity of copulating with them. Male brains become effectively rewired and addicted similarly to drug and alcohol abusers. He reduces this to the repetitive function of the click—clicking on content in an ever-refreshing feed of pornography—and describes this as a click-based addiction in the TED Talk that helped to popularize his ideas.[69] His TED Talk comes with a legal disclaimer from TED: "This talk contains several assertions that are not supported by academically respected studies in medicine and psychology. While some viewers might find advice provided in this talk to be helpful, please do not look to this talk for medical advice."[70] Funnily, it is TED's own addiction to click-based revenues that have led them to maintain a talk that requires such a disclaimer.

The problem here is that Wilson, like so many others, is taking a vague moral position, justifying it by appealing to normative gender roles, and then biologizing those gender roles. This is a paradox that Taylor and Jackson highlighted in their study of NoFap forums: NoFap requires men to "perform ostensibly innate characteristics."[71] In short, the problem with this discourse is that neither the morals nor the gender roles are universalizable. As Thomas Laqueur has demonstrated at great length, this conjuncture of universalized anti-masturbation sentiment is an essentially modern phenomenon in the Western world.[72] Laqueur found that masturbation was not seen as a serious problem for much of recorded history until the 1712 publication of *Onania: Or, the Heinous Sin of Self-Pollution, and All Its Frightful Consequences (in Both Sexes) Considered*.[73] *Onania* claimed that masturbation led to deleterious effects, like stunted growth, epilepsy, and the contraction of sexually transmitted infections.

The publication of *Onania* and its surrounding discourse is also deeply tied to the emergence of modern binary gender roles. Stephen Greenblatt neatly summarizes Laqueur's discoveries about this connection:

His book showed that in the seventeenth and eighteenth centuries people gradually shifted from a one-sex model—in which the woman's body was viewed as a providentially inferior version of a man's—to a two-sex model, in which the organs of generation were understood to be quite distinct. That is, they gave up the ancient idea that the vagina was in effect an unborn penis and grasped that what they had thought were the woman's undescended testicles were in fact something quite different, something they called ovaries.[74]

Thus, the emergence of procreative heteronormativity is not a millennia-old phenomenon but a thoroughly modern one in which the genders were articulated as different in kind, each with their own normative social and sexual roles. *Onania* thus successfully combined a historic religious and moral opposition to masturbation with misguided medical practice and scientificity, a heteronormative formula that would endure for generations.[75]

Onania had multiple American editions that were influential in the United States and imitated by many local authors.[76] Its line of argumentation was echoed by American founding father Benjamin Rush, who suggested "a vegetable diet, temperance, bodily labor, cold baths, avoidance of obscenity, music, a close study of mathematics, military glory, and, if all else failed, castor oil" to ward off masturbation.[77] The nineteenth and early twentieth centuries were filled with American physicians in the so-called "social hygiene movement" continuously inventing new ways to diagnose and temper the conditions that tempted people to masturbate, ranging from diets to devices.[78] These diets most notably included Sylvester Graham's famous crackers and J. H. Kellogg's cereal. Kellogg advocated not only serving his cold and bland cereal but also bandaging genitals and tying children's hands to their bedposts at night.[79] Other techniques included the use of straitjackets; wrapping children in cold, wet sheets at night; applying leeches to genitals; burning genital tissue with an iron; castration; and clitoridectomy. Technologies included genital cages, metal mittens, rings of metal spikes to cover the penis and stab it if it became erect, and metal vulva guards.[80] As Amy Wilkins, a professor of sociology at the University of Colorado–Boulder has noted in her interview for *New York Magazine*, this discourse tethers masculine identity to an ethic of self-control that actually reinforces heteronormativity—certain (heterosexual) desires are articulated as natural impulses in need of control through rigidly policed gender norms.[81] #NoFap needs to be understood in light of this. The men who predominate in its online discourse are participating in a form of masculinity tethered to self-control and traditional heteronormative biases.

In his 1904 book *Adolescence*, which is frequently cited as the origin of adolescent psychology as a field of scientific research, G. Stanley Hall examines the research supporting the argument that "self-abuse [i.e., mas-turbation] itself can be the cause of a distinct type of insanity"—namely, *sex perversion*.[82] Despite his other contributions to the field, Hall brought many of his heteronormative biases to bear on adolescent psychology and established them at the foundation of the field.[83] The strength of this dis-course is nowhere felt more strongly than in the *Boy Scout Handbook*, whose 1910 edition argued that "for an instructor to let his boys walk on this exceedingly thin ice without giving them a warning word owing to some prudish sentimentality, would be little short of a crime."[84] While psycholo-gists like Magnus Hirschfeld and Wilhelm Stekel would publish arguments that masturbation had no scientifically demonstrable negative effects on health in 1917, it wasn't until the late 1940s and 1950s that researchers like Virginia Johnson, William Masters, and Alfred Kinsey began in earnest to normalize masturbation, and scientific consensus wasn't reached until the 1970s. However, as Laqueur demonstrates, even after scientific consen-sus was reached, anti-masturbation sentiments flourished and continue to permeate our society through jokes and shame felt about masturbation, as well as in religious discourse. Tellingly, when asked about a leading propo-nent of the NoFap movement, Laqueur responded via email, "This guy is straight out of nineteenth century America. It warms a historian's heart."[85]

In his astute overview of the NoFap movement, Jesse Singal argues that NoFap offers "a version of anti-masturbation worries that has been tailored for an age in which *productivity* is the sort of buzzword that *piety* and *purity* were back when this panic first emerged."[86] This twenty-first-century anti-masturbation sentiment is fundamentally structured by an ambivalence about technology—and online pornography in particular. On the one hand, Rob-ert Weiss has argued that "the [NoFap] movement is less about not mas-turbating than it is about not engaging with 'sexnology' to the exclusion of in-the-flesh intimate encounters. In other words, these young men are rebelling against tech-sex; they are stepping away from their laptops and into the real world."[87] From this perspective, and following Singal, we can understand the NoFap movement as having a deep anxiety about nonpro-ductive sex, where productive sex might be read through either of the two historic heteronormative lenses of procreative sex or heterosexual inter-course to alleviate the biological impetus toward pleasure and sexual release. On the other hand, Sarah Sharma has critiqued the manosphere's emphasis on using technology for a *sexodus* in which feminist critiques and demands can be ignored because sex robots, toys, and pornography now prevent women from withholding sexual gratification from frustrated men—which to many in the manosphere is the only reason feminist demands might otherwise be negotiable.[88]

From this perspective, we can understand the NoFap movement as highly invested in sexual conservatism and particularly the maintenance of traditional gender roles, as well as technocapitalism. Here productivity might imply the felt urgency to continually press onward with the development of technology in a hypermasculine competitive marketplace without ever pausing to reflect, exercise hindsight, or invest time and energy into addressing feminist concerns. Why waste time learning how to make yourself and the world more inviting to women when you can build a robot sex slave? #NoFappers are not anti-orgasm, but they generally are decidedly anti-feminist.

PROUD BOYS

The violent ends of a movement toward an anti-pornography and anti-masturbation ethic can be more clearly seen in the case of the Proud Boys. The group began in the fall of 2016 when *VICE* magazine cofounder and libertarian provocateur Gavin McInnes and a group of fans gathered in a bar to laugh at videos about the Uhuru Solidarity Movement, which seeks to offer white reparations to African people, and to sing the song "Proud of Your Boy" from the Broadway adaptation of the Disney animated film *Aladdin*.[89] McInnes repeatedly articulates the Proud Boys as a fraternal social and drinking club open to any men, regardless of race or sexuality, willing to openly declare their commitment to what he calls "Western chauvinism."[90] While the term "Western chauvinism" is not clearly defined in the majority of Proud Boys materials, it is generally tied to a commitment to Western modernity and conservation of its values. These values center on a number of tenets:

- Minimal Government
- Maximum Freedom
- Anti-Political Correctness
- Anti-Drug War
- Closed Borders
- Anti-Racial Guilt
- Anti-Racism

- Pro-Free Speech (1st Amendment)
- Pro-Gun Rights (2nd Amendment)
- Glorifying the Entrepreneur
- Venerating the Housewife
- Reinstating a Spirit of Western Chauvinism[91]

All one has to do to join the Proud Boys is publicly declare one's Western chauvinism. By forgoing anonymity and facing the consequences of taking this stance, one achieves the "First Degree" of Proud Boydom.[92] This entry into Proud Boydom is often accompanied by the purchase of a black and gold Fred Perry polo shirt, which is the unofficial uniform of the Proud Boys.[93]

Simon Houpt, of Canada's *The Globe and Mail*, described McInnes's beliefs as "libertarian politics, *Father Knows Best* gender roles, closed borders, Islamophobia and something he calls 'Western chauvinism.'"[94] It was this combination of beliefs and the actions that they encouraged among Proud Boys that led the Southern Poverty Law Center to label the Proud Boys a hate group in 2018 and Canada to label them a terrorist group in 2021.[95] Proud Boy forums and online social networks were rife with white nationalist memes that, while they clash with the official positioning of the group, are in line with the alliances it has built and its affiliated media outlets. McInnes has published on hate sites like VDare.com and American Renaissance and in far-right publications like *Taki's Magazine*. He has made a series of racist, transphobic, and misogynistic statements in these media outlets and interviews for more mainstream publications.[96] For example, in 2003, McInnes told the *New York Times*, "I love being white and I think it's something to be very proud of. . . . I don't want our culture diluted. We need to close the borders now and let everyone assimilate to a Western, white, English-speaking way of life."[97] The ability to make these sorts of offensive statements itself is gendered and sexualized because it is associated with masculine potency, capacity to satisfy a sexual partner, and maintenance of "alpha" status. Conservatives who refuse to do so are referred to as *cuckservatives*, a term McInnes draws from Matt Forney's article for Return of Kings that associates such conservatives with cuckolds, men whose wives seek sexual gratification outside of marriage, often with racially othered male partners.[98] For McInnes, real conservatives would be better served by abandoning politically correct culture: "We keep clamoring for the youth vote, and the woman vote, and the minority vote when if we just accepted the dad vote we'd be fine."[99]

McInnes's commitments to heteronormativity are rendered even more transparent in light of his violent transphobia. In an article titled "Transphobia Is Perfectly Natural," McInnes wrote, "Womanhood is not on a shelf next to wigs and makeup. Similarly, being a dude is quite involved. Ripping your vaginal canal out of your fly doesn't mean you are going to start inventing shit and knowing how cement works. Being a man is awesome. So is being

a woman. We should revere these creations, not revel in their bastardiza-
tion."[100] He has similarly argued that transgender people are "mentally ill
gays" and has referred to them as "gender n★★★★★s" and "stupid lunatics."[101]
Though he argues that his transphobia is located in a respect for traditional
womanhood, McInnes is also an avowed anti-feminist and at times open sexist. On his YouTube show, McInnes has noted, "Maybe the reason I'm sexist
is because women are dumb. No, I'm just kidding, ladies. But you do tend
to not thrive in certain areas—like writing."[102] The Proud Boys use their
pro-Western posture to position themselves as promoting "Western values"
without ever acknowledging their perpetuation of the worst "Western" prejudices and intolerances around race, gender, and sexuality.

While the First Degree of Proud Boydom simply involves a public commitment to this ideology, the subsequent degrees involve taking concrete
actions. The Second Degree of Proud Boydom is twofold. First, members
must name five breakfast cereals while getting physically assaulted by at least
five men. According to McInnes, this serves as an exercise in "adrenaline
control" that comes in useful during both physical and verbal altercations.
Proud Boys need to maintain their composure at all times. This test also
works toward bonding and building camaraderie among Proud Boys.[103] Second, Proud Boys must commit to only watching pornography and masturbating once every thirty days, and when they do so, it can only be within one
yard of a woman and with her explicit consent. As McInnes notes, "[M]ost
Proud Boys will cite #NoWanks as what's improved their life the most. It
gets young men off the couch and talking to women and it gets married men
away from their computers and back into bed with their significant other."[104]
Interestingly, "Gay Proud Boys are exempt from #NoWanks because they
are doing just fine for intercourse."[105] This paradox is likely due to the Proud
Boys' emphasis on marriage and procreation as the ultimate goals for its
members.

The Proud Boys reproduce all of the same historically heteronormative
dimensions of anti-masturbation culture outlined previously in relation to
the NoFap movement, like the reification of binarized gender roles and thus
heterosexual normativity, the procreative ethic, a presumed entitlement
to access to women's bodies for sex, and an ambivalence about sexnology
that plays out poorly for women either way. However, the discourse of
self-control and its relation to heteronormativity is particularly important
in the case of the Proud Boys. This discourse has traditionally been used

to demonstrate the moral superiority and civilizational advancement of the white, heterosexual bourgeoisie and subsequently to justify the regulation and policing of sex by this same class of individuals. Time and again this rhetoric has been used to discriminate against and police people of color (POC) for deviations from heteronormativity.[106] This legacy manifests in the Proud Boys' tethering of sexual self-control to their commitment to "Western chauvinism," a combination that is amplified by collectivized policing mechanisms. As Wilkins has noted, similarly to historically Christian abstinence practices, the Proud Boys require "accountability partners" and their forums offer an opportunity to share stories of the struggle to control one's desire. In an interview with *New York Magazine*, she notes, "In this way they created a group culture of self-control that A) proved they were all red-blooded heterosexual young men and B) made sexuality central to their identities even when they weren't doing it."[107]

By collectively articulating their (predominantly heteronormative) sexuality in public and within the confines of an ideology that requires a commitment to sexual norms for membership and group approval, the Proud Boys have implicitly tethered heteronormativity to group identity. As Wilkins notes, "If one has to think about letting down the 'boys' every time he wants to jerk off, his association with his own, private sexuality becomes public, and twinned directly to a political ideology. There is no space between his body and the political apparatus that governs it."[108] A racialized heteronormativity thus becomes ingrained in Proud Boys' comportment toward their own bodies and private sexuality by the threat of social ostracization and community policing mechanisms.

Proud Boys can reach the Third Degree by getting a tattoo that reads "Proud Boy." The Fourth Degree, which was added later, requires a Proud Boy to have "endured a major conflict related to the cause."[109] According to McInnes, the Fourth Degree is not meant to encourage members to seek out physical confrontations with their enemies but is instead reserved for Proud Boys forced to defend themselves. He writes, "We don't start fights, we finish them. 4th degree is a consolation prize for being thrust into a shitty situation and surviving."[110] This latter clarification came alongside a number of initiatives to distance the Proud Boys from the alt-right after white supremacist and Proud Boy member Jason Kessler organized the infamous Unite the Right rally in Charlottesville, Virginia, in August 2017 that led to a number of skirmishes and the vehicular assault of many counterprotesters and murder of Heather Heyer by an alt-right extremist. Shortly after the Unite the Right rally, McInnes wrote a piece for *Proud Boy Magazine* in which he argued that the alt-right was trying to infiltrate the Proud Boys and frame them for crimes by wearing their shirts while doing terrible things in public. He then laid out some rules for how members might identify and excise members of the alt-right from the Proud Boy organization.[111]

Despite McInnes's attempts to distance his organization from the alt-right, the FBI identified members of the Proud Boys as extremist threats in the fall of 2018 and began warning local law enforcement agencies of their attempts to actively recruit members and their role in the escalation of violence at political rallies in Charlottesville, Portland, and Seattle.[112] That fall the Proud Boys also saw themselves banned from social media platforms like Facebook and Twitter and banned from using PayPal. Two days after the FBI's extremist group designation was made public, McInnes publicly quit the Proud Boys, though he claimed his actions were due to his lawyers advising him that his quitting could lessen the sentence of the "NYC nine," a group of Proud Boys then undergoing trial for fighting protesters in New York City.[113] Since then, McInnes has been banned from Amazon, PayPal, Twitter, Facebook, and YouTube.[114] Despite claiming to step down, he still maintains strong connections to the movement and participates in mobilizing it for extremist demonstrations, most notably the insurrection at the US Capitol Building in 2021. The Proud Boys may be the strongest of these movements in the manosphere at the time of writing after being specifically referenced by Donald Trump in the 2020 presidential debates, where they heard Trump tell them to "stand by" during the election.[115]

INCELS

The official incel wiki describes an incel as "someone who is or would be romantically and/or sexually rejected by the vast majority of the single members of the gender they are attracted to while approaching at random in spaces socially designated for dating, for at least a few years."[116] Hence the term *incel*, which is a shortened version of "involuntarily celibate." According to incel orthodoxy, inceldom is not a belief system, label, or ideology but instead a matter of fact, a phenomenon that occurs in both human society and the animal kingdom.[117] While their official wiki acknowledges that prejudice is widespread across incel forums, the wiki works to position this prejudice as nonessential to inceldom. The community makes widespread use of surveys of their forum users that show that only between 28 and 50 percent of the incel community is white—the largest minority population being what they refer to as (male) *currycels*, or incels whose ethnic background lies in the Indian subcontinent.[118]

Incels can trace a long genealogy for their community. In 1987, Brian Gilmartin published *Shyness & Love*, in which he argued that "love-shyness" ought to be treated as a medical condition—a term that he would use interchangeably with incel later in life.[119] Incels were active on the early internet in the alt.support.shyness newsgroup started in 1988 and the alt.seduction. fast newsgroup started in 1994, though the common term at the time was "socially anxious men," a term more accurate in part because it captures the male-centeredness of inceldom.[120] The term "incel" first entered popular usage in 1997 and achieved legitimacy through Denise Donnelly's 2001 academic study of involuntary celibacy published in the *Journal of Sex Research*.[121] The intervening years have seen the incel community flourish online, taking shape within a number of internet forums, including incels.co, r/Braincels on Reddit, Incelistan on Facebook, Incelistan.net, love-shy.com, and the forums Incelswithouthate and Foreveralone on the official incel wiki.[122]

Over these two decades, the incel community has also shifted from being an inclusive and somewhat woke support group to a set of frustrated men blaming women for their lack of access to women's bodies and calling for acts of extreme violence.[123] On May 23, 2014, Elliot Rodger, a self-identified incel, murdered six people and injured fourteen others outside a sorority house in Isla Vista, California, leaving behind a manifesto describing his involuntary celibacy and his desire for revenge after being rejected by women.[124] Rodger's acts were a direct inspiration to other frustrated men in the manosphere who have committed similar crimes and was cited in the murder of nine people and injury of eight at the Umpqua Community College in Roseburg, Oregon; the murder of two people in Aztec, New Mexico; the murder of seventeen people and injury of seventeen others at Stoneman Douglas High School in Parkland, Florida; the murder of ten people and injury of fourteen others in a vehicle-ramming attack in Toronto, Ontario; and the murder of two and injury of four at a hot yoga studio in Tallahassee, Florida.[125]

The incel community is notoriously and intentionally difficult to parse because of their use of *incelese*—their official glossary boasts over three hundred neologisms coined by the incel community. For instance, inceldom actually exists on a spectrum ranging from *nearcels*—who have some attributes of the incel but are also somewhat normal and may have dated in the past in between long dry spells—to tr*uecels*—who have "never even touched someone of the opposite sex," with incels serving as the intermediate step between the two.[126] Perhaps the most important neologism within inceldom is *blackpill*. This term is an incel-specific take on the familiar alt-right discourse on redpilling, drawn from the scene in the movie *The Matrix* where Neo is offered a choice between a blue pill that will let him wake up and forget all the events of the film or a red pill that will open his eyes to the world in its true form. While the red pill offers a call to action by presenting the vision of an ugly world that can be saved, the black pill offers only an awakening to the sexual dystopia of the modern world and at best some coping mechanisms and group solidarity.

While incels will sometimes attempt to discursively position the blackpill as being gender-neutral, it is without a doubt a masculine perspective of an inaccessible sexual marketplace. The blackpill consists of five essential truths:

1.   Looks are necessary to the formation of physical or romantic desire
2.   Looks are not distributed evenly among men
3.   Looks are not subjective
4.   "The Dualistic Mating Strategy"
5.   Hypergamy

The first truth describes a world in which women establish a minimum level of attractiveness for potential "mates" that they will then proceed to lie about and diminish the importance of. The second and third truths note that some men are disadvantaged by the uneven distribution of objective attractiveness across the population. The fourth truth largely positions incels as potential cuckolds that will be selected to raise the children of other men after women have lost the ability to cycle through more attractive partners—thus gaining "access to their genes." The fifth truth is that women are inclined to "trade up" for better men, and this tendency is catalyzed by a society with liberated women and sexuality.[127]

In their reading of A. J. Bateman's principles from evolutionary biology, incels argue that this hypergamy is understood as a biologically determined aspect of all females in the animal kingdom. Bateman derived his famous principles from a study of fruit fly mating in 1948 that for fifty years served as a touchstone for evolutionary biology.[128] His findings were basically that males are biologically driven to mate with as many females as possible, whereas females are biologically driven to be highly selective in their choices of mates—findings that he explicitly predicted would apply to humans.[129] For many years thereafter, evolutionary biologists faced what might be described as a confirmation bias as they took to the field looking for male animals exerting a lot of time and energy trying to mate with evasive and highly selective females. Inceldom's application of Bateman's principle is problematic for a number of reasons. First, recent empirical studies have failed to reproduce Bateman's experimental results.[130] Second, modern empirical data, like the results of DNA testing, produce results that are in conflict with Bateman's principle and often show female animals mating with multiple partners during a single mating season.[131] Third, mathematical models have demonstrated that intense competition for mates among one sex does not necessarily cause the opposite sex to increase their selectiveness.[132] And, finally, animals with higher intelligence, like primates, who can manipulate their social environments and/or reproductive physiology are marked by "female behavior and physiology (e.g. social strategizing, sexual solicitation or rejection, sexual advertisement or concealed ovulation, multiple mating, and reproductive failure)" that challenges Bateman's principle.[133] Sarah Blaffer Hrdy famously showed that female primates gained material benefits from mating with multiple partners, such as reduced risk of infanticide and increased assurance of fertilization.[134]

Humans in particular engage in all sorts of behaviors that make the application of Bateman's principles difficult and can lead to high variability across the species based on local contexts.[135] As Stevan J. Arnold has noted, evolutionary biologists have been too quick to assume that Bateman's principles can be universalized to all animals.[136] Perhaps the biggest complicating factor is that Bateman's principles apply exclusively to reproductive sexual behaviors—Bateman himself did not even analyze sexual encounters between fruit flies that did not produce offspring. The social scripts and strategies for nonreproductive sex are much more complicated than Bateman's principles might model, as sexual selection is not constrained by the time investment and difficulty of producing ova or rearing children. Regardless, incels leverage Bateman to commiserate with one another over their lack of access to women's bodies. Incels mourn their lack of access to women's bodies for sex writ large, not just reproductive sex, and thus are closer to Roosh's pickup artists than to Proud Boys.

The blackpill thus uses, at best, a reductive reading of scientific evidence to articulate a biologically determined sexual dystopia for men. It manages to combine the paradoxical pillars of heteronormativity, reproductive sex, and biological sex drives by mapping questionable research into reproductive sexual strategies from evolutionary biology onto a heterosexual libidinal economy, thus, even when women are not seeking to reproduce, their sexual selection is understood as being motivated by a biologically determined drive toward coyness, withholding sex, and cuckoldry. In this way, it reifies heteronormativity by grounding all sexual strategies within the evolutionary biology of reproduction. The blackpill philosophy is intended to awaken incels to the fact that "there's no personal solution to systematic dating problems for men and only societal hardship (such as mass poverty) can solve men's systemic dating issues."[137] In its least problematic interpretation, this fundamental truth is meant to protect incels from falling victim to "self-improvement" discourses, thus saving them the time, energy, and disappointment that would result from trying to improve their attractiveness to women. However, as we've seen, many men do not respond to the blackpill as an awakening to an unchangeable world and instead are driven to acts of mass murder that specifically target women to seek revenge on them for withholding sex from "unattractive" men.

FROM THE MANOSPHERE TO EVANGELICAL ANTI-PORN CRUSADERS
The extended analyses of these myriad movements in the manosphere demonstrate that despite their heterogeneity, in many instances, they all share a deep commitment to normative and biologically essentialized gender roles, heteronormative sexuality, and a tendency to lean on the rhetoric of science to produce pseudoscientific arguments about gender and sexuality. In the next chapter, I will show how a lot of these same comportments can be found among the male coders and executives in Silicon Valley, who often make eerily similar arguments as these online extremists, even if they prefer to site tamer and more publicly accessible intermediaries like the pop psychologist Jordan Peterson. Below, I would like to demonstrate how these same comportments are also frequently reproduced among evangelical conservatives who are crusading against online pornography. While an exhaustive analysis of these actors is outside the purview of this chapter, I will examine the case of Morality in Media, now rebranded as the National Center on Sexual Exploitation, in great detail. NCOSE is illuminating because it bridges the

gap between earlier Christian conservative anti-porn activism and today's form, as Morality in Media was founded in the 1970s, remained rather active through the decades, and through its rebranding has morphed into the most visible and successful Christian conservative crusader against porn. NCOSE is also particularly interesting for our case because it demonstrates a blend of alt-right arguments, woke Leftist arguments, pseudoscientific takes on scientific research, and traditional evangelical conservative positions on gender and sexuality. NCOSE thus perfectly demonstrates how crusades against pornography make for unlikely bedfellows.

THE NEO-CHRISTIAN CONSERVATIVE ANTI-PORN MOVEMENT

The popular narrative that conservatives have given up on regulating porn is a myth. Over the past twenty years, the proliferation of cyberporn has been coupled with the continued growth of preexisting and the emergence of new anti-porn grassroots campaigns, such Morality in Media/NCOSE, Pure Desires Ministries, the American Family Association, the National Law Center for Children and Families, the Family Research Council, the National Coalition for the Protection of Children and Families, Enough Is Enough, People Not Porn, Fight the New Drug, Truth About Porn, Your Brain on Porn, Culture Reframed, and the Fortify Program. While each of these groups differ in scale, effectiveness, and the depth of their explicit connections to Christian churches; they all commit to publicizing anti-pornography research and argumentation that draws on the language of addiction and argues for strong negative biological and psychological impacts of pornography use; they all frame their intervention through rhetorical appeals to the unwanted exposure of children to pornography and maintaining the sanctity of the family; they all call for heightened regulation of pornography and censorship of obscenity.

To my eye, Morality in Media—now NCOSE—has emerged at the forefront of the traditional conservative anti-porn movement in the United States. NCOSE has by far the most robust and sophisticated web presence of any of these groups, producing annual progress reports, sophisticated white papers, how-to guides for citizens to get involved and parents to better control their children's internet access and achieving headlines by being mentioned in media outlets like the *Today Show*, CNN News, the *New York Times*, BBC News, *USA Today*, and Fox News.[138] Their visibility is likely due to the inflammatory rhetoric that they use and their intentional blurring of the lines between pornography, prostitution, and sex trafficking, which together make for sensational headlines and easy click-bait on the web.

To get an overview of their take on pornography, one needs only look at their 2017 white paper, *Pornography & Public Health: Research Summary*, in which they describe pornography as "a social toxin that destroys relationships, steals innocence, erodes compassion, breeds violence, and kills love."[139] Their key argument is that pornography has become so ubiquitous that children are getting exposed to it at younger ages, that its pervasive use leads to addiction, that it negatively impacts women (they repeatedly leverage feminist rhetoric when useful), that its ubiquity infringes on individual rights by making it impossible to live a porn-free life, that private use of pornography has public consequences, that the combination of these last two facts means that it is unmanageable at the individual level and requires state regulation, and finally, that "pornography is prostitution for mass consumption."[140]

As is common in many of their reports, NCOSE loosely and reductively stitches together disparate academic research to draw their predetermined conclusions about pornography. As they note,

> While independently these studies do not prove that pornography *causes* harm, taken in totality, the converging evidence overwhelmingly suggests that pornography is correlated with a broad array of harms that adversely impact the public health of the nation. These include higher incidence of STIs, increased verbal and physical sexual aggression, acceptance of rape myths, risky sexual behaviors among adolescents, reduced impulse control and reckless decision making, increased sexual dysfunction, and more.[141]

It is worth noting that many of the studies they cite take place in cultural contexts outside the United States and have not been repeatedly verified by independent researchers. They are often preliminary results that are being read as objective facts and stitched together to make a leap toward totalization. This is not to say that none of their points are valid or in need of further research but only to bring these issues back into question rather than establishing them as axiomatic for all valid perspectives on pornography use. That said, it would take an entire book to rebut each of the claims that NCOSE makes about pornography, and here we might be best served by restricting ourselves to examining in more detail some of the more heteronormative claims that they establish at the foundation of their anti-pornography platform.

This platform mixes all of the familiar conservative tropes about protecting children, preserving the family, and combating sexual deviance with more contemporary feminist critiques of pornography, a legacy of the alliance between the Moral Majority and feminist porn critics from the twentieth century. The report argues that pornography harms children's brains, renders them more susceptible to addictions of all kinds as adults, weakens their emotional bonds with their parents, makes them more likely to engage in risky sexual behaviors, increases their chances of reporting being victims of physical and sexual violence, makes them more likely to commit crimes, lessens their sexual satisfaction, makes them more likely to have sex with younger adolescents, and increases their sexual uncertainty and casual sexual exploration.[142]

Much of the research supporting these arguments is up for debate, hasn't been reproduced across multiple studies, and often took place in contexts outside the United States. Beyond this, though, we can see a heteronormative perspective entrenched in the alignment of research. Sex is understood as a private and adult act that ought to be controlled and subsumed under structures like marital procreation or loving monogamous relationships. The core concern is deviation from heteronormativity. As the report notes, "More frequent use of sexually explicit Internet materials is shown to foster greater sexual uncertainty in the formation of sexual beliefs and values, as well as a shift away from sexual permissiveness with affection to attitudes supportive of uncommitted sexual exploration."[143] The development of a freer and more fluid sexuality is to be combated at all costs, as can be seen in the connections it draws to biological dysfunction, psychological trauma, and association with criminality—though even conservative media outlets like Reason have reported the factual inaccuracy of these links, particularly to crime, which has gone down in a near causal relation with the rise of online pornography.[144]

We can also see this entrenched heteronormativity in the emphasis on preserving the nuclear family. As the study notes under the heading "Risky Behaviors and Other Harms," "For males, increased pornography use is correlated with more sex partners, [. . .] greater acceptance of sex outside of marriage for married individuals, greater acceptance of sex before marriage, and less child centeredness during marriage."[145] It further correlates pornography use to paying for sex, increased casual sexual encounters, increased sexually transmitted infections (STIs), less condom use, earlier sexual debuts, increased relationship breakups, higher divorce rates, and riskier sexual practices.[146] Perhaps most tellingly, the report argues that marriage formation brings demographic and socioeconomic improvements to society, and that "pornography has been shown to significantly negatively impact marriage formation, and in light robust controls, the effect is likely causal."[147] The report thus reflects the standard devil's bargain of heteronormativity in which sex for pleasure is only acceptable within heterosexual, monogamous, amorous relationships, and, when this is pressed, the norm paradoxically reverts to procreative sex. Pornography is thus a social evil because it encourages libertinism and fuels sexual exploration and expressivity outside of the confines of heteronormative social scripts.

Ironically, despite feminism's well-established critiques of the nuclear family and an existence centered on child-rearing, a discursive alliance has been formed.[148] NCOSE argues that the paraphilic disorders and extreme sex in hard-core pornography teach women to enjoy sexual violence and degradation, instigate sexual offenses and perpetuate rape myths, increase verbal and physical aggression against women, increase female sexual victimization, and fuel the demand for sexual exploitation.[149] The study also notes that pornography leads to negative body images for women and pressure to perform the sex acts depicted in pornography: "As a result of viewing pornography, women reported lowered body image, criticism from their partners regarding their bodies, increased pressure to perform acts seen in pornographic films, and less actual sex."[150] While all of these are valid concerns worthy of further study and potential activism, it is clear that NCOSE has failed to engage any feminist thinkers after the early 1990s—with the possible exception of Gail Dines's radical anti-pornography writings. The report seems totally unaware of the discourse surrounding feminist and LGBTQIA+ pornography, instead understanding pornography as simply consisting of mainstream heteroporn and extremist deviant porn, like child sexual abuse images, incest pornography, zoophilia, coprophilia, urophilia, rape play, and torture.[151] In other words, the report takes a historically and culturally specific genre of pornography as the universal form of any and all possible pornography. It thus fails to recognize that a few dominant porn production companies are responsible for implementing and maintaining the dominant genre of mainstream heteroporn that potentially leads to such negative consequences for women. The report comes close to recognizing this but never follows through on its own insight: "Mainstream commercial pornography has coalesced around a relatively homogeneous script involving violence and female degradation."[152] Subsequently, NCOSE is unable to imagine that pornography could ever be different. This severely limits its analysis and shows that it cannot think of porn outside of heteroporn, perhaps another consequence of its entrenched heteronormative perspective.

The one exception to NCOSE's silence on more contemporary feminist discourse is their uptake of the term *intersectionality*. The term was coined by Black feminist theorist, lawyer, and civil rights activist Kimberlé Crenshaw in 1989 and has achieved public visibility through her 2016 TED Talk, "The Urgency of Intersectionality."[153] For Crenshaw, identity exists at the intersection of various cultural binaries and forms of marginalization. She draws on the experience of Black women to describe intersectionality, showing how Black women face the intersectional marginalization of being *both* marginalized as women *and* as Black people. In a staggering recontextualization of the term, NCOSE uses intersectionality as a foundational principle to interconnect sexual exploitation and abuse. As they explain, "Evidence supports the fact that child sexual abuse, prostitution, pornography, sex trafficking, sexual violence, and more, are not isolated phenomena occurring in a vacuum, but that these and other forms of sexual abuse and exploitation overlap and reinforce one another."[154] By articulating pornography, child sex abuse, prostitution, and sex trafficking as intersections of a singular social phenomenon, NCOSE is able to "promote a comprehensive umbrella of solutions."[155] As we will see in much greater detail in chapters 3 and 4, nowhere has this intersectional approach been more successful and more damaging to sex workers, adult entertainers, sex educators, and LGBTQIA+ content creators than in the 2017 passage of the FOSTA-SESTA act by the US Congress. At this point in time, though, it is worth reviewing some of the other effects that this intersectional and heteronormative approach has had on government and corporate policy in the United States.

NCOSE tends to overstate its impact on policy and regulation and downplay the small size of its funding.[156] For instance, the organization terminated all reported federal lobbying in 2006.[157] Despite this, NCOSE claims to host regular events in the US Capitol Building.[158] For example, in July of 2015, NCOSE held an anti-pornography summit on Capitol Hill titled "Pornography: A Public Health Crisis" that was meant to educate lawmakers on "how porn fuels sex trafficking, child exploitation, and sexual violence."[159] During the summit, NCOSE compared this health crisis to those of lead poisoning, asbestos exposure, smoking, and HIV/AIDS. The impact of these sorts of events is hard to gauge, but in 2012, NCOSE was able to get GOP presidential candidates Mitt Romney, Newt Gingrich, and Rick Santorum to commit on the record to cracking down on pornography, though the sincerity of these commitments was questionable.[160] In 2016, NCOSE saw the Republican National Committee include language from its summit in the official Republican platform for 2016: "The internet must not become a safe haven for predators. Pornography, with its harmful effects, especially on children, has become a public health crisis that is destroying the lives of millions. We encourage states to continue to fight this public menace and pledge our commitment to children's safety and well-being."[161] Between April of 2016 and March of 2018, NCOSE also managed to get draft legislation officially recognizing pornography as a public health concern passed by state legislative bodies in Utah, South Dakota, Tennessee, Arkansas, Louisiana, Virginia, Pennsylvania, and Florida, some even going so far as to describe pornography as a public health crisis.[162] A number of these legislative bodies passed these resolutions with upwards of 80 percent of the votes, sometimes unanimously. The effect has also been particularly noticeable in the military, which stopped all sales of pornography from military commissaries and now offers sex-trafficking training to all military service members "with the issue of pornography explained as a factor driving demand."[163]

NCOSE claims to have directly impacted the corporate policies of major US companies such as Comcast, Google, Walmart, Verizon, Starbucks, and McDonalds. Take Comcast for example, which in 2018 had more than twenty million television subscribers and was pressured to install much stronger parental controls and institute a "Common Sense" rating scheme to allow parents to automatically filter which programming and apps children have access to, including a "Kid's Zone" in which all content is vetted for children under the age of twelve. The company has also buried pornographic channels, blocked their voice remote from searching for pornographic content, and even sanitized the titles and descriptions of adult entertainment offerings to cut down on the unwanted exposure of children to pornography. Further, pornography has been completely removed from their mobile app. Comcast has committed to future meetings with NCOSE and has publicly noted, "We welcome dialogue on how to continually improve on these measures from third-party stakeholders in family safety and digital health, including the National Center on Sexual Exploitation."[164] Or take Google, which, one year after appearing on NCOSE's "Dirty Dozen" list, changed its corporate policy and banned all ads with pornographic content or that link to websites with sexually explicit content and further removed all pornographic and sexually explicit apps from its officially sanctioned Google Play store.[165] The company also agreed to make SafeSearch much more visible by placing it prominently in the upper righthand corner of Google Images.[166]

Even if NCOSE is not directly responsible for the number of government and corporate policy changes that they claim in their literature, the organization is representative of a wider and more powerful discourse on pornography and sexuality. Whether or not they originated the set of rhetorical strategies and arguments that they employ, they capture a common sentiment about and comportment toward sex and sexuality in the twenty-first century. This new discourse has selected the few bits of feminist and queer theory from the past twenty years that support their arguments to dress an old discourse up in new clothes. As we'll see in chapter 3, it is this discourse that has led to the most comprehensive changes in government and corporate policy toward pornography and sexual expression on the internet. It goes without saying that this demonstrates that heteronormativity still has deep roots in contemporary society and is deeply impacting not only the discourse surrounding the internet but also its very infrastructure.

CONCLUSION

Across the board, all of these contemporary anti-porn crusaders share a commitment to traditional gender roles and heteronormativity. They further share a commitment to leveraging pseudoscientific discourse and the rhetoric of protecting children and families to not only make their ideas palatable in the public forum but also to make it difficult for elected officials to be seen publicly opposing their political platforms. As we've seen concretely, the "Pandora's box of porn" myth is at least untrue insofar as anti-porn crusaders have never stopped organizing or acting in the public sphere to achieve increased censorship. The following chapters will further show how this perspective on gender, sexuality, and pornography permeates tech companies—and internet platforms in particular—and how the untamable flow of pornography has been dammed up through content moderation. These automated content filters have become so strong that they routinely overblock material that is not pornographic, including art, sex education,

LGBTQIA+ community discussions and resources, and a random assortment of other nonpornographic content. Further, even where the myth does hold true, for instance on tube sites like Pornhub, the untamable flow of pornography has been channeled into mainstream heteroporn productions, diminishing the heterogeneity of pornography to the point where it has become a rather banal stream of the same limited sex acts described by the same limited keywords. Both of these results of automated content filters are a signal victory for alt-right and Christian conservative activists who are willing to strike a devil's bargain to allow pornography to persist as long as it remains homogeneously heteronormative and who can use the content moderation infrastructure to systematically attack any low-budget or amateur pornographers who are making content that deviates from the heterosexual norm.

STRAIGHT CODE

LENNA AND THE ORIGINAL SIN OF COMPUTER VISION

In 1973, Alexander Sawchuk, the father of the JPEG image file format, was an electrical engineer working in the University of Southern California's Signal and Image Processing Institute (SIPI). Sawchuk was looking for the perfect image to scan to optimize the new image compression algorithms that SIPI was developing. He wanted an image that was glossy, had a complex mix of colors and textures, and one that contained a human face. The engineers at SIPI came across a *Playboy* centerfold of Swedish model Lena Söderberg—her name in the magazine spelled 'Lenna' to encourage its proper pronunciation. Lenna wore a feathered Panama hat, boots, stockings, and a pink boa, which seemed to offer the required image properties for testing their compression algorithms. The SIPI engineers took the top third of the centerfold only so that the image would be sized appropriately to be wrapped around the drum of their Muirhead wirephoto scanner and so that the resulting digital image would be 512px by 512px square. The scanner had custom analog-to-digital converters installed to capture the red, green, and blue channels of the scan in digital code that was then stored on a Hewlett Packard 2100 minicomputer.[1]

Emily Chang has referred to this moment as "tech's original sin."[2] By 1991, SIPI had made their scanned image of Lenna available for free to researchers across the world. It had quickly become the standard for evaluating image compression algorithms and could be frequently seen in the pages of image processing journals, books, and conference papers.[3] As Mar Hicks, historian of technology and author of *Programmed Inequality*, told *WIRED* magazine, "If they hadn't used a *Playboy* centerfold, they almost certainly would have used another picture of a pretty white woman. The *Playboy* thing gets our attention, but really what it's about is this world-building that's gone on in computing from the beginning—it's about building worlds for certain people

Figure 2.1
Lenna's Playboy centerfold scan by SIPI. Retrieved from https://en.wikipedia.org/wiki/File:Lenna_(test_image).png.

and not for others."[4] Hicks's comment captures well a sentiment that seems widespread among women working in computer science and engineering.

In 1997, Sunny Bains, a prominent scientist, tech journalist, and editor of engineering journals, wrote an op-ed for *Electronic Engineering Times* in which she argued that "the Lenna image grates because of its exclusivity. It's not difficult to feel isolated when you're a woman working in a male-dominated field. Seeing provocative images of women in learned journals can add to that feeling of non-inclusion."[5] This feeling has endured over time. In 2015, Maddie Zug published an op-ed in the *Washington Post* arguing that the use of the image in computer science curriculum led to sexual comments from male classmates and indicated a broader cultural problem that is at least partly responsible for the depressed numbers of women working in advanced computer science labs.[6] In 2013, Deanna Needell and Rachel Ward published a paper in which they used an image of the Italian-American model Fabio in place of Lenna for image compression research in hopes of motivating their field to reconsider the use of Lenna.[7] Jeff Seideman, an industry leader in image encoding, captured these critiques perfectly in his *defense* of the continued use of the Lenna image, telling the *Atlantic* in 2016 that "when you use a picture like that for so long, it's not a person anymore; it's just pixels."[8]

The use of the Lenna image fits into a long series of literal objectifications of women that have been central to the development of technology, ranging from the metaphorical objectification of the original labor of women computer operators whose function was automated by increasingly sophisticated circuitry to the literal objectification of women ranging from Kodak's use of "Shirley cards" to optimize their film and film processing technologies to the unauthorized use of Suzanne Vega's voice to perfect the sound compression algorithms that led to the MP3.[9] For nearly fifty years, Lenna has served as the benchmark of image-processing quality, shaping everything from the development of image compression formats like JPEG to the operations of smartphone cameras like Apple's iPhone to the operations of image software like Google Images.

The omnipresent use of the Lenna image is indicative of the unvoiced heteronormativity that permeates Silicon Valley. It harkens back to an earlier détente in the war on pornography in which *Playboy* was allowed to publish objectifications of a particular variety of female bodies and increasingly granted public legitimacy, while such open representations of alternative forms of desire—for different shapes, sizes, anatomies, and colors of bodies, perhaps in different contexts, performing different erotic acts, and so on— were denied such legitimacy and public visibility. It is the assumption of banality, the presumption that such an image was by default uncontroversial, that belies its heteronormativity. As I will show throughout this chapter, this "original sin" can be taken as symbolic of the gender and sexuality-based biases that ground the research and development of new technologies, where similar assumptions of banality, of shared norms, and an expected lack of controversy lead to heteronormative hardware and software.

In particular, we'll look at the history of Google's attempts to automate the censorship of "adult" content via its SafeSearch algorithms and image recognition technologies and Facebook's efforts to streamline the human review of content flagged as inappropriate and produce "human algorithms." While this critique is in no way confined to Google or Facebook—and I intend it to speak to the broader discursive community of computer programmers and software engineers, for which I will use the shorthand "coders"—I will draw heavily on case studies from the two companies to demonstrate the practical effects of this permeation of heteronormativity. The chapter considers this implicit heteronormativity from three perspectives: (1) its permeation into the discursive community of coders themselves, (2) its subsequent permeation into the parameters of the algorithms and datasets that currently shape computer vision as a field, and (3) its ongoing maintenance by "human algorithms," the people charged with performing the human labor of reviewing content flagged by the system for violating community standards. Across these three domains, we can see that heteronormative biases have a strong impact on the research, development, implementation, and everyday operation of content moderation algorithms.

THE HETERONORMATIVITY OF CODERS

In her article "Going to Work in Mommy's Basement," Sarah Sharma draws on the common Silicon Valley trope of "beta" coders whose conditions of existence are founded upon taking advantage of the unrecognized and feminized labor of their mommies, a twenty-first-century twist on the devaluation and rendering invisible of feminized reproductive and affective labor. She asks, "What kind of work is done in this 'coder's cave' of antisocial techbro culture? What kind of world gets programmed from a position of uncomplicated safety and abundance?"[10] This best of all possible worlds for male coders is what Emily Chang calls a *brotopia*.[11] In this brotopia, men who often identify as spurned lovers or borderline incels in their youth are finally recognized, courted by large tech companies, put in charge of cutting-edge start-ups, and through their power, prestige, and wealth can finally make up for lost time when it comes to sex. Sarah Banet-Weiser has described this as "toxic geek masculinity" and shown that it is not an isolated phenomenon but is instead undergirded by and connected to the broader cultural context of misogyny and heteronormativity online (examined in chapter 1).[12]

Toxic geeks understand themselves as being the victims of marginalization and alpha-male masculinity. Nathan Ensmenger has shown that the tech bros and toxic geeks referred to here are usually shaped by the historical injury of having been geeks, nerds, and socially awkward in their formative years.[13] As Kristina Bell, Christopher Kampe, and Nicholas Taylor explain, they thus understand themselves through the stereotype of being "weak, easily bullied, and socially awkward males who lack social skills, athletic abilities, and physical attractiveness," with their sole redeeming feature and claim to political, economic, and sexual agency being their "perceived [. . .] mastery over digital technologies."[14] Adrienne Shaw argues that because of this felt sense of victimhood, toxic geeks react hostilely to anyone who calls them out as being the perpetrators of abuses of power themselves. They seem totally incapable of recognizing their own privilege and in response receive feminist critiques as unwarranted attacks, even going so far as to define their identity as anti-feminist.[15] They are thus doubly injured by women, first through sexual rejection and second by feminist critique and women seeking entry into the workplace at technology companies. As Banet-Weiser notes, "This assemblage of features—technological prowess, social awkwardness, and cognitive dissonance about privilege—yields a contradictory subjectivity. According to this frame, geek men have been injured by the world and, more importantly, by women. The aggressive and violent regulation and exclusion of women is a way to regain masculine capacity."[16]

Sue Decker, former president of Yahoo, has used the metaphor of a fish being the last to discover water to describe the ubiquity of gender bias and heteronormative sexual harassment in Silicon Valley.[17] This bears out in what little comprehensive survey data we have from tech companies. Take, for instance, the infamous "Elephant in the Valley" study from 2017, which surveyed women of various ages and ranks that worked in tech companies about their experiences with sexism in the workplace. The study found that 90 percent of women surveyed had experienced sexist behavior at company off-sites or at industry conferences. Further, 60 percent of them had received unwanted sexual advances; most reported these advances were not one-time instances but instead repeated overtures, and more than half came from a superior at their company. A majority of those who reported sexual harassment were dissatisfied with how the company handled their case, and many ended up signing nondisparagement agreements to keep them from going public with their stories. Nearly 40 percent of women who experienced sexual harassment declined to report it for fear it would stunt their career advancement.[18]

This harassment takes place in both the materialized utopias of tech campuses and after work at off-site company events and industry conferences. Tech campuses are built to accommodate frat-like behaviors and to offer all the comforts of "mommy's basement." Most of them offer unlimited free alcohol and games like table tennis and foosball. They regularly keep free high-end food within fifty yards of every employee at all times and offer free dinners for employees who stay after 5 p.m. They contain services on-site ranging from gyms to doctors to hairdressers to laundry to pet care. All of this takes place within open floor plans that make it notably difficult for employees to avoid coworkers who might harass them. In short, their designs skew toward the desires of young, single men. This is perhaps nowhere more visible than in Apple's failure to include a daycare service in its new $5 billion Apple Park campus that opened in 2017.[19] As Emily Chang has found, "Few employers offer stipends for child care, and even fewer provide on-site child care. Sure, you can bring your dog to work, but you are (mostly) on your own with your baby."[20]

Silicon Valley tries to position itself as being on the cutting edge of both technological and sexual experimentation, with strong polyamorous communities and hookup culture buoyed by exclusive company sex parties hosted at private homes. As Chang has found, most of these events skew toward the fantasies of heterosexual men, as they are maintained with higher ratios of women (selected for their appearance) to encourage sexual encounters with tech bros and toxic geeks. While the Valley's progressivism extends to threesomes, these are almost exclusively a man and two women, with gay and bisexual sex acts conspicuously absent from the scene and little pressure on men to engage in this sort of progressive experimentation. In explaining his peers' behavior, Evan Williams, a cofounder of Twitter, has described polyamory as a "hack."[21] Thus, most of the rhetoric surrounding sex in the Valley is simply a convenient means for justifying the voracious and heteronormative sexual appetites of men who are finally able to get access to women's bodies in the ways they dreamed of as deprived adolescents.[22]

The liberation of this "progressive" scene is exclusively male. Women who participate in sexual exploration lose credibility and respect. They also gain a reputation of being open to any and all future advances, anywhere, and at any time. However, not attending has similarly bad consequences, as it can severely limit women's opportunities to network and advance their careers since work gets done at these sex parties.[23] The women at these parties are also kept at arm's length for fear that they might be "founder hounders," the Silicon Valley neologism for gold diggers. The rhetoric surrounding founder hounders is frequently used to justify predatory behavior toward these women, as it presumes that they are similarly engaging in predatory behavior by trying to trap rich men and extract capital from them. In a chilling interview, Chang spoke to an anonymous tech company founder about the rampant use of drugs to "lubricate" sex parties and the potential advantage tech bros were taking of women. He replied that "on the contrary, it's women who are taking advantage of him and his tribe, preying on them for their money."[24]

A culture like this was able to emerge because women's participation in the field significantly diminished leading up to the dot-com boom and tech's resurgence after the dot-com collapse. This was a particularly notable turn-around when it came to the development of software, which was dominated by women for many decades.[25] While in the early 1980s women were earning nearly 40 percent of all computer science degrees in the United States, that number decreased to closer to 20 percent by the time today's platforms were emerging and has remained relatively stable since. At companies like Google and Facebook, from what numbers are publicly available, women account for between 30 and 35 percent of the workforce, but only around 20 percent of the technical jobs.[26] This lack of representation is particularly acute in AI fields, where 80 percent of professors are men, as are 85 to 90 percent of the research staff at Google and Facebook.[27] During their formative years, many such companies employed aptitude tests like the IBM Programmer Aptitude Test and the Cannon-Perry Test that were biased toward the selection of antisocial, combative, and hubristic coders who just so happened to also be predominantly male. These tests included "brain teasers" that asked appli-cants to make wild speculations on the spot backed by some form of logic and calculation, like asking applicants how many windows are in New York City. Google, for instance, did not stop using these sorts of brainteasers until 2013. Its longtime former head of human resources, Laszlo Bock, then admitted to the *New York Times* that "brainteasers are a complete waste of time. . . . They don't predict anything."[28]

While companies began to wake up to this problem in the 2010s, much of their culture, corporate policies, and technological infrastructures had already been determined by largely male coding and legal teams. Companies like Google espoused a commitment to hiring more women early on, but this commitment was often half-hearted, as the company's organizational chart reads more like a soap opera script of interoffice affairs. CEO Eric Schmidt, cofounder Sergey Brin, and Andy Rubin, the lead technician who devel-oped Android, all engaged in relationships with women at the company who were their subordinates, and longtime executive Amit Singhal was given a golden parachute after sexually harassing a woman.[29] Despite this bad cor-porate behavior, the company did strive to implement fairer hiring practices. In 2008, Google established a secret hiring practice in which female appli-cants had their applications submitted to a second review committee called the "Revisit Committee" if the initial hiring committee found them unacceptable. The Revisit Committee was tasked with reviewing the applications of all potential diversity hires. Company policy stipulated that hiring committees remain silent about any interviews they conducted. Google also established a secret policy that all technical candidates' committees contain at least one woman, a practice that put undue burden on women already at the company.[30] This intense secrecy and the measures Google took to correct for bad hiring practices demonstrate a key antagonism within Silicon Valley that persists to this day: the antagonism between the myth of meritocracy and the use of hiring practices meant to combat unconscious bias.

Meritocracy may be the central myth around which Silicon Valley's culture is constructed. The problem with this is that belief in meritocracy most often requires a belief that brilliance is innate, and research shows that these cultural biases lead gatekeepers like teachers and hiring committees to assume that (white) men are more likely to possess innate talent. One university study found that "the extent to which practitioners of a discipline believe that success depends on sheer brilliance is a strong predictor of women's and African American's representation in that discipline."[31] Another empirical study found that "when an organization is explicitly presented as meritocratic, individuals in managerial positions favor a male employee over an equally qualified female employee."[32] The problem with meritocracy is that it doesn't recognize the cultural contexts within which "brilliance" is defined and emerges. In Silicon Valley, brilliance is defined in such a way that it privileges male coders, and the position of privilege from which male coders apply to jobs goes unrecognized in the application process. Even Michael Young, who brought the term into public discourse with his 1958 book *The Rise of Meritocracy*, recognized this problem.[33] He concluded that meritocracy could produce a new social stratification and sense of moral exceptionalism based on who had access to elite education and social networks. Further, meritocracy is always impossible to implement because it first needs to be defined, and the definition of meritocracy is most frequently founded on preferences for certain qualities, aptitudes, demeanors, and skill sets that are primarily available to wealthy white men.

True believers in meritocracy don't see these internal contradictions and instead use meritocracy as a logical explanation for the privilege that they enjoy. It gives them a smugness and overinflated sense of self-worth that can cause them to react violently to what they perceive as "discriminatory affirmative action" policies like the ones Google implemented to hire more women for technical positions. While incurring these violent backlashes may be worth it if diversity hiring actually leads to more equity in the workforce, this doesn't seem to be the case as the number of women in technical positions at technology companies has remained rather stagnant despite the past decade of attempts at fairer hiring practices. Most companies now implement some equivalent of unconscious bias training where they offer employees workshops on how their unconscious biases about race and gender might impact their thinking in the workplace, a new and revised version of earlier attempts at "sensitivity training." There is another problem, however, with how unconscious bias training actually plays out. In attempts to avoid shutting down dialogue by calling employees out on biased behavior, unconscious bias training begins with the premise that everyone has biases, that there is nothing wrong with having biases, and all one is responsible for is curbing them as much as possible. Studies have found that this essentially normalizes gender and racial bias by removing the cultural stigma around it. It can even cause people to accept these biases as unavoidable and make them more likely to exhibit these types of biases in the workplace.[34] Even Anthony Greenwald, the inventor of the Implicit Association Test that helps demonstrate to people the unconscious biases they hold, has expressed concern about unconscious bias training. He told an interviewer, "Understanding implicit bias does not actually provide you with the tools to do something about it."[35]

In short, much of the workforce that is charged with creating the algorithms that govern the internet hold heteronormative biases about gender and sexuality. They often come from a position of privilege, desiring to work from mommy's basement without recognizing the care and benefits that position gives them in the supposed meritocracy they believe themselves to be navigating. Their ideology tends toward the biologization of talent and the belief that brilliance is innate to individual coders. No other explanation could justify the hubris necessary to believe themselves as the ordained arbiters of the future. Further, much of this connects to an understanding of themselves as being ignored by the world, and women in particular, in their adolescence, as they were forced into the position of "betas" or beta males. They have pulled themselves up by their bootstraps and are ready for their just rewards after having proven the world's evaluation of them wrong. Those who disagree with this position are often structurally located in weaker positions in the corporate organizational chart and have little power to challenge the dominant culture of the valley. All of this looks eerily similar to the worldview espoused by the alt-right, particularly their anxieties around gender and sexuality. Nowhere is this clearer than in the case of the Google memo, to which we'll now turn.

JAMES DAMORE'S GOOGLE MEMO

The most infamous instance of the penetration of heteronormativity, misogyny, and contemporary alt-right ideology into Silicon Valley is easily James Damore's Google memo.[36] In 2017, Damore circulated a memo titled "Google's Ideological Echo Chamber: How Bias Clouds Our Thinking about Diversity and Inclusion" internally within the company that was quickly leaked to the press and became a media sensation. The memo is couched within the framework of human biodiversity, a hobby horse often used by alt-right writers to leverage the authority of scientific objectivity to support their arguments but which tends to produce politically motivated pseudo-scientific arguments. Damore begins the memo by writing, "I value diversity and inclusion, am not denying that sexism exists, and don't endorse using stereotypes. When addressing the gap in representation in the population, we need to look at population level differences in distributions."[37] According to Damore, men and women—N.B., he exclusively uses these terms cisnormatively—differ biologically at the statistical level of population. These differences include

- women being more open to feelings and aesthetics than ideas,
- women having a stronger interest in people than objects,
- women expressing extroversion through gregariousness rather than assertiveness, and
- women being more susceptible to "neuroticism," including having higher anxiety and lower stress tolerance.

For Damore, these differences explain the distribution of men and women into different professions, the gender pay gap, and the retention problem that tech companies have with female employees.

Damore is careful to note that while these biological differences hold at the population level, they do not map directly onto individual men and women. He further outlines some potentially useful "non-discriminatory ways to reduce the gender gap," such as making software engineering more people-oriented through pair programming and collaboration initiatives, making tech and leadership roles less stressful, and better facilitating work-life balance through options like part-time work. However, Damore's memo is more famous for its other suggestions that echo familiar cries of "reverse racism." Damore argues that it is discriminatory to foster diversity through

- diversity initiatives that offer programs, mentoring, and classes exclusively for women;
- using high priority queues and secondary reviews for female applicants;
- applying advanced scrutiny to groups of people not sufficiently diverse; and
- setting organizational-level objectives and key results for increased representation.

He follows these arguments with suggestions that Google de-moralize diversity, stop alienating conservatives, de-emphasize empathy ("being emotionally unengaged helps us better reason about the facts"), punish intentional sexism rather than unintentional transgressions and microaggressions (he argues here that there is no evidence that speech constitutes violence), be more open about the science of human biodiversity (e.g., IQ and anatomical sex differences), and reconsider making unconscious bias training mandatory for promotion committees, among other things.[38]

Damore describes Google as an "ideological echo chamber" with "extreme" and "authoritarian" elements. He argues that Google—and here he is referring specifically to the midlevel managerial and public relations teams instituting diversity initiatives—is "extreme" in its belief that representational disparities are due to structural injustice. Google is "authoritarian" because it engages in "discrimination"—or what critics like Damore often refer to as "reverse discrimination"—when it tries to institute policies to correct for structural injustice.[39] He understands Google as a "silent, psychologically unsafe environment" that has been invaded by the culture of "PC-authoritarians" (i.e., politically correct authoritarians).[40] Damore noted that he had received "many" messages from supporters within the company who thanked him for raising these issues and who noted that they would have been too afraid to speak out within the company.[41] Thus, Damore understood himself to be standing up for the voiceless inside the company and as taking an acknowledged risk in circulating the memo. Screenshots of

Google's internal message boards, interviews with employees, and an informal Twitter poll all showed that a significant number of Google employees agreed with the contents of Damore's memo.[42] At one point, the document was inaccessible because so many employees were attempting to view it concurrently.[43]

Many women who have worked or currently work for Google have spoken out since the memo to argue that Damore's ideas are endemic to the company. Kelly Ellis, a former Google employee who reported being sexually harassed at the company in 2015, noted that this rhetoric was common at Google, not just among coders but also among those doing performance reviews and on hiring committees.[44] She told *WIRED* that "Those guys like to pretend they're silenced and afraid, but they're not."[45] Another Google employee noted that the response to the memo inside Google was highly gendered, with men being much more likely to agree with Damore and see him as brave for speaking out.[46] A third Google employee noted of the memo, "It's not worth thinking about this as an isolated incident and instead a manifestation of what ails all of Silicon Valley."[47] Megan Smith, a former vice president at Google who also served as chief technology officer for the United States under Barack Obama, similarly noted that these perspectives are common across Silicon Valley and permeate its culture.[48]

If one were inclined to take this evidence as anecdotal, one could look to the 2017 lawsuit in which the US Department of Labor sued Google for the release of decades of employment data in an effort to combat gender bias within the company.[49] Janette Wipper, a Department of Labor regional director, testified in court that "we found systemic compensation disparities against women pretty much across the entire workforce."[50] Janet Herold, the regional solicitor for the Department of Labor, further noted, "The government's analysis at this point indicates that discrimination against women in Google is quite extreme, even in this industry."[51] The lawsuit against Google, in addition to a handful of other Department of Labor suits against Silicon Valley tech companies, was grounded on the fact that these companies were federal contractors.

Two months after they were filed, President Trump signed an executive order that effectively rolled back Obama-era protections for female workers.[52] It is worth noting that as of 2019, the Department of Labor has lost its lawsuit suing for the requisite data to demonstrate a long-term trend of gender bias within Google.[53] While this story was largely passed over silently in the press, Trump's executive order is reflective of repeated libertarian arguments that the gender pay gap is a myth and alt-right arguments that any gender pay gap is due to human biodiversity rather than cultural bias and structural injustice. Google made similar claims that it had closed the gender pay gap at all levels across the entire company when it refused to hand over the additional data that the Department of Labor requested. Thus, the context within which Damore wrote was one in which a number of female Google employees at both junior and senior levels were accusing the company of frequently harboring similar sexist beliefs and in which the best data available to the Department of Labor led them to believe there was a systemic gender pay gap across the entire company.

Damore was fired shortly after the memo was leaked—although a Harvard-Harris poll would show that 55 percent of surveyed voters said that Google was wrong to fire Damore.[54] In his op-ed for the *Wall Street Journal*, Damore described Google as seeking to placate the outraged mob that resulted from his memo being leaked. He wrote, "The mob would have set upon anyone who openly agreed with me or even tolerated my views."[55] Key Google executives and other Silicon Valley elites voiced their condemnation of the memo, including Danielle Brown, Google's VP of diversity; Sundar Pichai, Google's CEO; Sheryl Sandberg, COO of Facebook; Susan Wojcicki, CEO of YouTube; and Megan Smith, a former Google VP. However, even Pichai, the ultimate authority at Google, equivocated in his statement, writing, "[T]o suggest a group of our colleagues have traits that make them less biologically suited to that work is offensive and not OK. [. . .] At the same time, there are co-workers who are questioning whether they can safely express their views in the workplace (especially those with a minority viewpoint). They too feel under threat, and that is also not OK."[56] This equivocation remains to this day, as Google has barred its employees from protesting the company's actions in their official capacity as employees or anywhere near Google's Pride Parade float at the 2019 San Francisco Pride Parade.[57] In response, a number of employees have petitioned the San Francisco Pride board of directors to revoke Google's sponsorship of the 2019 Pride Parade.[58]

Following his firing, Damore mounted a publicity campaign in which he began to increasingly echo the public's interpretation of his message, quickly dropping his caveats about applying population statistics to individuals and his potentially helpful suggestions for reform and instead focusing on ramping up his image as a victim and his insistence on human biodiversity as a central cause of gender disparities in the workplace. In his Reddit Ask Me Anything (AMA), Damore noted, "I honestly haven't seen any valid criticism that disputes my claims."[59] Damore's positioning of himself as a Silicon Valley pariah has led to his adoption by the alt-right in North America.[60] This is perhaps nowhere more evident than in Damore's photoshoot with Peter Duke, who the *New York Times* has described as "the Annie Leibovitz of the alt-right."[61] In the resulting photo, Damore sits in a T-shirt that reads "Gulag" styled as the Google logo. Damore arranged to have this photo retweeted by Mike Cernovich, an alt-right conspiracy theorist who has previously claimed that date rape does not exist. Afterward, Damore claimed that he was unaware of Cernovich's politics and past statements and only did it to reach Cernovich's 300,000 followers.[62] Like many like-minded coders in Silicon Valley, Damore keeps his politics hard to pin down, hiding behind claims of ignorance, claims of centrism, reliance on the rhetoric of science, and caveats about his potentially having some form of undiagnosed autism as an excuse for any insensitivity in his statements. On his AMA, Damore described himself as "centrist" and a "liberal," but in a group for libertarian-leaning Google employees, he more accurately noted that his libertarianism "influenced a lot of the document."[63]

In his AMA, Damore also noted that a key influence on his thinking was University of Toronto pop psychologist Jordan Peterson, who blends vague and thus easily universalizable morals with antiquated Jungian analytical psychology and highly motivated readings of empirical evidence of the biological differences of anatomical sex. In the wake of the media campaign, Peterson interviewed Damore for his YouTube channel, ostensibly to provide an objective assessment of the Google memo. Despite Peterson's claims to scientific objectivity, he found nearly all Damore's ideas to be well supported by "the relevant psychological science." Peterson argues that Damore, in fact, holds what is the majority viewpoint and that Damore was only silenced and made to feel like a pariah because "social constructionists" are better organized—despite their being wrong factually, scientifically, and ethically. Peterson even describes affirmative action hiring practices as "racist." The result is a revivified Damore, who in the end argues that he has been proven right, that the entire culture is attempting to silence any dissenting viewpoints, and that we need a more "objective" way of looking at these issues.[64]

It is worth noting that others who have fact-checked Damore's memo have had very different takes and have found the scientific evidence for many of his claims to be either totally lacking or in contradiction to his statements.[65] Anatomical sex differences actually don't hold much explanatory power when it comes to people's different abilities, attitudes, and actions.[66] In a survey of nearly four thousand studies, boys do not perform better than girls at mathematics as children, and the advantages adolescent and adult men have in mathematical ability are much better explained by social conditioning and cultural biases.[67] And while differences in anatomical sex do correlate to different occupational interests—like an interest in STEM careers—these differences are not biological. They are much more likely because of the discourse in communities surrounding different occupations, as well as social conditioning.[68] These differences are exacerbated when it comes to working with computers, as it has long been known that males exhibit "greater sex-role stereotyping of computers, higher computer self-efficacy, and more positive affect about computers."[69] This is not only the consensus among researchers doing empirical studies of the very issues that Damore raises but also the standard position of the American Psychological Association.[70] As Diane Halpern, professor of psychology and past president of the American Psychological Association, has noted, the problem comes when these differences are understood as deficiencies and interpreted as biologically preordained, when in fact they result from a complex and continuous feedback loop between biology and environment.[71]

What we can learn from this is that while Google increasingly seeks to diversify its labor pool and offer a voice to women at the managerial level, it does not, and likely cannot, fully commit itself to these endeavors. Silencing the discourse on human biodiversity within the company potentially alienates too large a group of the essential talent pool of male coders that the company needs to keep happy in order to operate its global empire. At the top of the pyramid, Sundar Pichai equivocates about his commitment to gender equity in the company, and at the bottom, myriad coders express deep sympathies with Damore's position. This pseudoscientific biologizing of people's abilities, attitudes, and actions according to anatomical sex is not only inaccurate and reductive of the complexities of anatomical sex but also erases the hard-earned and central distinction between anatomical sex and gender. This erasure leads to a slippage in which gender roles are easily essentialized through the same pseudoscientific appeals to biology. By combining sex and gender, gender also becomes binarized. This cisnormativity, as we've seen, undergirds heteronormativity. It is only atop this cisnormative binarization that heterosexuality is semicoherent as a concept and available as a cultural norm. Further, it is only atop this binarization that homosexuality can emerge as a derivative and abnormal concept. Instead of individual bodies connected by desire, we have categorically distinct bodies connecting within pre-articulated matrices of desire ([male, female], [male, male], [female, female]).

Coders operating within this epistemological framework are ill-suited to ethically manage the vagaries of contemporary sexuality as it manifests itself through digital communications. And further, because of its pseudoscientific grounding and the increasing retrenchment that occurs after pariahs like Damore are turned into martyrs by alt-right media, we are left with a discourse community surer of its convictions. While we will continue to draw on internal case studies from Google, as we've seen, this conjuncture is in no way limited to a single corporation but instead is endemic to Silicon Valley. This problem is exacerbated by the ambiguous messages of CEOs, the often-toothless warnings of middle managers working toward diversity initiatives, and the very silence that Damore identified in his memo when it comes to internal dialogues about gender equity and diversity. As we will see in the next section of this chapter, when these biases and silences are combined with the hacker culture surrounding the implementation of new algorithms and curation of big data in Silicon Valley, it can lead to biased technological systems and platforms that carry with them a large amount of inertia that inhibits the full correction of biased functions after implementation.

THE HETERONORMATIVITY OF CODE

There is a hubris embedded at the core of Silicon Valley research and development practices that is frequently referred to as the *hacker ethic*. This ethic is unique to the conjuncture in which computer science arose, a cross-fertilization of military and academic research.[72] It was brought to popular awareness by Steven Levy in 1984 when he published *Hackers: Heroes of the Computer Revolution*, which celebrated a culture obsessed with openness, empowerment, and the fundamental maxim that "information wants to be free."[73] Levy's interlocutors made convincing counterarguments at the time, such as Dennis Hayes, who argued that the hacker ethic was a myth constructed by computer journalists and a highly misleading representation of the field. Instead, Hayes saw a culture that was blind to purposes and solely fixated on techniques, a necessity because of its need to bow to corporate and military priorities to achieve research and development funding. Hackers were so obsessed with manifesting the innovations they envisioned that they were blind to their potential impacts on society.[74] All systems had bugs that could not be predicted. The hacker's job was to build the technology and make ad hoc adjustments to it to fix any errors or ill effects that might emerge. Hackers have a strong confidence that only they can arbitrate the future of technology, and any attempts to regulate them or rein in "progress" are ill-conceived. As Noam Cohen noted, "There is the successful entrepreneur's belief that the disruption that has made him fabulously wealthy must be good for everyone."[75]

Few at the time recognized the gender bias that was being established at the foundation of tech culture. Levy described hackers as so obsessed with programming computers that they would ignore women. He wrote, "Not only an obsession and a lusty pleasure, hacking was a mission. You would hack, and you would live by the Hacker Ethic, and you knew that horribly inefficient and wasteful things like women burned too many cycles, occupied too much memory space."[76] One hacker that Levy quotes uncritically noted, "Women, even today, are considered grossly unpredictable. How can a hacker tolerate such an imperfect being?"[77] Instead, hackers gendered computers and experienced them as their ideal women whose hardware and software could be directly interacted with at will, perfectly controlled, and intimately known. As Noam Cohen has explained, "If this all sounds sort of sexual—or like an old-fashioned marriage—well, you aren't the first to notice."[78] As computer science pioneer John McCarthy noted, "What the user wants is a computer that he can have continuously at his beck and call for long periods of time."[79] The masculine generic in McCarthy's statement is emblematic of a culture that did not forbid women from participating but made a point of not accommodating or welcoming them into the field, increasingly discouraging women from participating in a field they had dominated during its infancy. This effacement of women's historic centrality to computation is deeply connected to the myth of meritocracy in Silicon Valley, as predominantly male, libertarian individualists continually perpetuate a narrative in which they arrive at fame and fortune without having had any special privileges or owing anything to anybody.[80]

This hacker ethic quickly cemented itself into what others have called "the Californian Ideology," an aggressive libertarian and narcissistic understanding of society that masquerades under the façade of chill nerds who just like to build cool things.[81] Whether this belief system is maintained in earnest by all programmers in the Valley is irrelevant. As scholars like Christian Fuchs and Nick Dyer-Witheford have pointed out, programmers are an increasingly precarious class because of their replaceability and are easily controlled by the corporate officers of their companies because of their desire to maintain the perks of their positions—prestige, high wages, utopic office spaces, and the ability to perform labor that they find meaningful.[82] Thus, those programmers who might develop an interest in the purposes of their work or find themselves critical of the social impacts their research might have on the world are left with little room to voice these qualms. Instead, the ruling ideology is one in which "progress"—here understood as advancements in practical technologies—is inevitable, and all one can do is try to capitalize on being the first to meet the bleeding edge of the future. This ideology is established on a fundamental heteronormativity that genders and sexualizes the computer as the perfect object for the masculine gaze and control. The narcissistic hubris that it establishes leads men to believe that no one can see the future better than them, that no one ought to prevent them from realizing their ideas, that any idea will inevitably be made manifest, and that all one is responsible for is hacking together the best operational prototype possible from available resources and patching it as problems emerge in the future. This is precisely the worldview that we will see in Google's development of SafeSearch and Facebook's content moderation practices (Facebook has gone so far as making the address of its campus 1 Hacker Way, Menlo Park, California). Both companies hack together available resources without clear plans or solicitation of outside feedback or criticism. Both companies consider progress to be inevitable and work to be at its cutting edge. And both companies end up embedding heteronormative and sexist bias into the foundations of their platforms that, as we'll see in the following chapters, can never be fully patched after the code has been hacked together.

In the next section, I'd like to turn to a closer examination of the datasets and algorithms behind the automation of content moderation online with a specific focus on Google SafeSearch. While the technical details in the section may be difficult and tedious to some, I think they are worth exploring in this level of detail for a number of reasons. First, if we want to make changes to the algorithms and datasets that shape large portions of the internet, we are going to need to be able to engage in discussions with computer scientists, and this necessitates working toward at least a basic command of their discourse. It is my hope that going into this level of detail and demonstrating at least a basic awareness of computer science discourse will help make my arguments more convincing to people at the levers of power. Second, I think that these analyses pay dividends, which readers will see if they persist through some of the denser paragraphs. I've done what I can to make things as clear and concise as possible, but the technical literature is dense and difficult to perfectly distill. That said, I've tried to distribute new and surprising findings throughout the extended case study that wouldn't have been possible for me to unearth without diving into this technical literature. Readers can rest assured, though, that the following section of the chapter—and the remainder of the book for that matter—return to less technical issues, like the human labor of content moderation here and the impact that overbroad censorship has on LGBTQIA+ communities in chapters 3 and 4.

GOOGLE SAFESEARCH AND THE CLOUD VISION API

The history of SafeSearch is nearly synonymous with the history of Google. At the turn of the millennium, Google was already more focused on obliging potential advertisers by censoring pornography from its search results than it was on Y2K. One of its earliest hires was Matt Cutts, who for nearly twenty years led the department at Google that fights spam and search engine optimizers to protect the integrity of Google's search results, one of the most important positions at the company. Yet Cutts's first job at the company was to develop SafeSearch. His first months at the company were spent crawling web porn looking for largely text-based classificatory signals that he could use to automate porn filtering and subsequently trying to recruit colleagues to search for porn that might have evaded his filter system.[83] It is worth noting that from the beginning, Google has understood web pornography through the lens of spam. Just like spam, porn has no fixed definition and requires vigilant updates.[84] For Google, porn is like a virus, constantly mutating in form and strategy to evade detection and infect the healthy body of search results.

In its earliest iterations, SafeSearch was focused on Boolean textual analysis almost exclusively. Cutts's web crawlers would analyze the text that appeared on porn sites to aggregate a set of weighted "trigger words" that could indicate the likelihood that any given site was pornography. The viral understanding is evident here, as, for instance, slang and misspellings were considered to be motivated—i.e., deliberate attempts to evade the filter—and thus were programmed to weigh in as indicators of pornographic content.[85] Google would then layer behavioral data from its users atop this textual data. By keeping track of what users actually clicked on when they were searching for pornography and how long they visited those links, Cutts was able to establish further patterns about what the context and content of websites were.[86] This was particularly important because, at the time, it was impossible to parse the content of images or videos on the web. One could only simulate an understanding of any given image's content through an analysis of the textual content it was embedded in and behavioral data on how users interacted with it. Analyses of images thus began with looking at the text and user behavior attached to them, and only later would these analyses become sophisticated enough to examine the pixel values of the images themselves.

The visual analysis of images pixel by pixel only started to pick up steam in 2008 as graphics processing units (GPUs) became cheaper and more powerful. The first iterations would index the RGB values of millions of images such that any given image could be correlated with nearly identical versions online. This was the origin of the broader capacity we all enjoy today of using an image as a search query on Google, an innovation brought about by Google's focus on porn censorship.[87] Shortly thereafter (c. 2012), Google began exploring the use of machine learning to train neural networks to detect pornographic content and developed what in April of 2016 it would make available to the public as its Cloud Vision API.[88] As Google explains it, "Google Cloud Vision API [application programming interface] enables developers to *understand the content of an image* by encapsulating *powerful machine learning models* in an easy to use REST API" (emphasis mine).[89] Cloud Vision's features include not only "Explicit Content Detection" but also "Label Detection," "Web Detection," "Face Detection," "Logo Detection," "Landmark Detection," "Image Attributes," and "Optical Character Recognition."[90] In my experience working with Cloud Vision, a number of these features remain severely limited, but the API's capacity to detect explicit content is uncannily accurate—provided we understand explicit content as being any and all nudity and that we understand nudity as female-presenting nipples and breasts, genitals, and (sometimes) buttocks.

Google actually has a much larger definition of explicitness that it has programmed into its Cloud Vision API. Images may be considered explicit based on their participation in any of five separate categories: (1) adult, (2) medical, (3) spoof, (4) violent, and (5) "racy" images can all be detected and blocked. Adult images may contain elements such as nudity, pornographic images or cartoons, or sexual activities.[91] The category is meant to focus solely on "explicit" or "pornographic" nudity, especially those images that focus on "strategic" parts of the anatomy. However, the system is trained to avoid flagging as adult content any medical, scientific, educational, or artistic nudity, as well as "racy" images that cover said "strategic" parts. Medical content consists of "explicit images of surgery, diseases, or body parts," and its classifier primarily searches for "graphic photographs of open wounds, genital close-ups, and egregious disease symptoms." Spoof content primarily looks for memes, which are indicated by the presence of text (often at the top and bottom of images) and typical meme faces, images, and backgrounds. Violent content consists of images flagged as depicting killing, shooting, or blood and gore.[92]

The fifth category was added only after launch and remains in a sort of beta state despite being available to any developers using Google's Cloud Vision API. "Racy" image detection is meant to capture all the content that escapes the adult content filter but might still be risqué enough to be worth censoring. In perhaps the only extant definition of what this content consists of, Google writes, "Racy content includes lewd or provocative poses, sheer or see-through clothing, closeups of sensitive regions, and more."[93] It appears to be most often triggered by images of nudity wherein "strategic" parts are just barely obscured or covered. This is perhaps Google's most nebulous classifier and demonstrates their orientation toward pornography as a virus needing eradication. In this metaphor, the broadness of the classifier indicates that it is more important to eradicate any viral pathogens than it is to preserve benign organisms. In more practical terms, blocking porn is more important than *not blocking* nonporn, including *art*. Take the Venus de Milo, for example. When I ran a Cloud Vision analysis of a standard Wikimedia Commons image of the statue—and keep in mind this is an image Google has certainly indexed, including its surrounding content and context—the API is convinced that it is likely a "racy" image (see figure 2.2).[94]

Before moving on to examine some examples of heteronormative biases that are hardcoded into the datasets that these algorithms are trained on, it is worth outlining some rudimentary results that I obtained by running sets of images through the Cloud Vision API to get a sense of how these sorts of heteronormative biases inflect content moderation on Google's platform. I did a simple Google Image Search for "female breasts" and gathered the first

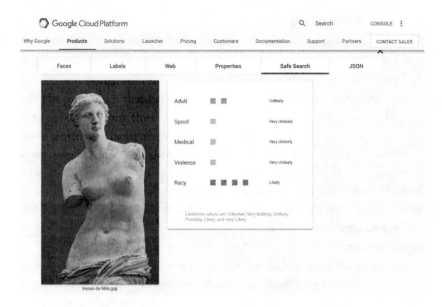

Figure 2.2
Venus de Milo being run through Google's Cloud Vision API.

one hundred relevant images—including a large number of pictures of fully clothed women, medical images and diagrams, and artistic renderings—and ran them through Cloud Vision. Of these images, exactly half of them were determined to "very likely" be "racy" images and thus would be censored in many instances through SafeSearch and in apps developed with the Cloud Vision API. Google SafeSearch seems to have learned the shape and texture of the average female-presenting—and lighter-skinned—breast. This was confirmed by running images of "nude paintings," "nude sculptures," and "hentai" (Japanese-styled nude and sexual drawings) through the system, all of which were frequently flagged as "racy" content when they contained any semblance of a female-presenting breast, again, even when clothed. Needless to say, this result was not repeated when I ran images of bare male-presenting chests through the system.

This betrays a particularly American, heteronormative interpretation of what breast tissue is and what it means. It exacerbates a sexualization of women's and female-presenting bodies that has been a problem for internet users with what platforms deem "female breasts" for decades. For instance, Tarleton Gillespie has excellently documented the decade-long struggle that people have faced in trying to post images of their breastfeeding online.[95] This problem is hardcoded into the datasets that algorithms like these are trained on, in the first instance by the decision to assume stable gender binaries. These assumptions have been productively challenged by trans women like Courtney Demone, whose #DoIHaveBoobsNow? campaign on Instagram showcased topless photos at different phases of her hormone therapy to beg the question of when her breasts became a content violation.[96] This sexism in the dataset allows for breasts that are coded as "female" to be associated with "pornography," "adult content," or "raciness," thus capturing and reinforcing a culturally singular cisnormative and heteronormative bias. It would take a team of much more capable researchers than me to fully catalogue the results of many of the sexual and gender biases in these datasets. While it is beyond the purview of this book to give a full demonstration of all their impacts, I will now turn to tracing some of the other biased sexual concepts that get captured and reinforced in both the primary datasets that image recognition and computer vision algorithms are trained on and tested against.

At this point, we need to take a detour through how a computer vision algorithm learns to detect adult content so that we can later understand how and where heteronormative biases can be hardcoded into the system. Many machine learning applications require a large dataset with consistent metadata from which they can then analyze and learn patterns to identify and classify new data. In the case of computer vision, this means that large repositories of images must be consistently tagged with appropriate metadata *before* any algorithms can learn to identify and classify new images. Since 2012, ImageNet has been the gold standard image dataset for training computer vision algorithms. ImageNet began as a conference poster presentation by Princeton University researchers in 2009.[97] By 2010, it already contained nearly fifteen million labeled images.[98] In that year, ImageNet also launched the annual ImageNet Large Scale Visual Recognition Challenge (ILSVRC), where computer scientists used a specified subset of the images as seed images to train algorithms to automatically identify and classify images not used in the seed set—you use half the dataset to train your algorithm and then test it on the other half of the images that it hasn't yet analyzed.[99] As we'll see shortly, it was in response to the ILSVRC that the first major breakthrough in the use of convolutional neural networks for computer vision was achieved, and this breakthrough serves as the bedrock for many of Google's computer vision applications today. Further, Google's Inception architecture and

GoogLeNet algorithm were developed atop ImageNet in 2014, later serving as the foundations for Google Photos and the Cloud Vision API.[100]

As noted above, each image in ImageNet needs to be consistently labeled with metadata. The metadata that each of these images can be labeled with, and thus the entire structure of the dataset, is extracted from WordNet, "a large lexical database of English."[101] WordNet also originated at Princeton in 1985 with funding by US Office of Naval Research, the National Science Foundation, the Defense Advanced Research Projects Agency, and the Disruptive Technology Office (formerly the Advanced Research and Development Activity). The goal of WordNet is to capture all of the distinct concepts in the English language and their interrelations. It does this by collecting all English nouns, verbs, adjectives, and adverbs and grouping them into sets of cognitive synonyms that it refers to as "synsets." As its site notes, "Synsets are interlinked by means of conceptual-semantic and lexical relations."[102] Take, for example, the WordNet entry for "sex": WordNet's understanding of sex is composed of four noun synsets, one for "noun.act" that looks at sex as an action and contains "sexual activity" and "sexual practice," one for "noun. group" that looks at anatomical sex, one for "noun.feeling" that looks at sex as an urge, and one for "noun.attribute" that looks at gender and sexuality.[103] The noun.act synset for sex is embedded within the parent synset for a "noun.process" composed of the terms "bodily process," "body process," "body function," and "activity," which themselves are contained within the parent synset "organic process" and "biological process." This latter synset is contained within the "noun.Tops" parent synset of "process" and "physical process" described as "a sustained phenomenon or one marked by gradual changes through a series of states."[104] It is embedded within two more generic noun.Tops synsets, the first being "physical entity," which describes "an entity that has physical existence" and "entity," which describes "that which is perceived or known or inferred to have its own distinct existence (living or nonliving)."[105] In short, WordNet provides the ontology for ImageNet, determining what can exist and how it can be related—with relations existing between parent, child, and sibling concepts.

WordNet's understanding of sex also subsumes the following child synsets:

> "bondage," "outercourse," "safe sex," "conception," "sexual intercourse," "intercourse,' "coitus," "sexual congress," "sexual relation," "relation," "carnal knowledge," "defloration," "fuck," "screw," "ass," "nookie," "piece of tail," "roll in the hay," "shag," "shtup," "hanky panky," [*sic*] "penetration," "unlawful carnal

knowledge," "criminal congress," "extramarital sex," "free love," "adultery," "criminal conversation," "fornication," "incest," "pleasure," "sexual love," "lovemaking," "love," "carnal abuse," "coupling," "mating," "conjugation," "sexual union," "assortative mating," "disassortative mating," "hybridization," "hybridisation," "crossbreeding," "crossing," "interbreeding," "hybridizing," "dihybrid cross," "monohybrid cross," "reciprocal cross," "reciprocal," "testcross," "testcross," "inbreeding," "servicing," "service," "reproduction," "procreation," "facts of life," "miscegenation," "crossbreeding," "interbreeding," "generation," "multiplication," "propagation," "biogenesis," "biogeny," "foreplay," "stimulation," "caressing," "cuddling," "hugging," "kissing," "petting," "smooching," "snogging," "feel," "perversion," "sexual perversion," "paraphilia," "exhibitionism," "immodesty," "fetishism," "pedophilia," "paedophilia," "voyeurism," "zoophilia," "zoophilism," "pederasty," "paederasty," "sodomy," "buggery," "anal sex," "anal intercourse," "oral sex," "cunnilingus," "cunnilinctus," "fellatio," "fellation," "cock sucking," "blowjob," "soixante-neuf," "sixty-nine," "autoeroticism," "autoerotism," "masturbation," "onanism," "self-stimulation," "self-abuse," "frottage," "jacking off," "jerking off," "hand job," "wank," "promiscuity," "promiscuousness," "sleeping around," "one-night stand," "lechery," "homosexuality," "homosexualism," "homoeroticism," "queerness," "inversion," "sexual inversion," "lesbianism," "sapphism," "tribadism," "bisexuality," "straightness," "bestiality," and "zooerastia."[106]

While it is hard to keep a data structure like this in your head—and I'd recommend taking a look at the term "sex" and others via WordNet's online platform to get a better sense of it—it is clear that WordNet is engaging in some pretty sophisticated ontological work. It essentially offers an entire linguistic and conceptual schematization of the world ready-made and in machine-readable form.

As Aylin Caliskan, Joanna J. Bryson, and Arvind Narayanan have shown, "language itself contains recoverable and accurate imprints of our historic biases, whether these are morally neutral as towards insects or flowers, problematic as towards race or gender, or even simply veridical, reflecting the *status quo* for the distribution of gender with respect to careers or first names. These regularities are captured by machine learning along with the rest of semantics."[107] This is certainly the case with WordNet, where we can find several standard conceptual biases about anatomical sex, gender, and sexuality embedded in the English-language semantics that are formalized in the synsets connected to "sex." For example, one synset for masturbation combines "self-stimulation" with "self-abuse," both defining "manual stimulation of your own genital organ for sexual pleasure."[108] Here we can see the theological concept of "onanism" go digital (see the introduction). Historical heteronormative biases surrounding masturbation and procreative sex are rendered in machine-readable form.

The term "sodomy" is found in two child synsets for the term "sex." The first synset also contains buggery, anal sex, and anal intercourse, while the second also contains bestiality and zooerastia.[109] Thus, sodomy forms a machine-readable bridge between anal sex with humans and sex with animals, a common trope in conservative fearmongering that surfaces in many debates surrounding LGBTQIA+ rights. It was in fact precisely these connections that Justice Antonin Scalia drew upon in his dissent in *Lawrence v. Texas* (2003), the case that legalized gay and lesbian sex in the United States.[110] The terms "crossbreeding" and "interbreeding" are found in two child synests for the term "sex." The first synset also contains the terms "hybridization," "hybridisation," "crossing," and "hybridizing" and is defined as "(genetics) the act of mixing different species or varieties of animals or plants and thus to produce hybrids."[111] The second synset also contains the term "miscegenation" and is defined as "reproduction by parents of different races (especially by white and non-white persons)."[112] Thus we can see not only the biological essentialism of sexuality that is a hallmark of heteronormativity but also the continued life of scientific racism in machine-readable form. Thomas F. Gossett has catalogued the United States' long legacy of besmirching scientific discourse by leveraging its ethos to peddle scientifically incorrect conflations of race and species. However, while Gossett hoped that Franz Boas, among others, largely delegitimated such nonsense in at least scientific if not popular discourse, here we can see it manifesting once again in a foundational dataset for computer science in the twenty-first century.[113]

These are just a few of the more glaring biases found in a cursory review of a single search result in the online version of WordNet. Others are certainly waiting to be found. It is unfortunately beyond the purview of this book to extend this analysis much further. However, it is essential that other interested researchers push this work forward by further connecting our legacy of critical and analytical knowledge to the analyses of semantic biases in machine learning platforms that are already being implemented by STEM scholars. Every facet of historical prejudice in English-language discourse is likely to rear its head in machine learning platforms and will largely go unaddressed if none of us are keeping track. Bias and prejudice surrounding sex and sexuality are perhaps most likely to take center stage, as the centrality of ad revenue—and thus of censoring pornography—will make definitions of sex and sexuality primary foci for machine learning moving forward.

While WordNet contains over 100,000 synsets, ImageNet primarily borrows the nouns, which account for over 80,000 of WordNet's synsets. As they note, "In ImageNet, we aim to provide on average 1000 images to illustrate each synset. Images of each concept are quality-controlled and human-annotated."[114] Ironically, this Anglocentric dataset is produced by using Amazon's Mechanical Turk to outsource most of the English-language labeling labor to (predominantly) non-native English speakers. Any linguistic barriers are overcome by redundancy and exploitation: have multiple people label the same images, use only the labels that the majority agree on, and only pay those who provided the labels consistent with the majority. The more obfuscated and thus potentially more nefarious problem that may exist here is the influence of Anglocentrism on the deep structure of the datasets. Researchers have pointed out some of the problems in the use of English as the root structure for translation algorithms.[115] To my knowledge, no one has yet sufficiently analyzed what the global effects might be of structuring our computer vision algorithms in accordance with English-language "conceptual-semantic" and "lexical" relations.

Today, ImageNet contains an estimated one hundred million images, and its maintainers hope to expand the dataset to trillions of images in the future.[116] This would make the visual dataset reach a similar scale to the linguistic and conceptual datasets already powering search algorithms—and particularly graph search functions like those at Facebook or Google.[117] This task shines new light on the willingness of companies like Google and Facebook to host infinite and increasingly high-resolution user images for free. And further, labeling the image datasets of the future will likely require some combination of the automation of image labeling, gamifying the practice to stimulate users to perform labeling labor for free, and continuing to hire out the labeling labor through services like Amazon's Mechanical Turk. The economic and political stakes of this increasing emphasis on extracting un- or underpaid labor and producing an objectified, alienating, privately owned, and blackboxed form of collective or social knowledge are already being explored by other scholars.[118]

In 2012, Alex Krizhevsky, Ilya Sutskever, and Geoffrey E. Hinton used ImageNet to make a breakthrough in machine vision at the University of

Toronto when working on an algorithm for the ILSVRC. They used a convolutional neural network (CNN or ConvNet), which is a specific kind of artificial neural network that has the benefits of having fewer connections and parameters and thus being easier to train with only slightly worse performance. The only drawback is that they require large amounts of nonserial or GPU processing power.[119] As Hinton, Sutskever, and Hinton noted, "Their capacity can be controlled by varying their depth and breadth, and they also make strong and mostly correct assumptions about the nature of images (namely, stationarity of statistics and locality of pixel dependencies)."[120] This power is afforded by the ability of CNNs to process convolutional data, which means building a function out of the integration of two other functions or variables. In essence, convolutions are capable of working with the fuzziness of visual data to make accurate identifications. Visual data comes in so many more permutations and positions than the linguistic-based conceptual data that many other artificial neural networks are trained to process. Whereas syntax, grammar, and spelling in English-language textual discourse provide a somewhat standardized conceptual topography (i.e., words are often in the same positions in sentences and rarely misspelled), the visual concept of "cat" as expressed in any given cat image could see that cat positioned in any part of the image, at any distance, in many colors, sizes, positions, fur lengths and textures, with various contexts and backgrounds, and so on.

To provide an unavoidably reductive explanation, Hinton, Sutskever, and Hinton's system was able to do this through the unique feed-forward model of a CNN, which connects three types of layers: (1) convolutional, (2) max pooling, and (3) fully connected (see figure 2.3). In this model, the essential component is the neuron, which is fed pixel values as its inputs and is triggered when it detects a particular pattern in those pixel values (such as a horizontal edge, a vertical edge, or a color contrast).[121] Convolutional layers use many identical copies of these neurons and cluster them together into various kernels that only get triggered when all of the neurons in that kernel are themselves triggered (thus, a kernel might be triggered when it detects a vertical edge, a particular texture, and a particular color contrast all together). Convolutional layers break individual images into small groups of pixels and feed each group of pixels into a set of kernels (itself a set of neurons). In a sense then, in the convolutional layers, the set of kernels the machine has learned range over the image one section at a time and fire when they detect particular patterns (boundaries, textures, shapes, and so on). The data from these convolutional

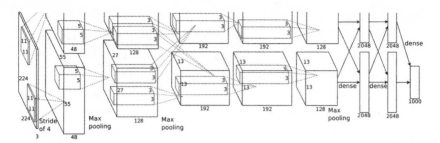

Figure 2.3
Example of layers in a CNN. *Source:* Alex Krizhevsky, Ilya Sutskever, and Geoffrey E. Hinton, "ImageNet Classification with Deep Convolutional Neural Networks," in *Advances in Neural Information Processing Systems* 25 (2012): 1101.

layers, which essentially consists of which kernels were triggered by which sections of the image being processed, is fed into a max-pooling layer, which can aggregate this local knowledge into a broader regional knowledge about specific types of patterns in the image. A max-pooling layer can thus determine where the edges of objects might be, what textures and colors objects might have, or what shapes they are composed of or contain. This data is then fed into fully connected layers that can create global patterns—and thus global knowledge—of the image based on the regional and local patterns that have been identified. In short, once the max-pooling layer passes on information about patterns across the entire image—like the center of this image has a round figure with a fuzzy texture with two pointy shapes atop it, two circles in it, and lines coming just off-center on either side to its exterior—the fully connected layer can identify this as an image of a cat's face by its shape, fur, pointy ears, round eyes, and whiskers.

The truly unique thing about CNNs though is not their capacity to identify new images but their ability to, when fed a set of seed images with consistent labels, *learn* which kernels of which neurons are useful for indicating which local patterns are useful for indicating which regional patterns, which are useful for identifying global patterns—and thus images themselves. Perhaps more simply, the neurons, kernels, and patterns that the machine uses to identify new images are not *programmed*, they are *learned* by the machine itself through massive and incredibly fast trial-and-error experiments. It is for this reason that CNNs are so hard for people to imagine, as they see images in ways that are very different from us, and that can only be roughly represented to us. For instance, they might identify an image of a cat based on the texture of their eyeballs, the curvature of their inner ears, the number and placement of whiskers, or even more difficult visual signifiers for humans to distinguish. That said, *what* they can identify is determined in advance by the WordNet labels and the ImageNet images—the algorithm cannot learn to identify things that it does not have images of or labels for. In short, no matter how sophisticated the system, if you feed it heteronormative data, it will produce heteronormative results.

Visual datasets have been shown to contain selection biases that lead to what in computer science lingo are referred to as "certain most discriminative instances" of image categories. We might think of these as certain images that best capture or represent the inherent biases of a particular dataset, and they can demonstrate to both algorithms and even the human eye the differences between visual datasets—things like average depth of focus, number of objects, position of identified objects within the frame, number of identified objects, and so on. For example, in 2011, Antonio Torralba and Alexei A. Efros published the results of some experiments that were inspired by a game called *Name That Dataset!* that they devised in their computer vision lab.[122] In the game, computer scientists working with different visual datasets like ImageNet were presented with three representative images from twelve popular visual datasets and asked if they could match each set of three images to the visual dataset they had been taken from (see figure 2.4). In their lab, most contestants were able to accurately attribute 75 percent of the images to their parent datasets. When they trained an image classifier to play *Name That Dataset!*, the best classifiers were able to achieve 39 percent accuracy—while random chance would have been 8 percent accuracy, thus demonstrating strong evidence of visual biases. Torralba and Efros argued that all datasets are *motivated* because they are pitched, funded, and developed as reactions against the deficits in their predecessors. These motivations tend to lead to biases in the visual data they aggregate, and this bias goes unnoticed because there is very little investigation of cross-dataset generalization. Or, in short, no one is paying much attention to dataset bias.

The biases of the images selected for visual datasets shape everything from the neurons and kernels to the schema and ontology of computer vision platforms. That said, the types of biases implicit in most visual data have less glaring politics and have to do with things like important objects occupying the center and focal middle ground of images, shaping the more banal aspects of what a machine vision system pays attention to. While we certainly need

Caltech101 ___   Tiny ___   LabelMe ___   15 Scenes ___
MSRC ___   Corel ___   COIL–100 ___   Caltech256 ___
UIUC ___   PASCAL 07 ___   ImageNet ___   SUN09 ___

Figure 1. Name That Dataset: Given three images from twelve popular object recognition datasets, can you match the images with the dataset? (answer key below)

Figure 2.4

Name That Dataset! (example of bias in visual datasets). Reproduced from Antonio Torralba and Alexei A. Efros, "An Unbiased Look at Dataset Bias," in *Proceedings of the IEEE Conference on Computer Vision and Pattern Recognition (CVPR)*, Colorado Springs, CO, June 20–25 (Piscataway, NJ: IEEE, 2011), 1521.

more humanists contributing to this body of analysis, many of these biases constitute a problem that computer scientists are at least economically motivated to solve because these biases can impact system performance in ways that tech companies care about.

Literally what can exist, how, and where for the system is shaped by these biases, which has repeatedly been demonstrated in terms of race. This was seen most publicly and hauntingly in the 2009 video of an HP facial recognition system failing to register Black Desi and track his face with its webcam.[123] Scholars like Joy Buolamwini and Timnit Gebru, who was unceremoniously fired in December 2020 for raising ethical concerns as co-lead of the Ethical Artificial Intelligence Team at Google, have demonstrated in great detail how racial and gender bias contained in the datasets and parameters of popular facial recognition systems lead to Black women being misclassified up to 34.4 percent of the time.[124] Race is deeply connected with adult content filters, as one of the primary strategies that computer scientists have employed since at least the 1990s to accurately filter pornographic images has been to focus on detecting skin tones through color and texture profiles.[125] Many scholars have noted the difficulty that these algorithms have in accurately assessing whether nudity is present in images, with error rates routinely ranging from 3 to 10 percent—which means a lot of false positives given that they are analyzing and making decisions about billions of images per day. That said, I've yet to find any scholars performing work like Buolamwini and Gebru's, and most of the assessments of skin tone detection accuracy do not break down error rates by either race/ethnicity or the standard Fitzpatrick skin typology.[126] Only one study examined a specific race/ethnicity in regard to skin tone detection algorithms and found that many systems performed poorly on people from the Indian subcontinent. Their improved system was only able to achieve accuracy rates between 88 and 91 percent.[127]

Based on prior evidence, we can expect that if the datasets these algorithms are trained on do not include representative samples of populations or include biased representations of certain populations the result will be algorithms that exhibit systematic errors when it comes to identifying and classifying POC.[128] It turns out that this is precisely the case with ImageNet. As I've demonstrated elsewhere, the synset on ImageNet that gathers images of Black people consists of images in low resolution that show few facial details, that have bodies positioned further away from the camera, that strongly feature celebrities (around 1 percent of the entire dataset is pictures of Barack Obama) and memes. Most inexcusable, however, is that over 6 percent of the entire category's dataset is composed of images of white people dressed in blackface, largely due to images of Dutch people dressed as Zwarte Piet (i.e., "Black Pete") during their Christmas celebrations.[129] While it is difficult to estimate the impact this might have on adult content filters without more systematic evidence, it is safe to assume that adult content filters will have higher error rates for images of POC and BIPOC women in particular. It is thus likely that POC are experiencing higher false-positive rates where their nonpornographic content is unjustly flagged by automated content moderation systems.

Another major bias that remains is the Western context of these visual datasets, which were largely compiled when images from the US dominated the internet. Google researchers have found that this has led to failures of image recognition systems to accurately identify scenes from other cultural contexts and geographic locations.[130] One of the most frequently

Figure 2.5
Wedding photographs with Google's label predictions based on Open Images. *Source:*
Tulsee Doshi, "Introducing the Inclusive Images Competition," *Google AI Blog,*
September 6, 2018. https://ai.googleblog.com/2018/09/introducing-inclusive
-images-competition.html.

cited examples is the ability to identify things like weddings, brides, and
grooms because of cultural and geographic differences in wedding attire and
locations (see figure 2.5). Facebook's AI lab has similarly found that image
recognition algorithms also demonstrate embedded cultural biases when
they label objects, as they are 15 to 20 percent more likely to incorrectly
identify objects from non-Western and low-income communities.[131] It is certainly the case that US- and Western-centric biases about what constitutes
obscenity and pornography are embedded in these algorithms as well, as most
exposed female-presenting breasts or buttocks and any genitalia will trigger the algorithm globally regardless of whether that particular community
would consider that nudity to be pornographic. It will perform even worse at
interpreting community standards regarding what constitutes artistic nudity.

Google has increasingly been trying to combat this US and Western bias
in its algorithms through its Crowdsource app, which asks users to contribute free labor akin to Amazon's Mechanical Turk with tasks like translation,
translation validation, handwriting recognition, sentiment evaluation, and
landmark recognition.[132] The company has plans to combat cultural bias in
image recognition systems with its Inclusive Images Competition, where
it challenges you to use its Open Images dataset to train an algorithm that
can successfully be applied to two challenge datasets that Google collected
from their global user community via Crowdsource.[133] Of the nearly 35,000
images, fewer than fifty could be described as depicting scantily clad bodies.
The most risqué image I found was an outline of Bart Simpson showing his

butt, and more often, the closest thing to racy or risqué images were images of men in tank tops or sleeveless shirts playing basketball. While the Inclusive Images Competition is a worthwhile endeavor, it certainly does not contain the correct images to properly train a machine learning algorithm to make higher-order distinctions about types of nudity based on cultural contexts— like what is artistic and what is culturally normalized versus what is censorable for its prurience.

Another important concern when it comes to the datasets specifically designed to train adult content filters is the consent of the people who are depicted in the images used to train the algorithms. While ImageNet and Open Images are the only publicly accessible image datasets that the image recognition algorithms at Google are known to employ, it is likely that they have propriety datasets in-house for this purpose as well. It is industry practice to ignore concerns over consent when collecting image datasets at this scale, and we might take an example from public adult image datasets used to train algorithms to produce deepfake porn as an example of the issues over consent that arise with these sorts of datasets. After scouring subreddits like r/GeneratedPorn and /AIGeneratedPorn and interviewing coders working on deepfake pornography, Motherboard found that many of these datasets included not only images without people's consent but also images of porn from producers who have been accused of lying to women and coercing them into having sex on camera. These include images from sites like Girls Do Porn, which stands accused of human trafficking and rape. Perhaps most notably, they include images from Czech Casting because each Czech Casting video came with a photoset that was extremely appealing to machine learning programmers. As Samantha Cole explains,

> Each video of a woman also comes with a uniform set of photographs. Each set includes a photograph of the woman holding a yellow sign with a number indicating her episode number, like a mugshot board. Each set also includes photographs of the women posing in a series of dressed and undressed shots on a white background: right side, left side, front, back, as well as extreme close ups of the face, individual nipples, and genitalia.[134]

The obsession with objectification in the mainstream heteroporn industry makes it a particularly appealing sample for adult image datasets, which, coupled with its sheer abundance and availability online, likely ensures that it is strongly over-represented in adult image datasets. Again, without stronger empirical evidence, it is hard to be certain, but this is a likely explanation for the high incidence of LGBTQIA+ content being unduly filtered by automated content moderation algorithms online that we'll see in chapter 3. Having more mainstream heteroporn in the dataset means not only that it is better at identifying mainstream heteroporn but also that it is better at distinguishing between what is heterosexual porn and what is not heterosexual porn. It is likely less accurate at making the distinction between pornography and nonpornography when it comes to LGBTQIA+ content.

While it is easily imaginable that Google's public relations department would try to externalize the causality of these biases by laying them at the feet of the social collective whose data they mine or the digital laborers working through platforms like Amazon's Mechanical Turk to label the data they train their algorithms on, this clearly is not the case. The meanings established for the dataset's categories prefigure what data will eventually populate them. Take, for example, the term "closet queen," one of three child synsets for the synset of "homosexual," "homophile," "homo," and "gay" in Word-Net. A closet queen is defined as "a negative term for a homosexual man who chooses not to reveal his sexual orientation."[135] In its 2011 dataset—the most easily accessible online—ImageNet had thirty-two images representing the term "closet queen" (see figure 2.6). While in its current instantiation, the "closet queen" category is not very threatening and perhaps even laughably bad, it is a very good indicator of the potential implications of such a dataset. Anonymous Mechanical Turk laborers are presented with images of human bodies and prompted to provide this derogatory label to those images based on the presumed sexual identity of the people depicted. The architecture of the dataset demands that stereotypes about what constitutes the successful performance of a particular sex, gender, and sexuality become hardwired into the visual dataset. Regardless of which images end up populating the category, the category's very existence determines the way a computer will see—it will see stereotypically. For example, two men hugging, especially from behind, is a key indicator of closeted homosexuality.

As Alexander Cho has shown, the "default publicness" of social media platforms can lead to LGBTQIA+ youth being outed by computers, which has tragic consequences and reinforces heteronormativity by encouraging youths with unsupportive families or communities to avoid producing or consuming any online content that might out them.[136] This is exacerbated by a system increasingly data mining not only their sexuality but also the sexual semantics

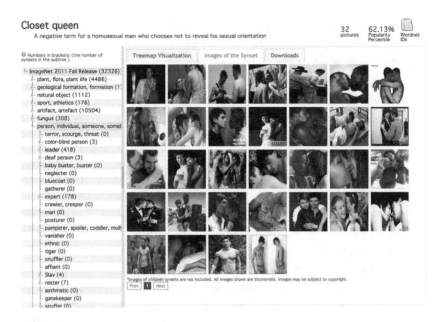

Figure 2.6
Images for "closet queen" synset on ImageNet.

of all the web content they interact with. Beyond this, it is easy to imagine a much more intentional and nefarious future application of such a technology for the automation of outing, where people performing machine-readable acts of closeted queerness become automatically identifiable. While some might view this as the imaginary of dystopic science fiction, I would caution against such a quick dismissal. In 2017, Yilun Wang and Michal Kosinski engineered a deep neural network to analyze images of people's faces and determine their sexual orientation. Their system used publicly available images from a dating site they have refused to name in hopes of slowing copycats.[137] Wang and Kosinski's system was able to accurately distinguish between "gay" and "heterosexual" men in 81 percent of cases and 74 percent of cases in women (compared to human success rates of 61 percent and 54 percent, respectively).[138] While a number of scholars posted critical responses online to the preprint version of the article, demonstrating the limitations of the system,[139] it is hard not to be frightened by the potential capacities of these systems, especially when their visual datasets include contextual data beyond faces (clothes, locations, comportments, other people, and so on), operate at web scale, and incorporate human semantic labeling through Amazon's Mechanical Turk.

The United States and the United Kingdom, in particular, have a long history of selling technology with few to no strings attached to oppressive regimes around the world, ranging from IBM's sale of tabulators to support the Third Reich's "final solution," as documented by Edwin Black, to more recent sales of metadata-based surveillance technologies by Britain's Government Communications Headquarters, an intelligence and security organization, to Honduras, Bahrain, Saudi Arabia, China, and Qatar.[140] And even if Western governments and companies were to exercise a previously unheard of self-restraint by refusing to sell computer vision technologies with such capabilities to regimes interested in the automation of outing, ImageNet is publicly available, as are many of the computer science write-ups of computer vision implementations built atop ImageNet. Anyone, from domestic neo-Nazi alt-right groups to oppressive governments abroad could build such a system themselves were it not available for purchase ready-made, provided ImageNet continues to build out its visual catalogue for terms like "closet queen." Even if this image data is not used to out people, the counting and classifying of LGBTQIA+ people has a long history of rendering them susceptible to dehumanization and violence.[141] This historical LGBTQIA+ precarity is only exacerbated now that private corporations control web-scale data collections and data analytics tools.[142]

In both WordNet and ImageNet, as well as in the image recognition algorithms built atop them, like Google's SafeSearch and Cloud Vision API, we can see the hacker ethic at work. Programmers are focused exclusively on implementing their ideas through the most practical means, largely ignoring the potential social harms these new technologies might cause or assuming that any ill effects can be patched on an ad hoc basis. The datasets that serve as the foundation for the majority of computer vision applications in the world today are riddled with biases, most notably biases about sex, gender, and sexuality. These biases deeply impact how the machine learning algorithms trained on them operate and likely can never be adequately patched after the fact. Biased data will always produce biased results. Without fostering interdisciplinary and diverse dialogue on what unbiased data might look like and large-scale investment in implementing less biased datasets, the infrastructure of the internet will continue to reinforce our preexisting prejudices and further marginalize LGBTQIA+ communities. Lastly, the most common industry response is that human reviewers are the answer for correcting these biases after the fact. However, as we'll see in the next section and chapter 3, these human reviewers put into practice just as much heteronormative bias as the algorithmic systems they are meant to correct.

THE HETERONORMATIVITY OF CONTENT REVIEW LABOR

FACEBOOK'S "HUMAN ALGORITHMS"

While few humanities and social sciences scholars have unpacked at length the operations of automated content filters, like those discussed above, a number of them have investigated their human counterparts, frequently composed of an underpaid, overburdened, and globalized labor force responsible for censoring broad swaths of the internet.[143] I would contest that this latter phenomenon can best be understood in relation to efforts to automate content moderation through machine learning algorithms like natural language processing systems and computer vision or image recognition systems. The way that major tech companies envision and situate this labor, structure and schematize it, and mask it behind confidentiality agreements and compartmentalization will all strongly reflect these companies' ideas and practices from designing algorithms. In fact, as we'll see, companies like Facebook even describe these laborers as "human algorithms." While the public archive surrounding Google's Cloud Vision API allowed for unique insight into their automated content moderation practices, we will now turn to Facebook's human content moderators because their response to criticism in the wake of the 2016 US election led to them opening up their content moderation practices to the public in unique ways that offer the best insight into how these "human algorithms" are at work within the company.

Facebook only began publishing data on the enforcement of its Community Standards in 2018. In their first report, they found that between seven and nine content views out of every ten thousand were of pieces of content that contained violations of its adult nudity and pornography standards.[144] In 2019, that number was up to eleven to fourteen views per ten thousand.[145] In their latest report, the company notes that since October of 2017, between 0.05 and 0.15 percent of all Facebook content contained flagged violations of the adult nudity and sexual activity clauses of the Community Standards. In each quarter since then, the company has censored between twenty to forty million pieces of content. Around 96 percent of all flagged content was caught by Facebook's automated content moderation system, with the remaining 4 percent being flagged by the user community.[146] Many of these determinations are considered by the company to be obvious, but the ones that fall into gray areas are kicked up to human reviewers whose labor has been formalized by the company such that they are sometimes referred to as "human algorithms."[147]

The labor force performing these reviews of flagged content is largely hired through a California-based outsourcing firm named oDesk, which farms out content moderation labor for both Google and Facebook, largely hiring from call centers. Around 2012, Facebook employed only fifty moderators for the entire platform, largely from Asia, Africa, and Central America. They were paid $1 per hour plus incentives for reviewing certain amounts of content during their four-hour shifts that could bring their total pay up to $4 an hour—this was the same year Facebook had its initial public offering at $100 billion.[148] In the wake of the 2016 election and Facebook's numerous scandals ranging from Russian trolls to Cambridge Analytica, the company was employing 4,500 content moderators.[149] By 2018, it was employing 7,500 with plans of increasing that number to 15,000.[150] While these numbers have been released, the company maintains secrecy about the number and location of its moderating hubs. As the content moderation labor force has been increased, training has been streamlined. New contract laborers receive two weeks of training and a set of prescriptive manuals for assessing content. They also are given access to Facebook's Single Review Tool (SRT), which allows them to act like human algorithms, categorizing content and checking whether it meets the appropriate sections of Facebook's Community Standards.[151]

These manuals and the SRT are created by young engineers and lawyers at the company who work to distill all content moderation into a series of yes-no decisions, thus producing an algorithm that can be run on the outsourced laborers' bodies and minds. While Facebook claims that there are no time constraints on these laborers, inside information indicates that moderators have eight to ten seconds to review each piece of content (longer for videos), and they have targets of around a thousand pieces of reviewed content per workday. The materials that have been released have all been in English, requiring laborers not fluent in English to use Google Translate throughout their daily work and increasing the difficulty of accurately moderating content.[152] It is worth noting as well that Facebook currently does not have enough training data prepared for its automated content flagging systems to be very accurate in languages other than English and Portuguese. Despite these linguistic difficulties, moderators are collectively required to review over ten million pieces of content per week and are expected to review every piece of flagged content on the platform within twenty-four hours. The company aims for a benchmark error rate of less than 1 percent, which means that there are still tens of thousands of moderation errors made each day by the platform's human algorithms.[153] As Max Fisher notes, "[M]oderators, at times relying on Google Translate, have mere seconds to recall countless rules and apply them to the hundreds of posts that dash across their screens each day."[154]

A number of these materials have been leaked to the press and can offer a small window into content moderation labor at Facebook. However, as Tarleton Gillespie notes, what is most shocking about the documents is not any aspect in particular that they reveal but the fact that they had to be leaked in the first place. As Gillespie notes,

> These are secret documents, designed not for consideration by users or regulators, but to instruct and manage the 3000+ independently contracted clickworkers who do the actual moderation work. These criteria, while perhaps crafted with input from experts, have not been made public to users, not benefited from public deliberation or even reaction. A single company—in fact a small team within that single company—have anointed themselves the arbiters of what is healthy, fair, harmful, obscene, risky, racist, artistic, intentional, and lewd.[155]

It is precisely at this point of hubris, where a small group of people thought that they could universalize determinations of obscenity in secret, that heteronormativity slipped into the foundation of Facebook's content moderation policies. This bias is only exacerbated in practice as an overworked and underpaid globally distributed set of laborers are charged with implementing them at scale. People performing this labor told the *Guardian* that "moderators often feel overwhelmed by the number of posts they have to review—and they make mistakes, particularly in the complicated area of permissible sexual content."[156]

The problem is that Facebook does not recognize analyzing sexual content as being among the content moderation tasks that are most difficult and time sensitive. The structure of its human algorithm is such that content like hate speech, conspiracy theorists preying on mass shootings, and content the media is focusing on, like Russian trolls, are "escalated" to better trained and longer-employed laborers. Sexual content more often remains de-escalated, handled by the least trained laborers. Sarah T. Roberts, a professor at UCLA who studies content moderation, told Motherboard, "The fundamental reason for content moderation—its root reason for existing—goes quite simply to the issue of brand protection and liability mitigation for the platform. It is ultimately and fundamentally in the service of the platforms themselves. It's the gatekeeping mechanisms the platforms use to control the nature of the user-generated content that flows over their branded spaces."[157] This is reflected in the training documents and guidelines that have been leaked to the press, which warn moderators against creating "PR fires" by making decisions about content removal that could "have a negative impact on Facebook's reputation or even put the company at legal risk."[158] Heteronormative bias does not often fit the bill for dedicated attention at the company and has never produced serious discussions among politicians about better regulating the platform. The few PR fires that ignite over LGBTQIA+ discrimination are more easily quelled by patronizing apologies and promises of changes and self-regulation that rarely manifest.

While specific examples of biased content moderation decisions will be overviewed in greater detail in chapter 3, it is worth taking a look briefly at two PR fires caused by content moderation decisions at the company to illustrate the point. For example, the first PR fire around heteronormative content moderation on the platform to catch the public's attention occurred in 2011 when Facebook moderators decided to censor an image of a gay kiss taken from the British television drama *Eastenders*. The company apologized profusely and reinstated the image, but there are no available public records or indications within leaked documentation of larger changes being made within its content moderation policies after this encounter.[159] In 2016, Facebook censored a famous image of the so-called napalm girl from the Vietnam War for violating its policies on depicted nudity, thus demonstrating that photorealism is so habitually associated with pornography that all nude bodies are liable to be considered sexually explicit unless proven otherwise after public outcry.[160] This demonstrates the default worldview of Facebook's content moderators in which all female-presenting bodies are sexualized. Facebook similarly apologized after the instance, and it now appears as an example in their training manuals, but this photo is allowed because of its credentials and historic importance. The next photo like it will still likely be censored on the platform until it has achieved enough awards, hung in enough museums, and climbed the Google Image search rankings.

Thus, Facebook's human algorithm is produced by a small set of predominantly white, straight, young men looking for the most practical solutions imaginable within their normative worldviews that minimally meet the company's desire to protect its brand value and avoid legal liabilities. Its outsourced labor force is made up of culturally heterogeneous contract laborers who receive little training, are given heteronormative guidelines, are under immense pressure to rapidly determine whether to censor content, and are instructed to default to censoring all potentially sexually explicit content, and the most highly trained and accurate of whom dedicate most of their time to reviewing escalated content exclusively. This leads to a lot of heteronormative bias in Facebook's content moderation practices and can have disastrous consequences for its users. Facebook Pages and Groups whose moderators have five pieces of content censored within ninety days or have more than two "elements" that can be considered sexual solicitation or nude imagery on their home pages are unpublished.[161] These policies similarly apply to personal accounts, with many users facing repeated and increasingly lengthy bans from the site. As we'll see in chapter 3, such biased content moderation policies are the norm on platforms like Facebook. They have dire consequences for all users, but particularly for LGBTQIA+ communities, and the adjudication mechanisms for correcting biased decisions are severely lacking. As evidence of this, I'd now like to turn to an examination of Facebook's Community Standards, particularly as they relate to key issues for the LGBTQIA+ community.

FACEBOOK'S COMMUNITY STANDARDS

Facebook maintains a detailed set of community standards and enforcement guidelines for moderating content on their platform. The company describes its mission as including the embrace of diversity in perspectives and notes that because of this, they err on the side of allowing content to persist on the site. This is in large part because Facebook regulates content via a single, global set of rules that are meant to be applied consistently to their entire Facebook community of some two billion users. They further reserve the right to deviate from the letter of these Community Standards and to enforce them based on the "spirit" of the policies.[162] As we'll see, this leads to a pervasive heteronormativity in Facebook's content moderation practices, despite their best efforts to combat this bias, as well as pervasive Western, and specifically US-centered, biases—a limitation particularly difficult to combat because the deliberations about content moderation policies and the publicly available information on these changes are in English.

Since 2016, Facebook has taken steps to make this deliberative process that results in changes to their Community Standards more transparent to the public. These meetings are prefaced by multiple working groups performing research within the company and engagements in discussions with "stakeholders" who provide input into proposed policy changes, all of which is aggregated and presented at Facebook's Product Policy Forum (previously called the Content Standards Forum) for comment before Facebook makes its final decision on policy changes. Since 2017, Facebook has publicly released the minutes and presentations from the Product Policy Forum on the Facebook Newsroom website, though the stakeholders and forum participants are anonymized in the publicly released documents.[163] A number of people performing content moderation review labor at Facebook have also leaked Facebook's guidelines to the press, particularly from the pre-2017 era in which their work was more thoroughly shrouded in secrecy. From these documents, we can piece together a rather clear picture of how content moderation labor is performed at the company and how the company's Community Standards get formalized into enforcement guidelines that can be run as "human algorithms" on human reviewers.

Currently, Facebook's Community Standards outline twenty-one different types of content that it moderates on its platform. Under the heading "Safety," Facebook's Community Standards list "Sexual Exploitation of Adults" as one type of content that they will moderate on their platform. This includes "content that depicts, threatens or promotes sexual violence, sexual assault, or sexual exploitation," and "content that displays, advocates for, or coordinates sexual acts with nonconsenting parties or commercial sexual services."[164] We can already see here the influence of NCOSE's concept of intersectional sexual exploitation, as sex work is definitionally conflated with sexual exploitation, thus removing agency from sex workers and reinforcing their historic positioning as the corrupted and helpless victims of the darker aspects of society in need of saving. This discourse is rooted in a heteronormative gender binary that historically understands women as being less compelled to seek sexual pleasure and personally and privately in charge of defending their sexual virtue from nonmonogamous or commercialized sexual activity. While it is certainly noble to guard against real sexual exploitation on a social media platform like Facebook, conflating that task with combating prostitution betrays deeply embedded normative and Christian conservative moral frameworks.

Under the heading of "Objectionable Content," Facebook also lists "Sexual Solicitation." Violations of this portion of the Community Standards include content that "facilitates, encourages or coordinates sexual encounters between adults."[165] This means that users cannot make posts that attempt to coordinate or recruit participants for filmed sexual activities, strip club shows, live sex performances, erotic dances, or sexual, erotic, or tantric massages. Facebook also considers content that explicitly and implicitly solicits sex to violate this standard. Explicit sexual solicitation includes offering or asking for sex or sexual partners, engaging in sex chat or conversations, or sending nude images. Implicit sexual solicitation is defined as an offer or request to engage in sexual activity combined with the use of suggestive statements, sexual hints, shared sexual content, and what Facebook calls "sexualized slang." While these policies officially apply to publicly posted content, Facebook has a history of scanning private messages as well and unclear policies about when and how it does so.[166] Essentially, Facebook does not want anyone to use its platform to arrange sex acts of any kind, including digital sex acts like sexting. As journalist Violet Blue notes, "Anything encouraging sex for pleasure between adults is now a bannable offense in public posts."[167] This anti-sex approach to content moderation should not be surprising, given Facebook's normative moral stance on pornography and sex writ large. In fact, Facebook was one of the first major tech companies to break ranks and support the passage of FOSTA-SESTA by the US Congress, a sweeping anti-sex and anti-pornography bill masquerading under the rhetoric of protecting children and preventing sex trafficking that will be analyzed in much greater detail in chapters 3 and 4.[168]

Facebook's most sweeping standard is its restriction of content displaying "adult nudity and sexual activity," which it considers as "objectionable content." Policies for regulating nudity as obscenity have always been difficult to formalize, and thus the company's definitions here more frequently come as lists of examples of censorable images. The current list of things you should not post images of on Facebook is as follows:

- Real nude adults, where nudity is defined as
  - visible genitalia except in the context of birth giving and after-birth moments or health-related situations (for example, gender confirmation surgery, examination for cancer or disease prevention/assessment);
  - visible anus and/or fully nude close-ups of buttocks unless photoshopped on a public figure; or
  - uncovered female nipples except in the context of breastfeeding, birth giving, and after-birth moments; health-related situations (for example, postmastectomy, breast cancer awareness, or gender confirmation surgery); or an act of protest.
- Sexual activity, including
  - sexual intercourse;
  - explicit sexual intercourse, defined as mouth or genitals entering or in contact with another person's genitals or anus, where at least one person's genitals are nude;
  - implied sexual intercourse, defined as mouth or genitals entering or in contact with another person's genitals or anus, even when the contact is not directly visible, except in cases of a sexual health context, advertisements, and recognized fictional images or with indicators of fiction; or
  - implied stimulation of genitalia/anus, defined as stimulating genitalia/anus or inserting objects into genitalia/anus, even when the activity is not directly visible, except in cases of sexual health context, advertisements, and recognized fictional images or with indicators of fiction.
- Other sexual activities including (but not limited to)
  - erections;
  - presence of by-products of sexual activity;
  - stimulating genitals or anus, even if above or under clothing;
  - use of sex toys, even if above or under clothing;
  - stimulation of naked human nipples; or
  - squeezing female breast except in breastfeeding context.
- Fetish content that involves
  - acts that are likely to lead to the death of a person or animal,
  - dismemberment,
  - cannibalism, or
  - feces, urine, spit, snot, menstruation, or vomit.[169]

They note that images are allowed that would otherwise violate these standards if the sexual activity is not directly visible or is not sufficiently detailed or if the image was posted in a satirical, humorous, educational, or scientific context. As we'll see below, these standards contain a number of heteronormative and Western biases that become apparent when they are put into practice. It is worth noting first that Facebook leverages the rhetoric of protecting children and the feminist discourse against revenge porn to justify their overbroad implementation of these standards. In short, the company defaults to removing any and all sexual imagery on the platform unless there is a specific "carve-out" that has been codified to allow that content.[170]

Each carve-out that the company has worked into its Community Standards and its "human algorithms" for reviewing flagged content is the result of a previous failure of the system and usually has only been implemented after strong grassroots organizing among Facebook users who have faced multiple account bans and had many pieces of content censored. Take, for example, the carve-out for images of breastfeeding, a hard-won victory by grassroots organizers well documented by Tarleton Gillespie in his book *Custodians of the Internet*. For more than a decade, Facebook censored all images of breastfeeding. As Gillespie notes, "Some women spoke of feeling ashamed and humiliated that their photos, and their experiences as new mothers, were being judged obscene. Removal of a photo was literally an erasure of the woman and her accomplishment, and could easily feel like a particularly personal violation of a deeply held conviction."[171] This censorship also synced up with people's experiences with the hypersexualization of female-presenting breasts that made breastfeeding in public a social taboo, extending these same restrictions into the digital world. In this example, we can see Facebook kowtowing to their advertisers, protecting their brand image, and appeasing heteronormative conservatives at the expense of breastfeeding parents. The policy was not changed until 2014, after a decade of parents politically organizing, engaging in political action, making negative headlines for the company, and engaging in acts of "platform disobedience," like purposefully posting images that violated this community standard and then documenting and sharing Facebook's responses—many people had their accounts banned multiple times to achieve this victory.

More recently, Facebook has been struggling to figure out how best to handle what it refers to as "cultural nudity," which is most often exemplified by photos of "aboriginal" peoples and religious figures and rituals. For

the people in these images, nudity is a cultural norm, and it would be difficult to impossible to visually represent them on the platform without violating Facebook's Community Standards. In 2019, the company convened
four cross-functional working groups, engaged in seventeen conversations
with external stakeholders, and made a presentation at their Product Policy
Forum without reaching a consensus on how to address this gap in their current policies. Facebook's current policy would be to ban any of these images
that contain visible female-presenting nipples or the genitalia of either sex,
but the company has considered allowing images of age-appropriate people
whose female-presenting nipples are exposed, provided the images are not
sexually suggestive and no genitalia are visible. This proposal produces some
problems, though, as it leads to value judgments of content, the problem of
having moderators attempt to interpret content, and would require a lot of
labor to overhaul the automated content moderation systems. The other pro-
posed change would add carve-outs for full nudity when there are indicators
that the nudity is "cultural/Indigenous" or is posted in the explicit context of
"pregnancy/motherhood." This latter proposal presented problems of determining the consent of the nude people depicted; produced the possibility for
false positives within the carve-outs; requires a definition of cultural nudity,
which is difficult to produce; may produce a slippery slope in which context
is used to justify more and more nudity on the platform; and requires an
overhaul of the automated system. In the end, the company failed to reach a
consensus on new changes and continued to analyze its options for the rest
of 2019 while the ban on depictions of genitalia or female-presenting nipples
remained the status quo.[172]

From this example, we can see a number of problems in the way content gets moderated on Facebook. First, the company's quest to produce a
universal—and English-language-based—set of standards runs into problems
when applied in practice. Here these problems consist of cultural variations
in what is considered "nudity" and in which contexts that nudity becomes
"obscene." While it is easy to see how a company with the practicality of an
entrenched hacker ethic would lean on the visibility of female-presenting
nipples as the sole determinant of whether an image is obscene, this comes
at the expense of hardcoding heteronormativity into the platform. It reinforces the sexualization of female-presenting bodies and produces an unfair
double standard that is disadvantageous for female-presenting people.[173] Further, even the proposed policy changes would not introduce toplessness for

female-presenting people and potentially achieve the hoped-for desexualization of female-presenting bodies among populations that have historically suppressed this behavior. As the company noted in its Product Policy Forum, "We are trying to focus on historic, social and cultural norms that exist across different groups of people, whether that's religious groups, racial groups, social groups."[174] This move is also grounded on a homogeneity across historic, social, or cultural opinions about female-presenting toplessness that does not exist. For example, in the United States, thirty-seven states do not have official policies on female-presenting toplessness, and it is more often legislated at the local level, producing a wide variety of local ordinances governing the exposure of female-presenting breasts in the United States.[175]

The most heteronormative aspect of this particular community standard, however, is the assumption that "female nipples" correlate with genitalia or that anatomical sex can be inferred in cases where genitalia are obscured from the shape and size of the breast tissue that visible nipples are attached to. Take, for example, Courtney Demone's #DoIHaveBoobsNow? Project, in which Demone, a transgender woman, posted photos of her exposed chest as she underwent hormone replacement therapy, challenging Facebook and Instagram to answer her very simple question, "At what point in my breast development do I need to start covering my nipples?"[176] Platforms cannot answer this question based on their cisnormative community standards. In other words, their policies turn out to be profoundly *im*practical for regulating the visibility of gender fluid, nonbinary, and trans bodies on the platform. With the current accuracy rates of computer vision-based automated content filtering, coupled with the "human algorithms" Facebook employs to sort out the content that slips through its automated filters, the company can quite accurately identify all images with exposed nipples. So why not just produce an overlaid filter that blurs an image until people confirm that they are willing to be exposed to it, as Facebook already does with violent and medical images posted to the site? Why not simply produce a nipples/no nipples toggle in a user's Facebook settings? It would be easy to implement such a solution and, since the company already verifies user identities and ages, it would be easy to gatekeep children from "unwanted exposure." Heteronormativity on a platform like Facebook is essentially this: to see biased filtering as the default, most practical solution to the problem of content moderation rather than recognizing the ease with which less normative filtering could be achieved across the platform.

Another recent point of contention in Facebook's Product Policy Forum has been how to moderate sexual activity in art. In late 2018 and early 2019, the company convened two working group meetings, consulted with fourteen external stakeholders, and held a presentation at their Product Policy Forum to reaffirm their status quo and formalize better operational guidelines to ensure more consistent enforcement by their "human algorithms." As the company notes, "Our policies distinguish between real world and digital art in the context of adult nudity and sexual activity because we have historically found that digital images are hypersexualized."[177] In essence, the company maintains a medium-specific set of standards. If your image is a photograph of an oil painting or a sculpture, Facebook assumes it is less likely to be hypersexualized than a digitally produced image. The company also is more likely to remove performance art and mass-produced, video-based content. Thus, content moderators are trained to look at whether an image is of a "real object" (paper, wood, canvas, wall) or composed in a "traditional medium" (water colors, pencil, marker, charcoal, spray, marble, bronze) and to use Google Image Search to check whether the art is "real or digital." They also look to see if an image has been altered by photo editing software through things like cut and paste signals and whether there are traces of paint programs, like vector shapes or 8-bit lines. This essentially reproduces a traditional classist distinction between "high" and "low" art in which Tom of Finland erotica is permissible because it's been made with oil paints on canvas but anonymously created digital nude portraits are not. While it might not be readily apparent how this connects to heteronormativity, one needs only remember the financially precarious existence of much of the LGBTQIA+ community, particularly a large section of the trans community. This makes it more difficult for the community to publicize its arts and culture, arbitrate and litigate censorship, and take in essential revenue to maintain and produce new artworks. As smartphones increasingly become a necessity for everyday life—essential for gaining employment, managing finances, obtaining housing, and so on—they are increasingly the windows through which arts and culture are accessed, disseminated in the public sphere, and marketed to generate revenue. Digital communications mediated by these smartphones and the social media platforms that dominate their internet usage can easily lead to a future in which artistic production is less viable for the LGBTQIA+ community. By producing a medium-specific set of community standards surrounding artistic nudity, Facebook is potentially leaning into a future in which LGBTQIA+ art bears an undue burden of censorship and risks being rendered invisible to the broader public.

Taken collectively, despite response to public pressure to improve their content moderation policies and practices, the operation of Facebook's "human algorithms" leaves much to be desired. The employees responsible for the moderation of content of central importance to LGBTQIA+ communities in the United States are largely the least experienced, operate from other cultural contexts, and are underpaid and overburdened, leading to uninformed, exceedingly fast decisions about censorship. As I've shown, these decisions are particularly impactful when it comes to content surrounding sex work, breastfeeding, nipple exposure more broadly, cultural nudity, and artistic expression. This creates an undue burden of censorship on LGBTQIA+ communities and disallows a large portion of content that many people would not find to be explicitly obscene or pornographic, ranging from community building, social activism and organizing, sex education, explorations of gendered embodiment, and artistic expression. As we'll see in chapter 3, these actions by Facebook are not the exception but the rule on the internet. LGBTQIA+ content is faced with undue censorship, account banning, and demonetization across the web.

CYBERPORN AND THE END OF REGULATION

The internet as we know it and many of the companies that dominate it were forged in the wake of a nationwide sex panic about children's access to pornography. This sex panic might be best exemplified by the August 3, 1995, *Time* magazine issue on *cyberporn* (see figure 3.1). In the issue's cover story, Philip Elmer-Dewitt reported on the findings of a later debunked study showing that 83.5 percent of the images stored online at Usenet newsgroups were pornographic.[1] Twenty years later, Elmer-Dewitt would describe this as his worst story "by far" and note that one *Time* researcher assigned to his story later recalled it as "one of the more shameful, fear-mongering and unscientific efforts that we ever gave attention to."[2] This sex panic surrounding "cyberporn" culminated in Congress passing the Children's Internet Protection Act (CIPA) in 2000. CIPA required public schools and libraries to install internet filters on all of their computers to block obscene content, child sexual abuse images, and content deemed harmful to minors in order to continue receiving federal funding. Similar to earlier moral panics surrounding the dissemination of pornography in the United States, CIPA also embodied a class-based anxiety over *who* had access to online pornography, as evidenced by the original extension of the ban to adult library patrons.[3]

Media scholar Henry Jenkins responded to the *Time* story in a 1997 article published in *Radical Teacher*. In a passage worth quoting at length, he wrote,

> The myth of "childhood innocence" "empties" children of any thoughts of their own, stripping them of their own political agency and social agendas so that they may become vehicles for adult needs, desires, and politics. . . . The "innocent" child is an increasingly dangerous abstraction when it starts to substitute in our thinking for actual children or when it helps justify efforts to restrict real children's minds and to regulate their bodies. The myth of "childhood innocence,"

Figure 3.1
Time magazine cover, August 3, 1995.

> which sees children only as potential victims of the adult world or as beneficiaries
> of paternalistic protection, opposes pedagogies that empower children as active
> agents in the educational process. We cannot teach children how to engage in
> critical thought by denying them access to challenging information or provoca-
> tive images.[4]

As we'll see in this chapter, so much of our lives as children and adults are
lived at the interstice between the sexual and the platonic, the prurient and
the pure. Critical thought requires us to learn how to navigate these gray
areas, and the development of this capacity takes many years of practice,
online or off. Overbroad filters stunt this development, blocking access to
everything from legitimate nonsexual speech to hard-core pornography and
all the gray areas in between. As we'll see, this problem is particularly acute
when it comes to LGBTQIA+ discourse. However, what little resistance there
was to CIPA maintained these black-and-white distinctions between legitimate and illegitimate speech, focusing on how nonsexual speech was blocked
by overbroad filters.

Prior to CIPA, the American Civil Liberties Union (ACLU) was already
publishing detailed white papers arguing against internet censorship based on
a broad interpretation of First Amendment rights.[5] In 2002 the Kaiser Family
Foundation published a study indicating that at moderate levels, internet

filters did not significantly impede access to online health information, but at their more restrictive levels, the filters would "block access to a substantial amount of health information, with only a minimal increase in blocked pornographic content."[6] CIPA was challenged in court by the American Library Association, also on First Amendment grounds, and appealed to the Supreme Court by 2003. It is worth noting that *none* of these free speech arguments against the implementation of porn filters were arguing that pornography ought not be filtered. Pornography has never constituted protected speech in the United States and has been especially vulnerable to censorship after *Miller v. California*.[7] The central fact of all these arguments was that porn filters are unreliable. They always *overblock*—they filter some portion of nonpornographic sites for one reason or another—and they always still let some porn through. The First Amendment claims against these filters were all based on the fact that they would necessarily be blocking some portion of nonpornographic content, which, precisely because it was not pornography, would qualify for free speech protections.

All nine Supreme Court justices agreed that restricting children's access to pornography posed no constitutional problem. They also agreed that all available filters were blunt instruments that inevitably block some portion of nonpornographic material.[8] The constitutional question was thus whether this overblocking constituted a violation of First Amendment rights. The Supreme Court ultimately decided in favor of CIPA by a margin of six to three. In the aftermath of this decision and the displacement of the cyberporn sex panic from center stage by 9/11 and the escalation of wars in Afghanistan and Iraq, the free speech concern of overblocking largely faded into the background. As Deborah Caldwell-Stone noted in her 2013 *American Libraries* article, "Debate over filtering became muted. . . . While researchers counted the number of libraries and schools using filters, little inquiry was made into how institutions were implementing CIPA or how filtering was affecting library users."[9]

While the critical discourse seeking to combat overblocking by internet filters has yet to fully resurface, this moral panic about access to pornography through public internet outlets, and particularly in schools, is alive and strong. For instance, in both 2017 and 2018, NCOSE (see chapter 1) added EBSCO Information Services to their annual "Dirty Dozen" list of smut peddlers. While CIPA remains in force and most American public schools filter internet pornography, the EBSCO databases that many students use to access educational materials are not subject to these same internet filters. Even after

EBSCO worked to scrub their elementary, middle, and high school databases of pornographic and sexually explicit materials, NCOSE found a number of materials on these databases that they objected to. NCOSE researchers found "sexually graphic written content on high school databases, including sexually graphic written descriptions and instructions for oral sex and other sexual acts" that they considered "salacious and not academic."[10] On the high school EBSCO database, they also objected to academic articles about gay porn, articles about pornography more broadly, and articles from magazines like *Cosmopolitan* and *Redbook* that provide sex advice. EBSCO's middle school database (Middle Search Plus) and elementary school database (Primary Search) contained articles on adult entertainer Bettie Page; teen activists working to make public nudity acceptable by posting nude protest images to Instagram; sex advice articles with information on oral sex, anal sex, and BDSM; and other sex education materials that NCOSE considered guilty of normalizing deviant sex and encouraging the use of pornography by children.[11]

EBSCO spokeswoman Kathleen McEvoy noted that schools are primarily responsible for setting up their own EBSCO filters for blocking objectionable content and that the NCOSE researchers were likely accessing these materials through their home computers that would not be subject to these school filters. However, she noted that EBSCO initiated an investigation after NCOSE's research findings. While EBSCO was not able to reproduce their findings, she noted that the company took NCOSE's findings very seriously and that the company has taken steps to ramp up its content filters for public school databases. She also concurred with NCOSE that magazine articles about sex practices like BDSM did not count as "sex education" and thus ought to be censored.[12] Despite EBSCO's response to these problems, at least one school district in Colorado discontinued its subscription to EBSCO Information Services for the foreseeable future.[13]

We can thus expect that overblocking will continue to be part of the daily lives of public school students in the United States for the foreseeable future as well. This inordinately impacts the most underprivileged students who might not have ready access to the internet via broadband or mobile devices outside of the school's internet filters. As we've repeatedly seen, moral panics over sex and pornography always have class dimensions to them, which are repeated both here and in another instance in which NCOSE, after joining forces with Enough Is Enough, was able to get both Starbucks and McDonald's to agree to filter sexually explicit content on their free Wi-Fi in locations nationwide.[14] The overblocking that results inordinately impacts poor and unhoused adults in the same way that it did when public libraries installed filters after CIPA.

This chapter will make the case that overblocking is a phenomenon common across the internet writ large and is not confined to public schools or free Wi-Fi hotspots. Nearly every major internet platform today engages in systematic overblocking of sexual expression, which by default reinforces heteronormativity. The primary focus will be on analyzing the impact of the Stop Enabling Sex Traffickers Act and Fight Online Sex Trafficking Act, collectively known as FOSTA-SESTA and hereafter referred to as FOSTA, which the US Congress passed in 2017. FOSTA was the first substantial change in legislation and regulative policy surrounding adult content that the United States has made since CIPA and has had the largest impact on the internet since the Communications Decency Act (CDA) was passed in 1996. We can essentially divide content moderation practices into pre-FOSTA and post-FOSTA eras. In the former, ISPs and content hosts, like social media platforms, were not liable for user-generated content disseminated by or hosted on their networks, which led to a lighter, but still quite repressive, censorship regime, as we'll see below. FOSTA, claimed as a marquee policy victory by NCOSE, has led to extreme crackdowns on sexual speech on the internet. It has adversely impacted many LGBTQIA+ communities and has been exploited by the manosphere (see chapter 1) to punish adult entertainers and sex workers online. In the aftermath of FOSTA, many adult entertainers and sex workers have faced serious consequences as both their livelihoods and their bodies were put at risk by the act. Additionally, the act has ramped up the overblocking of sex education materials, which is likely to have an inordinate impact on the adolescents coming of age during its reign over internet content. As I'll show in chapter 4, this victory of anti-porn crusaders has also led to a détente wherein pornography is allowed to continue proliferating online provided it is produced by multinational corporations and coheres to heteronormative genre conventions.

OVERBLOCKING IN THE RUNUP TO FOSTA-SESTA

Since 2016, LGBTQIA+ digital content and its creators have been increasingly under attack at a global scale. As Freedom House's annual "Freedom on the Net" report for 2016 states, "Posts related to the LGBTI community resulted in blocking, takedowns, or arrests for the first time in many settings. Authorities also demonstrated an increasing wariness of the power of images on today's internet."[15] The organization found attempts to block LGBTQIA+ content in eighteen countries, up from fourteen in 2015, ranging from South Korean regulators asking the Naver web portal to reconsider linking to gay dramas to the Turkish government blocking all the popular LGBTQIA+ websites in the country for a period during 2015.[16] Turkey regularly invokes legal provisions about protecting families, censoring obscenity, and preventing prostitution to block LGBTQIA+ websites and apps like Hadigayri.com, Transsick-o, and Grindr.[17] By 2017, Freedom House estimated that 47 percent of the global population lived in countries where LGBTQIA+ content was suppressed and sometimes punishable by law.[18]

It is worth noting that information on the overblocking of LGBTQIA+ content online was restricted to only a single page of both Freedom House's 2016 and 2017 reports and was entirely absent from their 2018 report. Reporting on the overblocking of LGBTQIA+ content is largely absent from contemporary discourse on content moderation. A large part of this is due to the pressing issues of social media spreading alt-right political propaganda and conspiracy theories, which leads to an inevitable focus on content moderation in terms of political speech. However, it may also be due to the false Pandora's box of porn narrative leading people to believe that LGBTQIA+ content flows freely across the global internet. My hope in this chapter is to convince you that this is a false assumption and that LGBTQIA+ content is regularly overblocked in the United States. This US-based overblocking has global implications. As many of the most prominent internet platforms are headquartered in the United States, its legislation has an inordinate impact on global internet traffic for two primary reasons. First, internet platforms rarely maintain separate content moderation standards for different national or cultural audiences. If a state has the power to influence these standards, that impact is frequently felt globally. Second, the proprietors of these internet platforms and many of their employees live in and are influenced by the same US norms that make legislation like FOSTA possible. The global impact of FOSTA is thus to doubly reinforce heteronormativity, first by subjecting LGBTQIA+ content to stricter scrutiny than heteronormative content and second because silencing sexual expression effectively preserves the status quo.

The majority of anti-porn discourse argues that content filters are the only way to protect children from unwanted exposure to pornography online, thus justifying overblocking. This, however, does not seem to be the case. For instance, after analyzing two separate datasets, researchers found that the use of internet filters "had inconsistent and practically insignificant links" with adolescents encountering sexually explicit content online.[19] The overblocking that results from internet filters thus does not have its desired effect. Mainstream heteroporn with wide distribution networks, advanced search engine optimization (SEO) techniques, and the capacity for mass-producing content still makes it through the filter, as we'll see in chapter 4. What is lost is always a combination of art, sex education, LGBTQIA+ community resources, and LGBTQIA+ pornography.

BAD BLOCKS/WEAK ADJUDICATION

It is difficult to retroactively construct a full catalogue of unduly censored content prior to FOSTA because few researchers were focused on content moderation and no centralized agencies were collecting archival examples of overblocking. For example, a paper from the Berkman Klein Center for Internet and Society at Harvard University examined Google SafeSearch in 2003 and found strong evidence that Google routinely blocked newspapers, government sites, educational resources, and even sites *about* controversial concepts and images.[20] However, since 2003, there have been no academic studies of SafeSearch censorship, and thus there is no real catalogue of what has been getting censored or how the adjudication mechanisms play out for those who believe their content was censored in error and are thus seeking to get it unblocked.[21] To stick with the case of Google, this censorship has dire consequences for content producers and website managers, as even a temporary block can do irreparable damage to their position in Google search rankings and thus can cause an unexpected and potentially prolonged cessation of revenue as web traffic slows to a halt. As we will see below, this is not unique to Google. Across the internet, content creators and website administrators, particularly those with less access to capital and representing niche and/or marginalized communities, are confronting undue censorship and loss of revenue. The adjudication channels provided to them are opaque, alienating, and often unsuccessful if they do not have national visibility or expensive legal counsel.

In lieu of a robust archive of unduly censored content pre-FOSTA, I will work to stitch together what has been documented with some experimental explorations of contemporary content moderation practices, both my own and those conducted by artists using their own convolutional neural networks—particularly what are termed "generative adversarial networks" that reverse engineer the operations of computer vision algorithms. What we'll find is that automated content moderation performed by computer vision and image recognition algorithms is not very good at parsing the context of nudity, which constitutes a significant problem when it comes to the censorship of art. While some of this lack of contextual knowledge can be compensated for by relaying the moderation decisions to *human algorithms*, they, too, will often err on the side of overblocking artistic nudity. While they may recognize and override blocks to canonical Western artistic nudity—the types of oil paintings hung in world-class museums—this same consideration is rarely extended to non-Western, noncanonized, or everyday artistic productions.

It is no wonder then that one of the most frequent victims of overblocking is the artistic representation of nudity. As we saw in chapter 2, even canonical works of art like the Venus de Milo are potentially subject to censorship by Google SafeSearch because automated content filters have trouble with higher-level differentiations like that between pornography and nude art. Several famous works of art have been subjected to censorship on platforms like Facebook. In 2018, Facebook flagged images of the Venus of Willendorf as pornography and censored them on its platform, which led to an online petition against art censorship.[22] Facebook also automatically flagged an image of the painting *The Origin of the World* posted by Gustave Courbet, who had his account deactivated as a result.[23] Facebook has also banned images of Gerhard Richter's 1992 painting *Ema*, a misted view of a nude woman descending a staircase; Evelyne Axell's 1964 painting *Ice Cream*, a pop art painting of a woman's head as she licks an ice-cream cone; and Edvard Erikson's 1913 public sculpture *The Little Mermaid*.[24]

This trend is even more impactful when it comes to photography. Take, for example, Michael Stokes's work, which often includes photographs of men in various stages of undress, including wounded, amputee veterans. Since 2013, Stokes's photographs have been repeatedly flagged on Facebook as violating their community standards, and he has been subjected to multiple bans from the platform (not to mention hate messages and threats from other users). Stokes compares this to Helmut Newton's ability to freely post his photograph of Venus Williams in the nude for *ESPN*'s 2014 Body Issue, which Facebook has allowed to circulate without challenge. Stokes writes, "Nude subjects have traditionally been reserved exclusively for the male gaze, so when a man poses nude, to some this implies that the image is homoerotic."[25] Thus, Stokes has found that images of women can be further undressed than those of men without triggering content filters (either automatically or by people reporting the images). Stokes argues that this trend has only accelerated in the past few years. In 2015, he posted a photo of two male police officers, fully dressed, kissing with a caption about censorship that was, ironically, quickly censored. He further notes that he recognized a strong shift in Instagram's content moderation after it was purchased by Facebook. He encountered few problems with the platform before its sale and afterward was regularly subject to warnings and takedown notices. More recently, after Tumblr announced that it would no longer host sexually explicit content on its platform, nearly 70 percent of his 900 photographs on the platform were flagged as violating the new community standards.

Photorealism does seem to be a key marker of the likelihood that an image will be automatically flagged as sexually explicit, at least via Google Safe-Search. For example, I ran the first one hundred images that resulted from Google Image searches for "nude sculpture" and "nude painting" through Google's Cloud Vision API and found evidence that photorealism was a key indicator for an image being flagged as "adult" or "racy."[26] For instance, of the sculptures, only one was flagged as likely or very likely to be adult, and thirty were flagged as likely or very likely to be racy. Similarly, of the paintings, only twelve were flagged as adult and sixty-seven as racy. The sculptures that were flagged often were realistic and had a sheen to them reminiscent of the sweat and oil often found on models' skin during filming, and paintings were much more likely to be flagged the less abstract they were. This bears out upon further testing. I ran the first one hundred images from The Vulva Gallery, an online site and printed book containing close-up illustrations of vulvas in the likeness of watercolor paintings. None of them were flagged as adult, and only fifteen of them were flagged as racy. Similarly, I ran two sets of hentai fanart from the site DeviantArt.com through Cloud Vision, fifty color illustrations and fifty line art illustrations. Of the color illustrations, thirty-four were flagged as adult and forty-eight as racy, while only one of the line art illustrations was flagged as adult and only thirty-three as racy. Lastly, I took the first forty-four images of Real Dolls, lifelike silicone sex dolls, from a Google Image Search and ran them through Cloud Vision and found that all forty-four of them were flagged as both adult and racy. These findings are borne out by computer science literature, which demonstrates that color and texture properties are key features in the detection of nudity by computer vision algorithms, as seen in chapter 2.

Yet what a computer "sees" as indicative color and textural features of nudity is not the same as what we would expect based on our own visual experience. This has been demonstrated by several artists who have been using machine learning to probe the limits of computer vision, image recognition, and adult content moderation as it relates to the arts. Take, for example, the work of Tom White, an artist and senior lecturer in media design at Victoria University of Wellington. White uses a generative adversarial network (GAN) to produce what the tech industry calls "adversarial examples" based on ImageNet classifiers. In essence, a GAN mirrors the CNN that powers an image recognition algorithm (see chapter 2 for a lengthy overview of CNNs), feeding abstract shapes, patterns, or amalgamations of images into the CNN, seeing what classifiers that image triggers, and then adjusting the shapes, patterns, or amalgamations of images iteratively until it outputs an image that will trigger a classifier despite looking nothing like what a human would recognize as an example of that particular classification. As White puts it, he uses abstract forms to "highlight the representations that are shared across neural network architectures—and perhaps across humans as well."[27]

In two exhibitions, *Synthetic Abstractions* and *Perception Engines*, White has generated shocking images that will trigger certain classifiers on Amazon, Google, and Yahoo's image recognition systems but to a human look nothing like an object that ought to trigger that classification.[28] Take, for example, figure 3.2, which depicts a series of black-and-white abstract shapes and lines on an orange and yellow background. Google SafeSearch recognizes this abstract image as "very likely" to be adult content, and both Amazon Web Services and Yahoo Open NSFW make similar determinations. White has a series of similar adversarial examples that to humans present as abstract shapes and colors but to image recognition systems look like concrete, identifiable objects. Images like these challenge the efficacy of image recognition systems, probing their boundaries to demonstrate the different ways in which they perceive the world. They also constitute a more practical problem, as White's work would likely be censored on most major platforms today, and he would be required to individually appeal each automatic flag applied to images on his accounts despite their (to human eyes) obviously "safe for work" status.

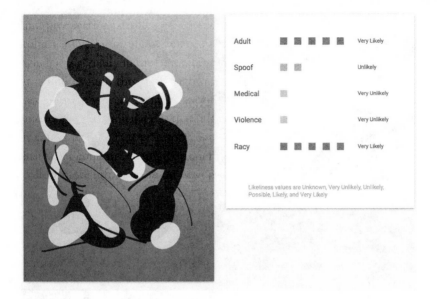

Figure 3.2
Mustard Dream by Tom White being run through Google's Cloud Vision API.

For another example, we can look to Mario Klingemann's eroGANous project, which stitches together elements from actual images into adversarial examples that will trigger image recognition systems.[29] These images are much more photorealistic than White's and, thus, while White's images may survive human review after the system has automatically flagged his content, the eroGANous images are more likely to be censored in the six- to eight-second window that human reviewers generally have to make censorship determinations on potentially sexually explicit content (see figure 3.3). As Klingemann notes, "When it comes to freedom, my choice will always be 'freedom to' and not 'freedom from,' and as such I strongly oppose any kind of censorship. Unfortunately in these times, the 'freedom from' proponents are gaining more and more influence in making this world a sterile, 'morally clean' place in which happy consumers will not be offended by anything anymore. What a boring future to look forward to."[30] As a side note, for those interested in escaping the boredom of this sterile visual regime, I'd recommend taking a look at Jake Elwes attempt at producing "machine learning porn," a two-minute video of computer vision pornography unrecognizable—yet uncannily evocative—to human vision.[31]

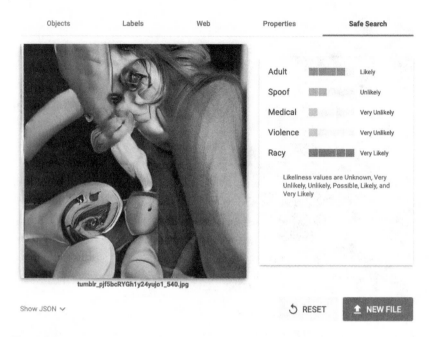

Figure 3.3
eroGANous image being run through Google's Cloud Vision API.

A similar example can be found in Robbie Barrat's work. Barrat fed images of ten thousand nude portraits into a GAN and used it to iteratively generate new "nude" images. As Barrat notes,

> So what happened with the *Nudes* is the generator figured out a way to fool the discriminator without actually getting good at generating nude portraits. The discriminator is stupid enough that if I feed it these blobs, it can't figure out the difference between that and people. So the generator can just do that instead of generating realistic portraits, which is a harder job. It can fall into this local-minima where it isn't the ideal solution, but it works for the generator, and discriminator doesn't know any better so it gets stuck there. And that is what is happening in the nude portraits.[32]

Thus, as Barrat's project demonstrates acutely, computer vision has a very peculiar and least-common-denominator approach to detecting nudity that totally collapses the context within which that nudity occurs. For many people, none of the images above would be considered obscene, and even if they were, they are most certainly contained within the realm of artistic nudity rather than pornography. Despite this, these images are routinely censored by all major computer vision algorithms.

These experiments with computer vision challenge the reliability of image recognition and produce an implicit challenge to content moderation. They also demonstrate the guiding role that the ethic of anti-porn crusaders plays in their production, as overbroad censorship is always preferable to even one pornographic image slipping through. This prioritization of anti-porn morality is, as I've shown, explicitly at odds with the needs, desires, and rights of the LGBTQIA+ community. Further, the artists above allow us to imagine a future in which new BigGAN production practices can obfuscate pornography from content moderation algorithms. As Klingemann notes,

> Luckily, the current automated censorship engines are more and more employing AI techniques to filter content. It is lucky because the same classifiers that are used to detect certain types of material can also be used to obfuscate that material in an adversarial way so that whilst humans will not see anything different, the image will not trigger those features anymore that the machine is looking for. This will of course start an arms race where the censors will have to retrain their models and harden them against these attacks and the freedom of expression forces will have to improve their obfuscation methods in return.[33]

What goes unnoted here is that these techniques will likely only be available to the most tech savvy of content producers or, in lieu of doing it themselves, those with either the access to capital to hire others to perform this labor or with large enough audiences to crowdsource it for free. A likely unintended effect of this will be that in this arms race between porn obfuscators and content moderators, the only people unable to keep up will be amateur and low-budget artists and pornographers, of which LGBTQIA+ content creators are likely to form a substantial portion. In short, if what computers view as "porn" really can be likened to spam, it seems inevitable that certain types of "porn" will mutate to exploit the weaknesses in image recognition systems. It also seems likely that the content producers that achieve this will be the well-resourced corporations peddling mainstream, heteronormative content.

IFFY BLOCKS/BAD CONSEQUENCES

As we saw earlier in this chapter, the discourse of moral panic that leverages the idea of unwanted and traumatic exposure of children to hard-core pornography to legitimate regimes of censorship, sexual discipline, and heteronormativity necessarily makes children and adolescents the most likely to have their internet traffic filtered—at school, college, the library, and at home. This filtration is likely to be under the direction of the people with the most authority at any of these locations, and thus the patterns of regulation of internet traffic are likely to draw upon the preexisting material relations of inequalities at these locations, which are often strongly heteronormative in the household.[34] By pandering to these moral panics and providing overbroad filters to ensure the smallest possibility of "unwanted exposure," filters like SafeSearch place themselves at odds with some of the more liberatory potentialities of the internet. Additionally, in the United States, some evidence suggests that adolescents who use online pornography are more likely to be African American and to come from less educated households with lower socioeconomic status.[35] There are thus always class and racial tensions that cut through these sex panics.[36]

A number of scholars have argued that the internet can be a very effective medium for disseminating educational information about sexual health, introducing sexuality, and fostering sex-positive attitudes in children and adolescents.[37] While people of any age can reap these benefits, it is more common for younger people to use the internet for information about sex and sexuality, and even more common for LGBTQIA+ youths to do so.[38] Keep in mind that this is precisely the age group meant to have its internet traffic censored by filters like SafeSearch. Overblocking frequently leads to the censorship of sex education materials. Take, for example, the case of the National Campaign to Prevent Teen and Unplanned Pregnancy's online campaign called "Bedsider," which was launched in 2012. This campaign was meant to be hipper so that it would have more appeal to young people. This is a common strategy in newer sex education social media campaigns. As Susan Gilbert, codirector of the National Coalition for Sexual Health, explains, "We have to make healthy behaviors desirable by using creative, humorous, and positive appeals."[39]

Bedsider made use of these standard social media strategies to try to entice teens to engage in safer sex practices. For instance, Bedsider tweeted, "98 percent of women have used birth control. Not one of them? Maybe it's time to upgrade your sex life."[40] In response, Twitter banned Bedsider from promoting its tweets for violating Twitter's ad policy, which prohibits the promotion of or linking to adult content and sexual products or services. A Twitter account strategist noted that the problem would persist as long as Bedsider's website continued to host the article "Condom Love: Find Out How Amazing Safer Sex Can Be."[41] Even though the article was focused on encouraging young people to engage in safe sex, the Twitter account strategist told Bedsider, "It still paints sex in a recreational/positive light versus being neutral and dry."[42] In 2017, Facebook banned advertisements from the National Campaign to Prevent Teen and Unwanted Pregnancy that promoted regular health checkups. Like others, their modern and catchy "You're so sexy when you're well" advertising campaign was deemed as profane or vulgar language. Similarly, journalist Sarah Lacy's advertisements for her book *The Uterus Is a Feature, Not a Bug* were rejected for containing the word "uterus."[43]

In response, Lawrence Swiader, Bedsider's director, told the *Atlantic*, "We need to be able to talk about sex in a real way: that it's fun, funny, sexy, awkward . . . all the things that the entertainment industry gets so well. How can we possibly compete with all of the not-so-healthy messages about sex if we have to speak like doctors and show stale pictures of people who look like they're shopping for insurance?"[44] This is not an isolated incident. The Keep A Breast Foundation, a youth-based organization that promotes breast cancer awareness and educates young people about their health, was banned from using Google AdWords because of their slogan, "I Love Boobies."[45] Both of these instances constitute a staggering reiteration of early Supreme Court bias in enforcing obscenity doctrine against LGBTQIA+ and sex education materials but *not* against *Playboy* magazine; *Playboy* has been allowed to advertise its content through its Twitter account and has even posted photos of bare breasts. And they have very real material consequences. In the last systematic study I could locate from 2013, the Pew Research Center found that 59 percent of Americans had turned to the internet for health information in the past year, with 77 percent of them starting at a search engine like Google, Bing, or Yahoo.[46]

The appeals process for banned content is too complex, time-consuming, and expensive for nonprofit organizations to successfully engage in. For instance, in 2014, the sex education organizations Spark and YTH (Youth+Tech+Health) had four of their sex education videos removed from YouTube. The organizations repeatedly contacted YouTube and filed two official appeals through the online process, all to no avail. They were only able to successfully get their videos reactivated after hiring a lawyer who happened to go to law school with another lawyer high up in YouTube's policy department. As Swiader noted, "While some organizations have had success getting content through after initial rejection, the process of winning that minor victory is tireless. Many smaller organizations just don't have the bandwidth to fight for each individual piece of content."[47] This has been a huge hindrance to online sex education campaigns, as at least forty sex educational content creators have had their YouTube videos demonetized, their channels deprioritized in search results, and their accounts shadow banned, including channels like Watts the Safe Word, Come Curious, Bria and Chrissy, and Evie Lupine.[48]

This overblocking is not confined to sex education though. Entire identity categories have been subject to overblocking, even when their online content is not sexually explicit. Take, for example, Google's understanding of the term *bisexual*. From 2009 to 2012, Google only understood the term "bisexual" as a query for mainstream heteroporn. While the effects of this oversight at Google and their slowness to address it are quite bad, it is easy to understand how their algorithms would have come to such a conclusion. In mainstream porn, the term "bisexual" is popularly appropriated heteronormatively to signal only scenes with females willing to engage in group sex with other women—for example, male-female-female (MFF) threesomes.[49] The term "bisexual" then is hugely popular in mainstream heteroporn, and mainstream heteroporn comprises a large percentage of internet pornography (if not of the web in its entirety). As such, the term "bisexual" actually *is* more likely to indicate pornography than not. And while it is a flagship term in the LGBTQIA+ marquee, bisexuals often speak of feeling underrepresented or even marginalized in LGBTQIA+ discourse. With the term often being collapsed into its container initialism, one can see how this usage would have been less compelling to the content filter's machine learning protocols. The result was Google adding the term "bisexual" to a list of banned search terms that could cause a website to be deprioritized in search rankings if any of these terms appeared on the site. Because of this, for three years, all bisexual organizations and community resources were either deprioritized in Google Search results or completely censored.[50]

I can find no comprehensive studies of the effects of Google's changes to its algorithms post-2012 to disallow the censorship of bisexual organizations and community resources. There are also no comprehensive studies on other such terms that have been designated as exclusively pornographic, though "gigolo" and "swinger" went through similar classifications between 2007 and 2015.[51] Without such studies, it is hard to determine how many online

LGBTQIA+ resources are still being prevented from reaching their intended audiences by Google's SafeSearch features. These sorts of resources are a particularly difficult issue to deal with from Google's regulatory framework, as the line between explicit and educational or identity-forming content is hazy. In communities that look to the performativity of sex, sexuality, and/ or sex acts for their communal identity formation, visuals and discourse that might be considered explicit in other contexts take on a new valence. Here "prurient" interest can be tethered to sexual education and individua-tion. "Hard-core" pornography is used—in particular by adolescents—for educational purposes.[52] There is some evidence of a correlation between prurience—in this case masturbation to online materials—and seeking information about sex and sexuality online. While, not surprisingly, mas-turbation also correlates to viewing these materials more favorably, more interestingly it also correlates to people reportedly being less disturbed by sexual material.[53]

The internet is well suited for offering a safe space to experiment with one's sexuality with few negative repercussions—people can "try on" and "test out" sexualities and practice coming out—and for building communi-ties for people with marginalized sexual identities.[54] As Nicola Döring notes, "The Internet can ameliorate social isolation, facilitate social networking, strengthen self-acceptance and self-identity, help to communicate practical information, and encourage political activism."[55] While the internet offers very promising opportunities for LGBTQIA+ individuation and commu-nity building, its heteronormative content moderation practices work to cir-cumvent those opportunities. As Attwood, Smith, and Barker note, "Young people appear to be using their encounters with pornography as part of their reflections upon their readiness for sex, what they might like to engage in, with whom, how and what might be ethical considerations for themselves and prospective partners."[56] As such, we need to be having a much more robust conversation about what constitutes pornography, in which contexts, when it is actually in the best interests of children and adolescents to censor it, and how, and this conversation needs to better reflect LGBTQIA+ and sex-positive voices. To facilitate this conversation, we need a more robust and longer duration dataset that tracks online censorship, particularly when it comes to LGBTQIA+ resources online so that we can better understand just what content is being considered "explicit." Additionally, we need to collect more information on how people (adolescents in particular) use the web for sexual education, experimentation, individuation, and community building.[57] Without this basic information, it is very difficult to provide a well-founded critique of content moderation or to advocate for precise interventions into how content moderation algorithms ought to be altered to better suit LGBTQIA+ communities online.

FOSTA-SESTA AND THE FINANCIAL INCENTIVE TO OVERBLOCK

As I noted briefly above, in March of 2018, the US Senate passed the Stop Enabling Sex Traffickers Act (SESTA) and the tacked-on Allow States and Victims to Fight Online Sex Trafficking Act (FOSTA) by a vote of ninety-seven to two. Collectively, these acts are known as FOSTA-SESTA and work to close off Section 230 of the CDA of 1996, which for two decades had allowed internet providers and content hosts to avoid legal culpability for obscenity and the facilitation of prostitution that at times may have been facilitated by their services. Under the pretense of protecting women from sex trafficking and cracking down on child sexual exploitation, FOSTA stopped the protections of Section 230 and instituted a new, very ambiguous definition of content and services that can be considered to facilitate sex trafficking and prostitution. For instance, under FOSTA, sex work and sex trafficking are the same thing, and content hosts and service providers can be held liable for "knowingly assisting, supporting, or facilitating" sex work in any way.[58] Congresswoman Ann Wagner, a key sponsor of the bill, has also explicitly conflated consensual sex work and sex trafficking in a speech on the House floor.[59]

FOSTA is a clear mark of heteronormative bias in the congressional agenda, or at least a pandering to it. As Violet Blue notes, "Lawmakers did not fact-check the bill's claims, research the religious neocons behind it, nor did they listen to constituents."[60] FOSTA was opposed by everyone from the ACLU to the Department of Justice.[61] The Electronic Frontier Foundation (EFF) published many dozens of articles condemning the act, as did law professors, anti-trafficking groups, and sex worker organizations.[62] Large internet companies like Amazon, Google, Facebook, Microsoft, and Twitter also unilaterally opposed the act under the guise of the Internet Association in August of 2017.[63] Though by November these companies had changed their minds—ostensibly after unspecified revisions to the legislation—and were thanking the same senators that they were testifying before in Congress about having facilitated Russian interference in the 2016 US presidential election.[64] Tech journalists writing in both conservative and liberal news forums attributed this shift to Facebook's breaking ranks and championing the legislation in the wake of their series of scandals ranging from Cambridge Analytica to Russian bots spreading pro-Trump propaganda and hate speech.[65]

FOSTA was immediately claimed as a significant victory for NCOSE, which wrote shortly after its passage, "This is as great a moment in the fight to free our country from sexual exploitation, as the Emancipation Proclamation was in ending the scourge of slavery."[66] It is unclear exactly how much credit can be reasonably attributed to NCOSE for FOSTA. As has been noted, between 2016 and 2018, NCOSE was able to get its language into the official Republican Party platform and saw a number of states pass resolutions declaring pornography a public health crisis. It is unclear exactly how much of this grassroots organizing had made its way into the US House of Representatives and Senate, but the time line of FOSTA overlaps significantly with this movement, and it is safe to assume that it is part of a growing consensus among legislators that pornography needs stronger regulation, though under the familiar guise of protecting children. What is clear is that the discursive conventions of NCOSE have become mainstream. Their so-called intersectional approach to sexual exploitation that considers pornography and human sex slavery to be different only in degree rather than different in kind has been taken up on both sides of the aisle and was echoed by the Internet Association and Facebook executives like Cheryl Sandberg in particular. This is a particularly dangerous conservative anti-sex apparatus that has been constructed. It can mobilize the ambiguity of its blurred definition of sexual exploitation—containing equally everything from soft-core pornography to sex slavery—to attack any and all forms of sexual expression from the unassailable rhetorical ground of protecting children from being sexually abused and exploited on the dark web. And further, as has repeatedly been the case in the past, these sorts of apparatuses often reach a détente with the untamable flow of erotic expression in which only the most industrialized, corporate, and heteronormative versions of pornography are able to persist.

Ron Wyden, the only senator besides Rand Paul to vote against FOSTA, noted that rather than preventing sex trafficking or helping child victims of abuse, the law would primarily create "an enormous chilling effect on speech in America."[67] We can already see that this is precisely the case. The new law incentivizes law enforcement to focus on intermediaries that facilitate prostitution rather than sex traffickers themselves. It thus shifts focus away from real criminals, and in shuttering these intermediaries, it cuts law enforcement off from essential tools that were previously used to locate and rescue victims. It similarly cuts law enforcement off from easily tracked evidence that can be used in criminal cases against sex traffickers. This is why the bill was also opposed almost universally by anti-trafficking groups and sex work organizations.[68] Chapter 4 will dig deeper into the impact that FOSTA has had on the finances and everyday lives of sex workers and adult entertainers, with a particular focus on those offering LGBTQIA+ services and content. Here it is worth exploring how a number of platforms responded to the shift in regulatory policy. Most major ISPs and internet platforms clamped down on sexual expression, ramped up their content moderation practices, and ended up overblocking more content than ever. In particular, we will look at the overblocking imposed by Apple through its App Store that serves as a gatekeeper to all iPhone users globally and at the Google platform, both of which have engaged in heteronormative overblocking in the wake of FOSTA-SESTA.

OVERBLOCKING IN APPLE'S APP STORE

The Apple App Store was set up to function as a sort of moral policing mechanism for mobile content. Steve Jobs famously said, "We do believe we have a moral responsibility to keep porn off the iPhone," and he further noted that "folks who want porn can buy an Android phone."[69] This anti-sex sentiment has been literally codified in both the community standards for the app store and the algorithmic procedures for policing iOS content. These policies have been claimed as a victory by NCOSE, which had been putting pressure on Apple for years.[70] This sentiment also permeated the iPhone's firmware at one point, as researchers discovered in 2013 that the following words were intentionally excluded from the iPhone's dictionary and thus also from autocorrect and auto-complete: abortion, abort, rape, arouse, virginity, cuckold, deflower, homoerotic, pornography, and prostitute.[71] In essence, the system was hardwired to be blind to these terms and thus to inhibit conversations mediated by iOS about abortion, rape, virginity, sex, homosexuality, pornography, and prostitution. The industry describes lists like these as *kill lists*, and many text input technologies like Android and the Swype keyboard contain them as well.[72]

This was not new for Apple, as in 2011, it was discovered that Siri could not answer simple questions about where people might go to get birth control or to receive an abortion. In the latter instance, Siri would instead direct iPhone users to antiabortion clinics.[73] In 2016, researchers in New Zealand found that Siri produced either no answer or answers from disreputable sources for 36 percent of the fifty sexual health–related questions they asked. In particular, Siri failed to produce visual illustrations, misinterpreted "STI" as a stock market quote, and when asked to tell them about menopause pulled up the Wikipedia page for the show *Menopause the Musical* that was then running in Las Vegas.[74] These findings were in line with previous research demonstrating that Siri trivialized many important inquiries about mental health, interpersonal violence, and physical health.[75] These discrepancies between voice search and desktop search have a disproportionate impact on communities that more frequently access the internet through these or similar vocal interfaces, including people with visual impairments, lower literacy rates, or whose only internet-enabled device is their phone. Nor are they exclusive to Apple. In 2016, *all* the top virtual assistants—Siri, Google Now, and S Voice—could not understand questions about what to do if you are raped or being abused in a relationship.[76] As Jillian York, then director of international freedom of expression at the EFF, told *The Daily Beast*, "I hate to say it, but I don't think this should surprise anyone. Apple is one of the most censorious companies out there."[77] Apple's commitment to an anti-sex and anti-pornography regime of censorship is particularly important because so many technology companies, and platforms in particular, require the intermediation of the App Store to interact with iPhone users.

Take Instagram for example. As Instagram cofounder and former CEO Kevin Sysntrom explained, much of the platform's focus on censoring explicit content is meant to maintain its 12+ rating in the Apple App Store and thus capture a larger youth market share.[78] Instagram largely achieves this by operating two types of censorship based on hashtag use. The first type permanently blocks all content with particular hashtags from ever appearing in a search. It contains over one hundred hashtags that have been applied to millions of photos, mostly having to do with nudity, pornography, pro-anorexia, and self-harm. These hashtags range from the expected—#anal, #bigtits, #blowjob, #porn, and so on—to the vaguely sexual and somewhat surprising—#cleavage, #sexual, #femdom, #fetish, #footfetish,

#freethenips, #gstring, #nipple, #shirtless, #twink, #wtf, and the like.[79] These banned hashtags betray a general anti-sex comportment that sexualizes and objectifies female bodies by banning images of female-presenting people with cleavage and thongs that would be legally permissible to wear in public settings. They also work to foreclose politically sexual speech, like the famous Free the Nipple campaign in which males and females posted close-up photos of their nipples so that Instagram would have trouble determining whether they were sexually explicit or not according to its policies. The campaign began in 2014 to protest the double standard in which female nipples are eroticized and legally required to be covered in public under most state and local laws in the United States. The campaign grew immensely on Instagram and even attracted attention and support from celebrities like Miley Cyrus and Chelsea Handler. Lastly, Instagram bends its own rules to render images of feet censorable as sexually explicit solely based on the context clue of a hashtag indicating that users might masturbate to the images. This demonstrates a stronger commitment to preserving the spirit of heteronormativity rather than the letter of their community standards.

The second type of censorship is a soft ban in which a select number of hashtags return only thirty or so results. Users searching for these hashtags receive the following message from Instagram: "Recent posts from #[hashtag] are currently hidden because the community has reported some content that may not meet Instagram's community guidelines."[80] While Instagram implies that these soft bans are only temporary, research has shown that many have remained censored for at least several months at a time. Some of the soft-banned hashtags include #bi, #curvy, #everybodyisbeautiful, #iamgay, #lesbian, #mexicangirl, and #woman.[81] This demonstrates an even more insidious policing of queer expression on the platform, as it reinforces body normativity, reproduces Google's earlier obfuscation of bisexual discourse, and shuts down the sharing of images from LGBTQIA+ users because of the potential association of these hashtags with pornography. More recently, Instagram has soft-banned hashtags in a way that reaffirms cisnormativity. For example, in 2018, the hashtags #woman, #strippers, and #femalestrippers were all banned but hashtags like #man and #malestrippers were not.[82] In the wake of FOSTA, the company also banned the hashtag #sexworkersrightsday, further marginalizing and stigmatizing sex workers in the United States.

While these two forms of censoring images from appearing in search results based on hashtag use are Instagram's most proactive efforts to censor nudity on its platform, it also uses some rather clunky computer vision algorithms to automate content moderation and community reporting procedures that are exploitable by alt-right misogynists (as we'll see in chapter 4). While there is little to no publicly available data on these systems, it is fair to assume that they internalize a lot of the same biases as Google's SafeSearch and Cloud Vision API. What is available are many instances of Instagram's algorithms failing to appropriately identify objects in images. Sometimes this leads to quite funny and ridiculous results, such as in 2019 when Instagram censored a photograph of a potato.[83] Other times the results are much more appalling.

In 2018, internet studies researchers Stefanie Duguay, Jean Burgess, and Nicolas Suzor interviewed queer female Instagram users and found that they experienced Instagram's content moderation as overly stringent.[84] That same year, journalist and sex worker Alexander Cheves reached out to his network on Twitter and received over one hundred messages from other sex workers and adult performers whose accounts on Instagram had been flagged, disabled, or shadow banned in 2018.[85] Here are just a few of the particularly egregious examples of Instagram censoring (nonpornographic) LGBTQIA+ content. In 2019, Instagram banned the account of Tom Bianchi, a male erotic photographer and HIV activist who has helped to document the history of gay men's lives on Fire Island and elsewhere in the United States since the 1970s.[86] Speaking about his photography, Bianchi told *LGBTQ Nation*,

> Fire Island was, for me, a little utopia away from everything. It's literally an island. And even for me, my photos were an idealization. . . . Stonewall happened right before I got to New York and shortly before I started doing all of this at Fire Island. The image of the homosexual was that of degenerates working in shadows and perverts trying to seduce children. So healthy young American boys playing on the beach? Early game changer. . . . Basically I saw myself as the supporter of and encourager of the whole gay consciousness that was emerging at that time in a very positive way. . . . What's special about it is remembering the affection that we all had for each other. We were all best buddies. We played together, we partied together, we adored each other. We danced with each other.[87]

In 2018, Instagram also censored a photo of *Queer Eye*'s Antoni Porowski in his underwear.[88] Also in 2018, the Warwick Rowers, a rowing team that highlights advocacy and allyship for women and queer communities, had yet another of their posts censored on Instagram. This time, the photo was of the rowers nude but with no exposure of their genitals, the cover for their upcoming charity calendar whose proceeds support LGBTQIA+ inclusivity in sports.[89] Perhaps most egregiously, in late 2017, Instagram censored a photo of two lesbian women cuddling in bed with their child.[90] All of these efforts are solely meant to prevent nudity from becoming easily visible on the platform so that Instagram can maintain its market share of iPhone users. This market share is more valuable to the company than the intermittent public relations crises that result from its stifling of LGBTQIA+ expression.

Apple's aggressive anti-porn censorship regime even impacts large independent companies like Barnes & Noble and Amazon, both of whom rely on the Apple App Store to disseminate e-reading apps. For instance, in 2017, Barnes & Noble began terminating the accounts of erotica writers on their Nook platform without warning.[91] Similarly, in 2018, Amazon followed suit and began shadow-banning authors of romance, erotica, and similar books considered to be sexual content. A number of authors had their books stripped of their best-seller rankings with no warning or notice from Amazon. While this alteration may seem mild to some, it is worth noting that many of Amazon's algorithms use best-seller rankings to determine how content appears in searches, whether the book shows up in advertisements, and whether the book can be served up as a recommendation for buyers who have purchased similar titles.[92] These changes only took effect on the US Amazon site and thus demonstrate that Amazon was likely introducing these changes in anticipation of FOSTA's enactment.[93] However, the focus on eliminating erotica from the Nook and Kindle stores also betrays a focus on censoring mobile content likely meant to assuage Apple and keeping their mobile apps in the Apple App Store. This marks a radical divergence from past precedent in the United States where the last major attempt to censor an "obscene" literary text was William S. Burroughs's *Naked Lunch*, which reached the Massachusetts Supreme Court in 1965 before being overturned with testimony from Allen Ginsberg and Norman Mailer. Since then it has been presumed that establishing the negative impact of literary texts and demonstrating their obscenity was too high a bar to clear, and censorship was largely reserved for audiovisual texts going forward. While Amazon is a private company and does not have to adhere to these precedents in managing its digital storefront, it is shocking to see them take such a conservative and anti-sex stance on literotica. Further, self-publishing e-books presents a low barrier of entry for authors—it is cheap and easy to do—and thus literotica is a haven for LGBTQIA+ and other non-normative sexual content. Shadow-banning literotica from the Kindle and Nook platforms makes queer content harder to produce, locate, and afford for authors and readers alike.

Reddit similarly had a number of its apps pulled from the App Store in 2016 because they contained a NSFW toggle that allowed users to search for porn subreddits and view them on their iPhones. Reddit was forced to remove the toggle and make it extremely difficult to view any pornographic content through its apps to get them fully reinstated in the App Store.[94] In 2018, Microsoft banned nudity and profanity platform-wide, including on Skype, in Office 365 documents, and in Microsoft Outlook, a move likely connected to Microsoft's move to integrate these services into the mobile app ecosystem on iOS.[95] In fact, all major platforms and app providers are forced to bow before Apple's anti-sex morals, as Apple gatekeeps access to between 20 and 25 percent of all mobile phone users globally.[96] FOSTA simply gave Apple yet another financial excuse and set of rhetorical tools to justify its heteronormative policing of sex and sexuality.

We might similarly read Facebook's dedication to policing sexual expression, as was examined in chapter 2, as another result of Apple's gatekeeping given the large portion of Facebook users who access the platform primarily through its mobile app. However, while there is plenty of evidence of Facebook overblocking LGBTQIA+ content, there is less documentation directly connecting it to Apple's standards for its App Store. While we've already examined Facebook's heteronormative content moderation policies and some of their impacts on sex education, it is worth adding a few explicit examples of them censoring LGBTQIA+ speech before moving on to examining the Google platform. In 2018, several site admins for the sex education group SEXx Interactive on Facebook were banned the day after their biggest annual conference for an "offending image," which turned about to be their logo, which was simply the word SEXx in bold black text on a solid peach background.[97] Cyndee Clay, executive director of sexual health and harm reduction advocacy group HIPS told Motherboard that they were seeing a lot of content getting blocked or removed from Facebook for violating community standards, including a post from a friend of hers asking to interview sex workers for an article.[98]

In a 2018 story, the *Washington Post* found dozens of LGBTQIA+-themed advertisements that were blocked on Facebook for supposedly being "political," getting caught in the crossfire of Facebook's attempt to moderate political content after the 2016 election and alleged Russian misinformation campaign. These included advertisements for pride parades, beach concerts, pride-themed nights at a sports arena, an LGBT youth prom, an NAACP-sponsored conference on LGBTQIA POC, a Lyft ad raising money for an LGBT community center, an LGBT-themed tourist expedition to Antarctica, gay social groups, a gay comedian's stand-up event, senior-friendly housing options, and perhaps most notably an advertisement for a panel discussion with an LGBT radio station in Washington on the history of Stonewall.[99]

OVERBLOCKING ON THE GOOGLE PLATFORM

Steve Jobs's recommendation that pornography enthusiasts turn to Android was misleading at best. The Google platform has largely kept pace with Apple in the race to see which can be the most anti-sex and anti-pornography. For example, Google maintains its own "kill list" for Android. In 2013, researchers found that Android's firmware filtered words like intercourse, coitus, screwing, lovemaking, most terms for genitalia (with special attention paid to female anatomy), panty, braless, Tampax, lactation, preggers, uterus, STI, and condom.[100] These words were not contained in its dictionary and not available for autocorrect or auto-complete functions. This essentially made it more difficult for Android users to talk about sex and about their bodies, betraying a sex negativity whose silence helped reinforce heteronormativity. In the same time period that Apple was pointing the finger at Google as being pro-pornography, Google was systematically censoring it across their entire platform. Google banned pornography on Google+ at its rollout in 2011, on Blogger in 2013, in Google Glass apps in 2013, on Chromecast in 2014, on AdWords in 2014, and in the Google Play app store in 2014.[101]

Since then, people have reported Google Drive automatically deleting pornography stored on Google's servers without warning.[102] For a period in 2018, Google News censored all articles with the word "porn" in them, including legitimate articles that simply happened to be about or to mention porn, like stories on revenge porn or on the suicide of adult entertainers that were published in mainstream newspapers and magazines.[103] In July of 2018, Google AdSense blacklisted a page on GovTrack.us for hosting legislative information about a then thirty-two-year-old bill called the "Child Sexual Abuse and Pornography Act of 1986." The site's admin submitted a request to review the violation to Google but was quickly given a response that the request to unflag the page was denied and that the page would remain unable to display AdSense ads to generate revenue.[104] Today, you can even purchase a Google router and use Google Family Wi-Fi to filter all web traffic passing through that router with Google SafeSearch.[105]

Each of these bans produced instances of overblocking, most notably the shift to the content policies at Blogger. In 2013, Google announced that it had changed the content policy for the site, which had provided free blog hosting since 1999. The changes included a policy shift that would ban and begin deleting blogs "displaying advertisements to adult websites" without offering any definition of what constituted "adult" content. As Violet Blue reported, at the time, the blogs that Blogger marked for deletion included "personal diaries, erotic writers, romance book editors and reviewers, sex toy reviewers, art nude photographers, film-makers, artists such as painters and comic illustrators, text-only fiction writers, sex news and porn gossip writers, LGBT sex activism, sex education and information outlets, fetish fashion, feminist porn blogs, and much, much more."[106] In 2015, Google made additional changes, removing adult blogs from its search index, hiding them from public discovery without a direct invitation and Google login, and providing content warnings to visitors before they land on the page.[107] After these changes, bloggers were left with few alternatives to host their content. WordPress.com may host what Google considers "adult" content but does not offer options to monetize that content. Until 2018, Tumblr was a popular option, but its blogs were not indexed by Google Search and monetization was also difficult. The only real option was for bloggers to pay to host their own blogs, which produced financial and technical barriers for content producers.

Nowhere has overblocking been more visible on Google's platform than on YouTube. As digital media researchers Jean Burgess and Joshua Green note,

> Advertiser-friendly content regulation—particularly using automated methods—can just as effectively smooth the edges off radical progressive politics or the witnessing of human rights abuses as it can work for the intended purpose of dampening abuse, hate speech, and extremist activity. And the conflation of sexual content and harmful speech in content regulation can often end up inadvertently discriminating against sexual and gender minorities.[108]

This became readily apparent in what is popularly referred to as YouTube's *adpocalypse* in 2017. Advertisers realized that their ads were popping up on videos of white nationalists, hate preachers, and sexually explicit content.

Major advertisers like Coca-Cola and Amazon pulled their ads from the platform and ad revenues plummeted.[109] YouTube acted swiftly to implement a system to automatically demonetize any videos violating its new "Advertiser-Friendly Content Guidelines," therefore preventing ads from appearing alongside them. The criteria it used to make these determinations were vague and expansive, including videos whose main topics included inappropriate language, violence, adult content, harmful or dangerous acts, hateful content, incendiary and demeaning content, recreational drugs and drug-related content, tobacco-related content, firearms-related content, adult themes in family content, and controversial issues and sensitive events like politics, war, and tragedies, regardless of if they were presented "for news or documentary purposes," as well as a lot of LGBTQIA+-related content.[110]

YouTube's system is unique because its censorship is based fully on machine learning–based automated content filters and does not incorporate community flagging or reporting. As YouTube notes, "In the first few hours of a video upload, we use machine learning to determine if a video meets our advertiser-friendly guidelines. This also applies to scheduled live streams, where our systems look at the title, description, thumbnail, and tags even before the stream goes live."[111] YouTube acknowledged that the system was imperfect and implemented an appeal system in which creators of demonetized videos can get their cases reviewed, but only if they have been viewed 1,000 times in the past seven days. This requirement effectively prevents niche YouTubers from ever successfully appealing the demonetization of their videos and puts an unfair burden on smaller-scale content creators.[112] While these changes continue to cause significant damage to LGBTQIA+ content creators, they successfully appeased advertisers who quickly began returning to the platform.[113]

For example, Erika Lust, an erotic filmmaker, had her account shut down and was permanently banned from the platform after posting a series of video interviews with sex workers about their trade.[114] Lust wrote on her website, "There was NO explicit content, NO sex, NO naked bodies, NO (female) nipples or anything else that breaks YouTube's strict guidelines in the series. [. . .] It was simply sex workers speaking about their work and experiences."[115] In 2018, the YouTube channel for Recon, a fetish dating site for gay men, was suspended yet again, only being reinstated after a negative backlash on Twitter and in the press.[116] YouTube demonetized many of Sal Bardo's films, including *Sam*, a film about a bullied trans boy's journey of self-discovery, despite the fact that the film has been screened at festivals and in classrooms around the world and had over six million views on YouTube.[117] Queer YouTuber Stevie Boebi reported that all of her lesbian sex videos were completely demonetized on the platform.[118] Gaby Dunn similarly reported that YouTube had demonetized all of the LGBTQIA+ and mental health content on her and Allison Raskin's channel Just Between Us.[119] YouTubers Amp Somers and Kristofer Weston of Watts the Safeword have also had their content flagged and/or demonetized on YouTube.[120]

A number of YouTubers noted that simply including the word "trans" in a video title was enough to flag the video for demonetization.[121] On the last day of Pride Month in 2018, YouTube took to Twitter to apologize to the LGBTQIA+ community, noting that they were proud to have their voices on the platform and to facilitate the role they play in the lives of young people and promising that they would do better in the future.[122] This apology rang hollow to many, however, particularly the portion about the role these YouTubers play in the lives of young people given the previous year's rampant problems with YouTube censoring LGBTQIA+ content for adolescents and children. To my knowledge, YouTube has made no announcement of specific changes that have or will be implemented to date.

YouTube has offered a *Restricted Mode* since 2010, which is meant to be used by libraries, schools, public institutions, and users "who choose to have a more limited viewing experience on YouTube."[123] There are only two ways that a video can become censored in Restricted Mode: (1) the content's creator can apply an age restriction to any of their videos, and (2) an "automated system checks signals like the video's metadata, title, and the language used in the video."[124] Videos that deal with drugs and alcohol, violence, mature subjects, use profane and mature language, contain incendiary and demeaning content, and, most importantly for our purposes, sexual situations are subject to restriction. YouTube describes these sexual situations as follows: "Overly detailed conversations about or depictions of sex or sexual activity. Some educational, straightforward content about sexual education, affection, or identity may be included in Restricted Mode, as well as kissing or affection that's not overly sexualized or the focal point of the video."[125] This poses a key problem for people creating youth content on sexual health and sexual identity, especially when they attempt to make this material appealing to young people, as we've already seen in the instances with sex educators on Twitter and Facebook. Further, videos suffering from restriction offer a much more damning portrait of the company since, as their site notes, the only way a video can be restricted is by content creators self-selecting an age restriction or by an internal, automated content filter. In each of the cases we will examine, this is worth bearing in mind. This is *not* caused by an army of misogynist trolls flagging LGBTQIA+ videos as inappropriate—this is a fully automated function on YouTube's platform betraying its hardcoded heteronormativity.

In 2017, a number of LGBTQIA+ content creators noticed that their videos were now being censored on Restricted Mode, and their hashtag #YouTubeIsOverParty trended on Twitter as content creators commiserated with one another and began protesting YouTube's biased censorship.[126] If you notice the timing, this came shortly after the passage of FOSTA, a veil behind which all internet platforms were ramping up their censorship of LGBTQIA+ content. For example, Rowan Ellis, a feminist and queer YouTuber who makes videos about pop culture, activism, and self-care, found that forty of her videos were now being censored under Restricted Mode. In her video on the subject, Ellis noted, "The sexualization of queer and trans people is still rampant. This kind of insidious poison which makes us seem inappropriate is still around. It is still having an effect."[127] In another example, Calum McSwiggan, an LGBTQIA+ lifestyle vlogger, found that *all* of his videos had been censored under Restricted Mode except for one. McSwiggan acknowledges that a number of his videos include inappropriate content for children but notes that even videos with clean language and no explicit sexual themes were taken down without cause. Examples of such videos include one explaining gay pride and why LGBTQIA+ individuals march every year, a video celebrating the gay marriage of two of his friends, a video he made in collaboration with Tom Daley in which they interview celebrities who speak about who their pride heroes are, and a spoken-word video detailing how McSwiggan came out as gay to his grandmother.[128]

A popular LGBTQIA+ YouTuber named Tyler Oakley similarly complained on Twitter that his video "8 Black LGBTQIA+ Trailblazers Who Inspire Me" was blocked by YouTube's Restricted Mode.[129] A number of Sal Bardo's videos were restricted, including his contribution to It Gets Better, a campaign meant to prevent at-risk youth suicide.[130] Bisexual YouTuber neonfiona noted that on her channel, all the videos about her girlfriends were blocked while all the videos about her boyfriends remained visible in Restricted Mode—thus toggling the Restricted Mode settings effectively transforms neonfiona from a bisexual woman into a straight woman.[131] Another bisexual YouTuber named Melanie Murphy reported the exact same thing happening to her channel.[132] YouTuber Gigi Lazzarato had all of her videos about coming out as transgender and many that discussed gender identity and sexuality restricted. She notes, "[I]t's scary on so many levels because I know when I was younger, YouTube was my family, YouTube was the place where I found a community of people that understood what I was going through."[133] Seaine Love's video about coming out as transgender was restricted as well.[134]

In response to the complaints of these YouTubers, the company sent out a tweet noting that "LGBTQ+ videos are available in Restricted Mode, but videos that discuss more sensitive issues may not be."[135] In an emailed statement, YouTube representatives noted that their automated system may be incorrectly labeling some LGBTQIA+ videos as violating their community guidelines for Restricted Mode. They noted, "[W]e realize it's very important to get this right. We're working hard to make some improvements."[136] Within a month, YouTube claimed to have fixed a problem on the "engineering side" that was incorrectly filtering twelve million videos, hundreds of thousands of which featured LGBTQIA+ content.[137]

In 2018, a year after YouTube apologized for "accidentally" blocking, demonetizing, and/or age-gating the content of YouTubers like Rowan Ellis, Tyler Oakley, Stevie Boebi, and neonfiona, Chase Ross noted that any of his videos that contained the words "trans" or "transgender" in their titles were being demonetized or removed completely—the same videos with different titles were left alone. Ty Turner similarly tweeted that his channel was penalized for a video he posted about picking up his prescribed testosterone.[138] Not only do LGBTQIA+ videos continue to be censored, demonetized, and age-gated on YouTube, but the company has also since allowed extremist anti-LGBTQIA+ advertisements to be posted alongside LGBTQIA+ content on its platforms—a number of which came from the Alliance Defending Freedom, which has been deemed a hate group by the Southern Poverty Law Center.[139]

The Women of Sex Tech conference, which contains presentations and talks by a group of entrepreneurs in sex and technology industries, had its first-ever, live-streamed conference censored by YouTube in 2020. SX Noir, the vice president of Women of Sex Tech, told Motherboard, "I think this indicates that there will always be a moral judgment on these platforms. . . . When cis, heterosexual white men create these digital worlds, you see these moral judgments leading to more discrimination for people who are brown, black and queer."[140] In 2021, YouTube's overblocking of LGBTQIA+ content is still palpable, and LGBTQIA+ content creators still complain of censorship. For instance, as I write, you can still go to neonfiona's channel, toggle the Restricted Mode, and watch as her sexual identity appears to shift from bi to straight. By leveraging the rhetoric of protecting children and combating criminality and sexual deviance, YouTube is complicit in silencing LGBTQIA+ discourse for the youth and anyone poor enough to need to access YouTube through public computers. And, from their own admission, this is an instance of pure algorithmic bias.

CONCLUSION/ASMR

One of the oddest victims of FOSTA has been creators of autonomous sensory meridian response (ASMR) videos, called "ASMRtists." ASMR is a sensory phenomenon "in which individuals experience a tingling, static-like sensation across the scalp, back of the neck and at times further areas in response to specific triggering audio and visual stimuli."[141] These auditory phenomena are wide-ranging and most often nonsexual. Browsing the most frequently viewed ASMR videos on YouTube brings up content like whispering, ear cleaning, massage, tapping, peeling, brushing, crunching, squishing, and eating sounds. People who experience ASMR report a pleasant feeling and relaxation while listening to and/or viewing ASMR content, and this is its primary purpose rather than supposed sexual enjoyment. For instance, research has shown that these same people experience reduced heart rate and increased skin conductance levels while listening to or viewing ASMR content, which may indicate that it has therapeutic benefits.[142] There is evidence it may be useful in treating everything from depression to chronic pain.[143] This is the most frequently cited reason for accessing ASMR content online. In one survey, 82 percent of people used ASMR content to help them sleep, 70 percent to deal with stress, and only 5 percent for sexual stimulation.[144] It has also become remarkably mainstream. Rapper Cardi B noted that she listens to ASMR content every night, Ikea made ASMR advertisements for its furniture, and automaker Renault made an ASMR advertisement for one of its new cars.[145] Michelob even ran an ASMR ad for its Ultra Pure Gold beer during the 2019 Super Bowl.[146]

ASMRtists have long had to contend with the assumption that ASMR is a sexual fetish, and it has recently become a new target of the war on porn. In 2018, China cracked down on ASMR, calling for its leading video sites to "thoroughly clean up vulgar and pornographic ASMR content," a directive that sites like Youku, Bilivili, and Douyu complied with by removing all ASMR content writ large.[147] While the response in the United States has not been as extreme, it has certainly been troubling and betrays a heteronormative paranoia about queerness. YouTube began demonetizing the genre in 2018. For example, the YouTube channel ASMR with MJ got a notice from YouTube for violating its community guidelines, as nearly a third of its videos were suddenly considered improper for monetization.[148] In another example, the woman running the channel Be calm with Becca took to Reddit after having a number of her videos demonetized, such as videos where she is fully clothed and talking about clothes. As she notes, YouTube's appeals policy requires a video to get 1,000 views in a week before they will review it, a near impossibility for many ASMR videos that were banned because they are older and have niche audiences.[149]

This reaction quickly spread to PayPal, which began banning ASMRtists for life and freezing their funds for 180 days. Content creators like Sharon DuBois (ASMR Glow), Scottish Murmurs, Creative Calm, and RoseASMR all had their PayPal accounts banned and funds frozen, though two of them were able to successfully appeal the decision.[150] As Violet Blue has explained, there was an odd correlation between the ASMR accounts being demonetized, censored, and banned online and the gender of the content creators that can only be explained by looking to the manosphere, which had begun mobilizing against (female) ASMRtists on an 8chan forum called "PayPal Lowering the Hammer on ASMRtits [sic]."[151] The 8chan forum's name is a pun on the term ASMRtists, used to describe the predominantly female content creators. The censorship of ASMRtists betrays an assumption that all LGBTQIA+ and female-created content is automatically sexual and ought to be subject to stricter scrutiny on the part of internet platforms, which is all too easy for alt-right misogynists to exploit.

Despite the censorship crackdown, a number of companies have rushed to begin capitalizing on ASMR content.[152] The recent app and ASMR platform Tingles is rushing in to supplant both YouTube and Patreon, hosting ASMR content and monetizing it for ASMRtists on the same platform. Tingles tries to lure ASMRtists to its platform by promising to quadruple their ad revenue and offering incentive gifts for reaching certain numbers of supporters.[153] However, ASMRtists have reported that the company is a scam. By registering, content producers automatically have their entire YouTube portfolio uploaded to the Tingles platform, which disables their YouTube ad revenues and severely decreases their overall income.[154] Another similar attempt at commercialization is Monclarity's integration of ASMR content into their Mindwell meditation app, which is produced in-house. Mindwell now offers voices that pan across speakers to make users feel a sense of companionship that can aid with calming and relaxation, often offset by music.[155] It is worth noting that neither of these apps has been banned in the Apple App Store or the Google Play Store, and there are no murmurs among the alt-right community of targeting them to get them censored in app stores. Perhaps this is because both companies are owned and operated by men? In a heteronormative internet rife with biased censorship, it seems only men are allowed to control the sufficiently vertically integrated and capitalized companies that can push their content through the content filters and community guidelines to reach a user base at web scale. Anti-porn organizers only rest once digital prostitution is placed under the control of digital pimps.

PORNOTOPIA BOUND

WHEN TUMBLR BECAME STRAIGHT

On December 17, 2018, the social media site Tumblr banned "adult content" from its platform. For many years, Tumblr had been a safe haven for purveyors of alternative, feminist, and LGBTQIA+ porn, most commonly referred to collectively as "alt-porn." It also offered sex-positive and body-positive blogs and several curated archives of sexual expression not readily available elsewhere on the web. The changes worked to eradicate this safe space and renew a long-standing effort to cleanse the platform and better monetize it. Tumblr had been purchased by Yahoo in 2013 for $1.1 billion dollars with the promise that Yahoo would not "screw it up" by altering the platform.[1] Despite this pledge, shortly thereafter Yahoo moved to shadow-ban adult content on the site, with Yahoo CEO Marissa Mayer describing adult Tumblrs as not being "brand safe."[2] This was despite Tumblr supporting a robust alt-porn community, with its own analysts at the time reporting that less than 1 percent of its adult blogs were spam-based mainstream heteroporn advertisements.[3] Despite this, Yahoo exiled its adult blogs to what Violet Blue has referred to as a "nonsearchable ghetto," de-indexing them from both internal and external searches and making an estimated 12.5 million adult Tumblrs unfindable. At the same time, Tumblr rolled out its app for iPhone, which led to even more intense efforts to combat pornography on the platform, banning the hashtags #gay, #lesbian, and #bisexual from the app because it associated these terms with searches for pornography.[4] As we've seen, this heteronormative overblocking that so sexualizes people's existences that they can be considered pornographic is nothing new. After severe backlash from its user community, Yahoo announced that it would roll back these policies. By many accounts, Yahoo did not understand Tumblr or its users and ended up leaving the platform to its own devices after the failed attempt to cleanse it.[5]

This changed when Verizon acquired Yahoo for $4.48 billion in the summer of 2017 and began attempts to better monetize its holdings.[6] From the beginning, it was expected that Verizon would again look to crack down on sexual content on the platform. As Katrin Tiidenberg, a professor at Tallinn University in Estonia who studies adult content on Tumblr told *Quartz*, Tumblr's new owners understood the intermittent adult content as making it more difficult to sell ad space to potential advertisers.[7] This is despite the fact that adult content constitutes over 20 percent of all the content clicked on by Tumblr's desktop users, demonstrating the deep entanglement of the platform with pornography.[8] Within months of its purchase by Verizon, Tumblr rolled out a new "Safe Mode" on the platform so that users could browse content on the site without running into pornography. However, it appears that this did not suffice. In November of 2018, the company got the chance to further ramp up its censorship efforts when Tumblr's app was removed from the Apple App Store after child pornography was found on the platform.[9] As we've seen in the previous chapter, Apple maintains a strict anti-pornography and more generally anti-sex moral stance and polices its App Store based on those morals. Apple forces companies like Tumblr that want access to iPhone users to regulate their platforms in accordance with Apple's biases. As a recently purchased company looking to better monetize its platform, Tumblr had the excuse to ramp up content moderation on its platform and ban all adult content whatsoever, though, oddly, far-right extremist content continued to proliferate unchecked on the platform.[10]

Tumblr's new definition of adult content primarily included "photos, videos, or GIFs that show real-life human genitals or female-presenting nipples, and any content—including photos, videos, GIFs and illustrations—that depicts sex acts."[11] The company made exceptions for images of breastfeeding, people giving birth, and "health-related situations" like mastectomy and gender confirmation surgery, as well as for written content, nudity as political speech, and nudity in art. Tumblr acknowledged that its content moderation system was being implemented on the fly and that there would certainly be mistakes as it worked to develop automated features to cut down on the human review labor necessary to maintain its platform.[12] Its computer vision-based automated content moderation system led to a comedy of errors in its debut, likely due to the short time frame in which it was implemented. The system flagged user drawings of dragons, images of crocheted candles, of tights, a vase, and of NHL-player Alex Ovechkin sleeping with the Stanley Cup trophy, among others.[13] A number of art and anatomy Tumblrs had a large portion of their posts censored on the site.[14] Even a post *about* LGBTQIA+ content getting censored on Tumblr that was posted to the platform got flagged for violating its new adult content policies.[15] As we've seen, overblocking is a frequent result of any attempt to filter or moderate digital content and one that inordinately impacts LGBTQIA+ communities in its failure to distinguish the context of sexual speech and nudity, as well as its hypersexualization of female-presenting bodies. And similarly, this overblocking can have disastrous consequences, as having too many pieces of flagged content on your Tumblr will de-index it from Google Search and thus hurt your ability to monetize your digital content.[16]

Tumblr presents a unique case, however, because of its long history of being used as a queer-friendly safe space that incorporated sexuality and pornography into its open LGBTQIA+ discourse. Alexander Cho, a digital media anthropologist at UC Santa Barbara, has described Tumblr as a "queer ecosystem" in which LGBTQIA+ users felt free from having to articulate their identities in relation to heterosexual norms and, because Tumblr is such an image-based platform, of course, these communities flirted with edgy and sexual images.[17] He further points out that because Tumblr offers pseudonymous accounts and reblogging features, it avoids the "default publicness" of social media like Facebook that makes LGBTQIA+ youth fear being outed. Stephanie Duguay, professor of communication at Concordia University, noted that these communities on Tumblr "share GIFs and videos and content around queer celebrities, queer characters, and fanfiction. Sometimes nudity and adult content is in this. . . . It's a general part of people's self-discovery, especially when you're a young person and you're determining things about yourself and your sexual identity."[18] Duguay notes that it is important for these youths to *see* representations of queer identities in the context of relationships, embraces, kisses, and sex so that they can imagine these scenarios as possibilities in their future, a process that heterosexual people are privileged to take advantage of in most popular media. By fragmenting these communities, young people will have a more difficult time finding these materials and experiencing content that represents their identities and everyday lives. In the wake of these changes, a number of LGBTQIA+ Tumblr users have given testimony to the role that the platform played in shaping their sexual identities as they used the site to discover and imagine new possibilities for their futures. Many of them expressed their worries about a future in which LGBTQIA+ youth don't have access to these communities and this content.[19]

Internet studies researchers Tim Highfield and Stefanie Duguay have shown that by sharing edgy and explicit looping GIFs, LGBTQIA+ users are able to produce a sense of irreverence and play that builds communities and signals to people that they are in a safe space for sexual expression.[20] In interviews with queer women, Duguay has found that this visibility of queer sexuality may also dissuade homophobic harassment and lead to less discrimination on the platform.[21] For instance, trans Tumblr users engage in self-representation on the platform through sophisticated hashtagging practices that make their community dialogue visible to one another on the platform, often including sexual expression that challenges cisgender norms.[22] A lot of LGBTQIA+ history was also archived and catalogued on the site and has now been rendered invisible. For example, the anonymously authored Tumblr Bijou World curated photos of vintage gay porn, old magazine covers, and newspaper clippings to capture the history of LGBTQIA+ erotica and culture.[23] These losses may be irreparable to the community, as a number of artists have noted that not only were their images flagged, but their accounts were permanently banned, leading to them losing entire archives of their work that they had not backed up elsewhere because they trusted the long-standing reputation of Tumblr as a safe space for sexual expression.[24] Perhaps most importantly, however, this entails a forfeiture of the space for digital pornography to mainstream heteroporn conglomerates.[25]

For many years, Tumblr was the perfect solution for people who found "tube sites" like Pornhub or XHampster to be too flooded with misogynistic, mainstream heteroporn and who could not reliably find alt-porn through Google Search. As Ashley Vex, an adult entertainer and curator of a DIY porn Tumblr, noted in her eulogy for Tumblr,

> Sex wasn't this separate, shameful thing.... **We shared it, discussed it, debated it and *curated it*.** Porn on Tumblr wasn't treated as disposable, something just to be immediately purged from your browser history, but an aesthetic, artistic component of your page and your life, alongside your complementary colours of sunsets and song lyrics and personal posts. It was out in the open. **It allowed you to become a collector of your own desires, displaying them and celebrating them proudly, rather than having them spoon fed by a tube site algorithm.** [...] **It allowed for sex in a space that didn't feel like it was dominated by male desire.** [...] **It helped young, queer people find their communities and sexualities represented, to take control and represent them themselves.** [...] **It allowed people with disabilities, young parents,**

people of colour, trans and gender non conforming folk (identities that make up a large majority of the community of sex workers and who are too often ostracised by a traditional, capitalist workplace) to make rent. [. . .] If we push our depictions of sexuality into the shadows, we allow them to continue be defined and co-opted by the status quo.[26]

Vex's article is worth quoting at length because this sentiment abounds in nearly all of the reporting on the changes to Tumblr. For instance, *WIRED* conducted interviews with more than thirty sex workers, pornographers, and porn viewers who collectively lamented the loss of the site and the unique safe space that it curated for exploring sexuality. The magazine noted that these interviewees "described the site as notably more empowering and friendly than more traditional venues for explicit content."[27] Liara Roux, a sex worker and online political organizer, told the magazine that "the options for finding adult content online are diminishing, and consolidating with big companies," making it more difficult for LGBTQIA+ communities to find a space for their online existences.[28] With Tumblr cleansed of pornography, tube sites and Google are the foremost remaining options for finding digital pornography, and thus the bulk of this chapter will be dedicated to examining them. The first section looks at the political economy of tube sites and the heteronormative biases they reinforce, with an added focus on the recent moves in the United Kingdom to make all porn sites use the services of MindGeek, which maintains a monopoly on tube sites, to age verify all of their visitors. The second section looks at Google's move in 2012 to an always-on version of SafeSearch that only allows pornography to appear when users both turn SafeSearch off *and* use specific pornographic keywords in their search query. It goes on to show how the current political economy of "independent" porn sites is dominated by mainstream heteroporn whose influence sets genre standards that permeate even amateur porn and altporn. Lastly, this chapter will examine the financial impact that FOSTA-SESTA has had on sex workers and adult entertainers, and it will demonstrate how it has put pressure predominantly on low-budget and amateur pornographers, which results in an inordinate impact on LGBTQIA+ content.

TUBE SITES AND THE VICIOUS CIRCLE OF HETERONORMATIVITY

In 2013, David Cameron centered his election campaign on censoring pornography, which he argued was "corroding childhood" and doing irreparable harm to the minds of an entire generation of British children.[29] In 2014, the United Kingdom advanced David Cameron's anti-pornography crusade by amending the 2003 Communications Act. The new Audiovisual Media Services Regulations 2014 requires that online pornography now adhere to the same guidelines laid out for traditional video and DVD pornography by the British Board of Film Censors (BBFC). The act effectively bans pornography from containing acts of spanking, caning, aggressive whipping, penetration by any object "associated with violence," physical or verbal abuse even if consensual, urolagnia or "water sports," role-playing as nonadults, physical restraint, humiliation, female ejaculation, strangulation, facesitting, and fisting, noting that these final three are potentially life-threatening.[30] The BBFC argues that these restrictions are a "tried and tested" method for protecting children, though adult performers argue that they are more aimed at regulating women's pleasure with the odd inclusion of things like female ejaculation and facesitting.[31]

This sweeping set of regulations was just the prelude to the introduction of the Digital Economy Act 2017, which was introduced the next year and meant to require all online distributors of pornography to age verify every visitor to their website. The BBFC was to be in charge of enforcing the new regulations and holding sites accountable for any minors who viewed their content, with consequences including withdrawing advertising services, pressuring payment service providers to deny service to the websites, and requiring ISPs and mobile network operators to block access to these websites writ large.[32] Independent adult content producers feared the regulation would turn all erotic film in the United Kingdom into "boring, unrealistic male fantasy."[33] This is largely because many independent pornographers would not have been able to afford to age verify every visitor to their site. As feminist pornographer Pandora Blake, who runs the site Dreams of Spanking, noted in an interview, "There's no way sites like mine could afford to verify every visitor. We'll all go under."[34]

The United Kingdom's new age verification requirements were originally set to take effect in April 2018 but were pushed back twice with no clear date of implementation as the United Kingdom attempts to pass the laws through Brussels at the same time as it is managing Brexit.[35] As of 2019, Nicky Morgan, the fifth culture secretary, noted that the government no longer intended to enforce this component of the law but stated that its objectives might still be obtained by the new regulator set forth by similar legislation.[36] A large reason why the United Kingdom's porn blocker was repeatedly delayed before being canceled was the practical problem of implementing age verification. The BBFC intended to create a certification scheme for age verification systems that websites could've used but was never planning to create a nationwide scheme free of charge. Instead, it intended to leave this to the free market, with each site being responsible for implementing its own age verification scheme and, in most cases, doing so by purchasing schemes from third-party vendors that the BBFC had certified.[37] The frontrunner that stood to gain a near monopoly on the age verification market in the United Kingdom was the AgeID system being developed by MindGeek.

While sizable portions of the porn-blocking legislation appear to be defeated for the moment—thanks in part to organizers who demonstrated the collateral damage that it would have in terms of overblocking nonpornographic materials like charities, schools, and social support websites[38]— this incident helps to demonstrate the international reach, lobbying power, and adaptability when faced with government regulation of the most highly capitalized segments of the mainstream heteroporn industry. If you remember from the introduction, MindGeek owns Pornhub, as well as many of the other most popular tube sites on the web, like RedTube, YouPorn, GayTube, Xtube, ExtremeTube, SpankWire, and Tube8. MindGeek's platform boasts 115 million daily hits and consumes more bandwidth than Twitter, Facebook, or Amazon.[39] The average visitor to these tube sites spends at least ten minutes on them.[40] The frequency and duration of the visits have allowed MindGeek to create its own highly profitable advertising network, TrafficJunky, to serve targeted ads to the people consuming its free pornographic content. With its soaring profits, MindGeek has bought up several top pornography studios at discounted rates, including Brazzers, Digital Playground, Mofos, MyDirtyHobby, Reality Kings, and Twistys.[41] MindGeek and its subsidiaries also spend lavishly on advertising in *Adult Video News* and other industry news outlets, in trade publications, and at events, allowing them to effectively shape the discourse within the pornography industry.[42] As Shira Tarrant, professor of women's, gender, and sexuality studies at Cal State Long Beach and author of *The Pornography Industry*, told the *Atlantic*, MindGeek's business model "features vertical integration and horizontal integration, so they're really monopolizing the industry."[43]

In an interview with the Daily Dot, Adult Empire director of business development Colin Allerton noted that "every major studio and star is now partnered with MindGeek or has worked for a studio that MindGeek purchased."[44] In fact, studios and stars are so entangled with MindGeek that they are afraid to speak out about the company's practices for fear of being blacklisted.[45] One of these practices is hosting pirated pornography across their tube sites and requiring owners of that content to file individual Digital Millennium Copyright Act takedown requests for each pirated video on each tube site, an onerous burden and one that many smaller and independent studios don't have the financial resources to keep up with. As adult film star Siri noted, the tube sites "force copyright holders to jump through hoops to get our content removed."[46] This rampant pirating of content is occurring within an economy in which production, subscriptions to, and sales of pornography are all trending downward. As David Auerbach has explained, "The result has been a vampiric ecosystem: MindGeek's producers make porn films mostly for the sake of being uploaded on to MindGeek's free tube sites, with lower returns for the producers but higher returns for MindGeek, which makes money off of the tube ads that does not go to anyone involved in the production side."[47]

MindGeek, originally known as "Manwin," has served to reinforce patriarchy and heteronormativity for twenty-first-century pornography. We can see how this plays out if we look to three communities impacted by this shift toward tube sites in the political economy of pornography: professional adult entertainers, amateur adult entertainers, and consumers. In terms of professional adult entertainers, it has reinstated the traditional subjugation of female porn stars in a political economy in which they had been making strides toward equality as more women opened and ran pornography studios and websites. MindGeek has essentially instituted a "freemium" economic model in which adult entertainers make pornographic videos as advertisements for their other lines of business, like camming, stripping, or escorting. Adult entertainers make increasingly diminished returns off their pornographic videos, which requires them to bank on a small minority of consumers of that free content who will pay for additional services.[48] This pushes adult entertainers to heighten their performances and engage in more extreme sex acts, since they are essentially advertisements for niche audiences, and may explain the trend toward increasingly exploitative and misogynistic sex acts in mainstream heteroporn. It also has radically increased the number of adult entertainers who engage in escorting to supplement their income. According to *Salon*, while it would have been taboo within the industry to engage in escorting at the turn of the century, it is now considered normal. One porn star told *Salon*, "If you look at the escort sites, pretty much every porn star is on there."[49] Thus, the economics of tube sites and its subsequent impoverishment of adult entertainers has led to an escalation of misogyny in pornography and of adult entertainers engaging in escorting, a risky endeavor given state and federal anti-prostitution laws.

The same is also true of amateur adult entertainers, who similarly use their pornographic content on tube sites as advertisements for their camming, personal websites, one-on-one Skype sessions, and similar paid features. Even more so than professionals, amateurs must make use of tube sites to advertise their other content and services if they want to generate enough income to live off of. Tube sites are dominated by mainstream heteroporn, and the titles and metadata for their content reflect this. To generate clicks, amateur models often use similar titles and language to describe their videos, and they use similar tags to apply metadata to their content, all of which produce a normative effect on the actual content that they produce.[50] Similarly, a quantitative study by French researchers of tube sites Xnxx and xHamster found that while the sites do host a wide variety of material, just 5 percent of the tags (e.g., "blowjob," "teens," "big boobs," "cumshot," "anal") used to categorize pornography cover over 90 percent of the videos on the sites.[51] In broad-ranging quantitative studies, computational neuroscientists Ogi Ogas and Sai Gaddam have similarly found porn to be increasingly heteronormative.[52] As Shira Tarrant explains, the stereotypical, often sexist and racist, keywords that most people use to find pornography end up working as a feedback mechanism that subsequently influences what porn gets made.[53] Tarrant describes this as a chicken-and-egg problem, but we might better think of it as a vicious circle of heteronormativity inscribed into the political economy and algorithmic infrastructure of the internet.

Lastly, MindGeek reinforces patriarchy and heteronormativity among its consumers as well. It operates sophisticated recommendation engines that are trained on the heteronormative titles, descriptions, and metadata of mainstream heteroporn. As Tarrant explains,

> In addition, MindGeek, for example, uses algorithms to create highly curated personalized sites that are based on the user's search history. It's a lot like Amazon, where you look for a couple of books and they say, "You might also be interested in this." Then you're being spoon-fed a limited range of pornography based on the keywords you use, based on your geographic location, based on their algorithms and the information that they're processing about time of day. They're doing a lot of data collection. Online-porn users don't necessarily realize that

their porn-use patterns are largely molded by a corporation. We talk about the construction of wants and needs in other aspects of the economy, but that applies just as well to pornography.[54]

Thus, tube sites do not just lock porn producers into making content that corresponds with the view of the genre embedded in their recommendation engines; they also lock users into it as well. This is an opinion shared by Pandora Blake, who argues that MindGeek homogenizes pornography in accordance with the "male gaze" and objectifies all sex, leading to "clickable, sensationalistic" porn. She notes, "It's a power law distribution—the more something is viewed, the easier it is to find and the more views it gets, and then producers make more porn like it because they know it's popular. There's so much diverse, alternative material out there on the open internet, but as MindGeek's monopoly increases I fear it will become less and less visible."[55] These mainstream tube sites thus deflate their consumers' sexual imaginations and capacities to experience new pleasures and form new desires at the same time that they harm sex workers' livelihoods and push them toward more dangerous and unstable sources of revenue.

It is no wonder that professional and amateur adult entertainers alongside many consumers of pornography in the United Kingdom were fearful of handing over a monopoly on age verification to MindGeek. This monopoly would have quickly put most small-scale pornographers out of business and made it even easier for MindGeek's tube sites and affiliate networks to strengthen their monopoly. According to a Freedom of Information request, MindGeek met with the British government five times between the critical months of September 2016 and January 2017 as the act was being crafted and lobbied for the government to shut down their competitors.[56] They expected to sign up twenty to twenty-five million sites in the first month alone after the act went into effect on an initially traffic-based pricing schema, but there would be nothing to prevent them from increasing the rent once they have a monopoly on an age verification market. Further, there were no protections in the act for the massive amounts of user data that MindGeek would have been able to collect as it gained insight into the pornography consumption patterns of an entire nation.[57] Lastly, it should be noted that the act let search engines and social networks off the hook, classifying them as ancillary service providers and focusing instead on regulating "pornographic websites."[58] Perhaps it ought to be expected that internet platforms would have the clout to escape regulation, but it demonstrates a bias in the regulation schema toward censoring those sites without the capital to fight back.

While nothing on this scale has been seriously considered to this point in the United States, it is increasingly possible. The end of net neutrality in combination with FOSTA making ISPs potentially financially liable for facilitating vaguely defined sexual services makes it easy to imagine a world in which content filters will be applied at the level of ISPs rather than individual platforms. Violet Blue goes farther and even imagines a future in which classifications of "pornography" are broadened to include any speech that the government doesn't like and looks to examples like Kuwait and the United Arab Emirates, which classify the World Health Organization's website as "pornography" in order to censor it under national law.[59] As we've seen in chapter 3 and will continue to see in the rest of this chapter, however, even without heteronormative content filtering at the ISP level, the United States' increasing reliance on internet platforms and payment services creates a technological infrastructure and political economy in which mainstream hetero-porn can continue to dominate not only the porn we see but also the porn we can imagine.

GOOGLE SAFESEARCH AND THE INVISIBILITY OF ALT-PORN

As we have already seen, the tube sites that now dominate online pornography consumption operate heteronormatively in a number of ways. Many critics, like Pandora Blake, compare this to an idealized version of the open internet in which all content, no matter how niche or queer, was readily available to users. These ideal versions of the web as a pornotopia largely require us to view Google Search as an unbiased gateway to that pornotopia, else the content might exist, but everyday users would have no means of ever stumbling upon it. Or at least, if this imagined pornotopia can make room for just a little bias on Google's part, like allowing the most visited porn sites, which are by default heteroporn, to show up first in its search results, it would require a sort of pornoliteracy in which adept users might manipulate the search results to get past the wall of heteroporn and discover the feminist and queer pornography cached all across the web. In reality, both of these axioms for a pornotopia are immensely flawed.

First, while some readers—especially adult readers with a longer history of seeking and finding alt-porn online—will think that this pornoliteracy is widespread and easily obtained, I am not convinced that we should be so hopeful. It requires that internet users be able to make rather sophisticated determinations about search content, such as what content is the result of paid advertising or SEO techniques. In 2017, the Federal Trade Commission conducted a study on how advertising might be better distinguished online to help people make these sorts of determinations and found that in its default state, only 45 percent of the Americans they tested were able to correctly identify advertisements in search results and social media feeds.[60] A larger private study found that nearly 60 percent of people were unable to recognize paid ads on Google in 2018.[61] Similarly, the Pew Research Center found in 2019 that 59 percent of Americans reported that they understood little to nothing about what companies do with the data they collect.[62] Not only does this sort of pornoliteracy require the capacity to navigate around advertisements and search engine optimized heteroporn, but it also requires the impetus to do so in the first place. It requires the capacity to imagine that porn could be other than it is, a capacity severely diminished in our current pornographic ecology. This capacity requires practice to develop, which, as we will see, means that during the normative phase in which adolescents internalize archetypes of pornography and the possibilities for their sexuality represented in that pornography, they are most often stuck with mainstream heteroporn, at least until they develop a more sophisticated online pornoliteracy.

Second, Google has never offered an unbiased gateway to any content online, and certainly not pornography. Instead, it has always privileged mainstream heteroporn, a trend that has become radically amplified since Google's SafeSearch algorithms were changed in 2012 when SafeSearch became an always-on feature in Google Search. Turning SafeSearch off only opens up the *possibility* for pornography to appear in search results, but in actuality, Google will still censor pornography from search results in most instances. In actuality, SafeSearch is now only turned off by the use of pornographic keywords.[63] What this means is that unless your query signals to Google that you are intending to locate pornography, it will not present you with pornography in your results. By tethering the appearance of pornography—or more broadly nude or fleshy bodies—to this limited set of keywords, Google has essentially guaranteed the continual reification of the current political economy and genre hegemony of mainstream heteroporn. Mainstream heteroporn companies currently possess a dominant position in the link topography of the web, with well-established digital presences and vast systems of interlinking subdomains and companion sites, guaranteeing high positions in any Google Search results. Since 2012, they now have an easily identified and limited set of keywords that they need to perform SEO for and the upfront capital to hire top SEO firms to perpetually maintain their position atop the search rankings. As Safiya Noble has demonstrated, the porn industry is one of the most sophisticated users of SEO, particularly the American mainstream heteroporn industry.[64] What this means is that in ensuring that you only get porn when you want it, Google has additionally ensured that you will always get *the same kind of porn*. And that same kind of porn will be made by the same people in the same political economy and set of power relations that have been the subject of an endless series of critical porn exposés over the past few decades.

Political economic research on mainstream heteroporn has shown that the industry shows a strong capacity for constructing global networks through new dissemination technologies and adaptable business models.[65] As Jennifer Johnson has shown empirically, today's mainstream heteroporn operates something like an online platform.[66] Large corporations maintain closed networks of "affiliate websites" that are often independently run. These affiliate websites offer niche content to a limited set of users, but they purchase that content from a larger distributor. They also link to and sometimes share login credentials with other affiliate sites on the network, thus reinforcing that network and circulating porn users within their own online pornography platform. These affiliate programs allow large corporations and local webmasters to work collaboratively to use minimally differentiated content to cover a maximal number of established niche audiences and thus also capture maximal web traffic and economic expenditure. As Johnson explains,

> By circulating consumers inside a never-ending series of click manoeuvres and interrelated websites, constantly updated gonzo content and strategic targeting of addictive behaviour, the industry views consumers not as sexual beings with authentic desire but rather as dehumanized "traffic" to be manipulated and maximally exploited.[67]

Rather than offering a system in which niche content differentiates to match the evolving sexual proclivities of its audience, mainstream heteroporn circumscribes that audience and uses affiliate networks hegemonically to constrain its pornographic tastes to prescribed, revenue-generating niches. Google's algorithms are perfectly tailored to foster the digital hegemony of mainstream heteroporn, as their ranking metrics are highly sensitive to link topologies and expensive professional web design that meets their quality standards. By further limiting pornographic results to a limited set of pornographic keywords, SafeSearch only makes it that much easier for these affiliate networks to engage in SEO and further reify their hegemony over digital porn consumption.

While it may be true that sophisticated porn consumers figure out ways to escape mainstream heteroporn's hegemonic networks online, doing so requires the cultivation of what I have called a "pornoliteracy" above. While Kath Albury has described "porn literacies" as an ability to critique misogyny, homophobia, and racism in mainstream pornography that might be a useful addition to sex education, here we need to think of pornoliteracy as something more basic and widespread among porn users.[68] At its most basic, pornoliteracy is the capacity to navigate the world of available pornography, matching pornographic representation to one's own internal desires and imagination. There is a sexual and media literacy implicit in all porn use.[69] Porn users are active agents in their consumption processes. They select, reject, interpret, and cocreate the online pornography that they engage with.[70] Porn users acquire skills through viewing practice and come to view themselves almost as hobbyists with tastes and preferences, likes, and dislikes.[71] More than this though, pornoliteracy includes as well everything from viewing habits to a familiarity with the topography of online pornography— where the good stuff is and how to find more. What is important for our purposes here is that pornoliteracy is almost a *style* of porn use, and like any style, it takes cultivation.[72] As Attwood, Smith, and Barker note of one user, "porn begins as unknown and monolithic—an 'it'—but becomes 'kinds' over time and with the investment of browsing."[73] It is very likely that this monolithic version of porn will be the mainstream heteroporn variety. Mainstream heteroporn's hegemony over online porn consumption through strategies like affiliate networks ensures that people will find it first and most often. They will only come to escape it by developing their own pornoliteracy. And finally, even once more mature users learn to escape mainstream heteroporn, it has been granted the opportunity to serve a normalizing function. The research indicates that repeated viewing of certain sexual behavior does normalize that behavior and increases the viewers' positive evaluation of that behavior over time.[74] This capacity for normalization is only enhanced by the compulsive or addictive usage patterns that researchers have found in porn users.[75] This addiction occurs by design, as the content, web platforms, and affiliate networks are all engineered to stimulate it. As people stay enrapt in mainstream heteroporn, its normative influence grows.

Mainstream heteroporn thus constitutes the default pornography online, and its hegemony is only reified by SafeSearch making it easier for major players in the industry to game Google's search results for pornographic keywords. Thus, while SafeSearch does not really seem to have ever succeeded in preventing adolescents from accessing pornography online according to most studies, it is successful in heteronormatively channeling adolescent porn use.[76] The case of adolescents is again important, as adolescent porn use often precedes first sexual encounters and thus has a potentially socializing role on adolescents.[77] It is very difficult to accurately assess the precise stakes of this heteronormative, commodified, and sometimes misogynistic socialization that SafeSearch helps to reinforce. As a number of scholars have pointed out, research on pornography tends to be binarized into an anti-pornography perspective that focuses on negative media effects of pornography and an anti-censorship perspective that rebuffs prudery and celebrates sexuality by embracing pornography perhaps too enthusiastically.[78]

Many anti-pornography studies are motivated by conservative Christian morals, are often tethered to pro-censorship policy advocacy, and, even when more rigorous, often operationalize an oversimplified "media effects" theory of how people interact with pornographic texts in which texts unilaterally and homogeneously impact their readers or viewers.[79] Social science research on the subject is also deeply tethered to class and racial tensions. Pornography scholar Laura Kipnis perhaps puts it best when she reminds us that "researchers aren't busy wiring Shakespeare viewers up to electrodes measuring their penile tumescence or their galvanic skin responses to the violence or misogyny there."[80] Keeping that in mind, there are some common findings in media effects research on the negative impacts of pornography use that warrant attention, especially now that SafeSearch helps to reify the centrality of mainstream heteroporn online. Many studies suggest that mainstream heteroporn—and particularly pornography depicting violence, pain, or suffering during sexual activity—may be a risk factor for sexually aggressive behavior or sexual violence.[81] There also may be connections between mainstream heteroporn use and sexual risk taking, like having unprotected sex.[82] More broadly, there are also potential connections between mainstream heteroporn use and subscription to stereotypical beliefs about women, their sexual roles, and the acceptability of objectification.[83] Again, while none of these studies allow us to infer causation and many may contain implicit social biases, they are worth engaging so that we can better articulate the stakes of SafeSearch's censorship.

There have been only a handful of studies to empirically consider the potential positive effects of pornography use alongside its negative effects, even though these positive effects might outweigh the negative effects.[84] For example, Nicola Döring has described the positive effects as potentially including "increased pleasure, self acceptance, inclusion of handicapped people, improved communication between sexual partners, in addition to the widening of traditional gender roles and sexual scripts."[85] Within the media effects model of social scientific research, we need more balanced data so that we can effectively assess the overall impact of pornography use. Beyond that, more knowledge on the positive effects of the use of different types of pornography would be particularly useful in advocating for specific changes to content filters like the SafeSearch algorithm that might make more diverse porn more easily accessible.

Conversely, many anti-censorship studies look to celebrate the production and consumption of pornography. In particular, they focus on feminist porn, LGBTQIA+ porn, alt-porn, or Netporn. Looking at these pornographic texts, scholars argue that the internet has made possible new forms of amateur, low-budget, and/or niche pornography that can showcase empowered female agents, alternative body types, amorphous and queer sexualities, and BDSM, fetish, and other "grotesque" forms of sex.[86] These new forms of pornography challenge everything from the political economy of mainstream porn production to the heteronormativity of sexuality as presented on the screen. However, a number of scholars have pointed out that we now are left with very little critical research on mainstream heteroporn.[87] Pornography scholars tend to agree that mainstream heteroporn is "racist, classist, ableist, and heterosexist" and seem willing to leave it at that.[88] As Mark Jancovich has argued, there is a class tension in its decision as well, which assumes that mainstream porn is uninteresting and rote because of its popularity and mass production.[89] In short, anti-censorship studies need to be less automatically pro-pornography. To understand the impact that SafeSearch is having by directing users first to mainstream heteroporn, we need more critical scholarship on mainstream heteroporn that can help situate social scientific data on pornography use within broader analyses of its cultural context, as well as alternative interpretations of pornographic texts. As Kipnis has noted, "Pornography [. . .] is profoundly and paradoxically social, but even more than that, it's acutely historical."[90] Beyond this, a number of porn studies scholars have argued that we need to be more critical of more celebrated alternative pornographies also.[91]

As I have noted above, mainstream heteroporn operates normatively on porn users as they (in the best of cases) develop the requisite pornoliteracy to escape, first, SafeSearch and, second, the mainstream heteroporn affiliate networks. This dynamic is duplicated at the industry level, as the normativity of mainstream heteroporn also influences a large portion of alt-porn, as one might expect from porn genres that define themselves over and against mainstream heteroporn. A number of porn studies scholars have demonstrated how the genre conventions of mainstream heteroporn continue to shape the production of what is often collectively referred to as "alt-porn."[92] Here, we can understand alt-porn as an aggregation of alternative pornographies whose main similarity is their positioning as outside the mainstream. Aside from that similarity, they are incredibly heterogeneous, ranging from niche fetish pornography to LGBTQIA+ pornography to feminist pornography. The influence of mainstream heteroporn on alt-porn is only complicated by the increasing professionalization of amateur porn.[93] Cramer and Home have gone so far as to call indie porn "the research and development arm of the porn industry."[94] The hegemony of mainstream heteroporn that SafeSearch helps to maintain has consequences even outside of its affiliate networks, as it constrains the possibilities for alt-porn in many ways. For example, a study of YouPorn.com has shown that amateur videos on the site follow a heteronormative "pornoscript" that focuses on dichotomized sexual and gender differences as the primary source of visual pleasure and almost always from a male subject position.[95] Some, but certainly not all, alt-porn falls under the critique that Kipnis made of mainstream heteroporn: that it "creates a fantastical world composed of two sexes but one gender," where that one gender is male.[96] This is particularly true of amateur porn posted to these sites because, as Paasonen notes, "amateur porn that is shared online needs to fit into already established subcategories to be recognized as porn."[97] This is particularly problematic because amateur porn signals "realness" or "real life" and thus can further naturalize heteronormativity.[98] As Shoshana Magnet argues, alt-porn's emancipatory potential is limited by its commercialization.[99]

Alt-porn needs clicks and views to garner revenue. Clicks and views require high ranking by indexes and search algorithms. Achieving a high ranking in search indexes requires conforming to that search engine's definitions of the genre.[100] Their definitions of the genre are the extracted lowest common denominators across all pornography. These definitions also operate with inertia, meaning that each successive index influences the web traffic that the next index extracts its data from. SafeSearch greatly exacerbates this problem of index inertia by greatly restricting web traffic to pornographic websites that are not tailored to a limited set of largely heteronormative pornographic keywords. As Döring notes, there are few social scientific studies of how people select and process pornography at cognitive and emotional levels or how they might develop a unique style or pornoliteracy in doing so.[101] Without this type of research, it will be hard to empirically assess the impact of SafeSearch on porn consumption. In addition, we need much more expansive data collection on exactly which keywords can trigger pornographic results in different Google Search algorithms at different times, places, and by different users. Without this data, it is hard to articulate exactly what norms are being perpetuated by SafeSearch's filtration efforts. At this point though, it is safe to assume that these keywords will reflect the heteronormativity so deeply ingrained in our pornography, in SafeSearch's schema and ontology, and on the internet writ large, as we've seen throughout this book.

As Susanna Paasonen argues, "Pornography is a multifaceted assemblage—a historically evolving media genre. It is a field of labor, technological innovations, monetary exchange, carnal acts and sensations, regulatory practices, verbal definitions, and interpretations."[102] She notes that this evolution has no predictable direction or trajectory, as it continually tries to connect new genre conventions, technologies, body styles, and values in such a way that it will affect users, both materially and symbolically.[103] By affording mainstream heteroporn companies the capacity for ongoing digital hegemony, Google has essentially limited the possibility for pornography to evolve by limiting our ability to take random walks through and engage in serendipitous discovery of new materials in our digital pornographic milieu. It has essentially shut down what could have been a freer and more open space for explorations of human sexuality. The alternative, avant-garde, and experimental pornography that is the focus of much of porn studies may find itself continually and increasingly marginalized. If porn is where we go for a safe space not only to be affected—materially, symbolically, and sexually—but also *to discover what affects us*, this space has been sold for the sake of ad revenues. The outcry over unfiltered porn will always outweigh the outcry over filtered art.

FOSTA-SESTA AND THE NEW POLITICAL ECONOMY OF SEX WORK

While we've seen the impact that FOSTA has had on nonpornographic content online in chapter 3, I would now like to turn to its impact on sex workers, particularly LGBTQIA+ sex workers. Not only is FOSTA ineffective, but its real purposes are transparent. Essential tools that sex workers used to find clients and thus protect themselves from having to solicit sex in person and to verify clients to screen out those who have abused sex workers in the past have been shuttered, including Backpage, NightShift, CityVibe, the Erotic Review, VerifyHim, HungAngels, YourDominatrix, Pounced, and Yellow Pages.[104] In an article that traces her history of soliciting sex in person, using print-based personal ads in newspapers, and dealing with exploitative but safer online personal ad sites like Craigslist and Backpage, Caty Simon notes,

> What we've been telling the media over and over again is plainly true: many of us will die, some of us have already died because of the damage SESTA's done, and especially because of the loss of Backpage. And the victims will more often be trans workers, disabled workers, workers of color, and trafficking survivors—those of us who never had many options to begin with. We are without allies.[105]

This is by design in the ambiguous language of FOSTA, which conflates sex work with sex trafficking and holds companies culpable for acting as intermediaries, even if all they do is host a link to another website where a transaction may take place. As Simon notes, its most immediate victims are often doubly marginalized, as they are not only sex workers but also disproportionately LGBTQIA+, disabled, POC, and trafficking survivors. This has been confirmed repeatedly. Emily McCombs interviewed dozens of sex workers for a *Huffington Post* article on FOSTA and reported that many of them noted that opportunistic clients and pimps were already trying to take advantage of this window where sex workers didn't have access to online personals and client screening resources.[106] She also interviewed sex worker and adult film star Arabelle Raphael, who pointed out that "it is so far mostly free and low-cost sites that are disappearing, which she says largely affects those who can't afford more expensive platforms or who can't 'class pass'—that is, adopt the markers of a higher socioeconomic class—enough to get work on them."[107] Performer Ginger Banks told Motherboard that FOSTA has made it more difficult for those working in the adult industry to speak out about abuses and misconduct in their industry, such as the wave of revelations in summer 2020 primarily focused on Ryan Madison's abuses while shooting scenes for Porn Fidelity and Teen Fidelity—both owned by his wife's company, Kelly Madison Media. People working in the industry are concerned that their revelations will be used by anti-porn activists to further argue for the "abolition" of pornography, and thus they may be disinclined to report abuse to protect their livelihood.[108]

While Ann Wagner claims that FOSTA has shut down nearly 90 percent of online sex trafficking business and ads, the *Washington Post* has fact-checked that claim and found it to be inaccurate. Online personals were already back to nearly 75 percent of their pre-FOSTA levels within six months of the bill's passage.[109] As McCombs notes, those with the privilege of disposable income and technoliteracy have been migrating toward encrypted communication technologies and cryptocurrencies.[110] A number of services have also cropped up to help sex workers in the wake of FOSTA, like Red Umbrella Hosting, an Iceland-based, sex worker–owned and operated web hosting service and Switter, a sex worker–oriented Twitter-like platform run out of Austria. Switter's hosting service, Cloudflare, determined it necessary to refuse service to the site after it had amassed 49,000 uses, despite Cloudflare having campaigned against FOSTA and having since described it as "a very bad law." Switter was able to find alternative hosting; however, Cloudflare did this without notice and without ever replying to emails from Switter or providing any kind of explanation.[111] Even nonprofit organizations that aim to help sex workers and sex trafficking victims have been negatively impacted by FOSTA. For example, the Woodhull Freedom Foundation notes that FOSTA caused them to censor information on their site that could assist sex workers.[112] Similarly, the Sex Worker Outreach Project had to cancel the "acquisition and development of an electronic tool for sex workers to report violence, harassment and other harmful behavior."[113] To my knowledge, the digital tools that sex workers used to protect themselves have not been fully recovered in the wake of FOSTA.

FOSTA does not stop sex work or trafficking. It pushes it offline, where it is more difficult to track, and leads to more negative material ramifications for sex workers. It also inordinately impacts the already marginalized who may not be able to wait out the law or invest in new technologies and platforms to recover their lost income. They instead face the prospects of financial, mental, and physical tragedy in the interim. For instance, in 2017, researchers studied the impact that Craigslist's erotic services section had on violence against women in the United States between its opening in 2002 and its closing in 2010. They found a 17.4 percent decrease in the female homicide rate as a causal effect of Craigslist's erotic services section during the years it was active.[114] It is difficult to establish the impact of FOSTA empirically, as such studies are rare in my experience. Further, FOSTA has led to the legitimation of discrimination based on sex, sexuality, and sexual expression, and this legitimacy is being taken advantage of by nearly every internet platform from financial service providers to content hosts to social networks. The passage of FOSTA essentially established a financial incentive for internet companies and service providers to maximize overblocking.

Sex workers' income has long been under attack by traditional financial entities like JPMorgan Chase, Visa, and MasterCard, which have routinely denied their services not only to sex workers (thus forcing them into the dangerous position of having to conduct cash transactions) but also any small business, artist, or independent contractor whose business happens to center on sex. A number of legal porn actors, including Stoya, Teagan Presley, Dakota Skye, Layton Benton, Tieran Lee, Bonnie Rotten, and Veronica Avluv, have been denied Chase accounts or had their services terminated because they were considered to be in a "high-risk" line of work.[115] More shocking yet, Chase refused to process payments for Lovability, a condom company that stresses gender equality and safe sex.[116] Chase only relented and agreed to process Lovability's payments when the refusal made headlines, and it was pointed out that Chase handles mergers and acquisitions for Trojan condoms.[117] Chase similarly refused to process payments for New York Toy Collective, a company focused on giving people access to safe, high-quality, and self-affirming sex toys to help foster a sex-positive culture safe for all forms of gender expression.[118] These practices are heteronormative not only in their explicitly anti-sex disposition but also more subtly in that they produce a political economy in which smaller-scale and niche-oriented sexual commerce is strangled and only large-scale industrialized corporations like Trojan can survive, which by their very scale tend to be heteronormative in orientation because of their imagined majority audience.

In December 2020, both Visa and Mastercard pulled their services from Pornhub, partially in response to a *New York Times* opinion column by Nicholas Kristof that argued the companies were indirectly supporting child sexual abuse images and exploitation by providing financial services to Pornhub.[119] Not only is this argument specious—far more nonconsensual abusive imagery is shared on platforms like Facebook, Instagram, or Twitter than on Pornhub—it also aligned with the messaging of anti-pornography crusaders, particularly the anti-Pornhub Traffickinghub campaign backed by Exodus Cry and NCOSE, which Kristof mentions explicitly. As Samantha Cole notes for *Motherboard*, this is yet another expansion of the demonetization of sexual speech on the internet—from more niche pornography like blood play and water sports to pornography writ large—that harms sex workers' ability to access financial services.[120]

In response to being denied more traditional financial services, many sex workers and sex-oriented businesses have turned to Silicon Valley for financial management, using services like PayPal, Square, WePay, Patreon, and even Amazon wish lists to facilitate the transfer of money and goods as payment to sex workers. All of these services have begun targeting sex workers for denial of service in the wake of FOSTA. Nowhere have these practices been more prevalent than at PayPal, which routinely denies service, seizes accounts, and freezes funds indefinitely for account holders associated with online sexual content, including art and sex education.[121] Violet Blue has catalogued some of these practices, which include

- banning dominatrix January Seraph for life,
- freezing the account and seizing the funds of Dee Dennis Tess Danesi for publishing the New York City Sex Blogger Calendar,
- banning blogger and adult industry writer Cara Sutra for selling a corset,
- banning former escort Vicky Gallas for processing payments for her memoirs,
- freezing the account of the Seattle Erotic Art Festival for processing fine art submission fees, and
- freezing the account porn performer and producer Maggie Mayhem made to raise charity funds for relief work in Haiti because she linked to it from her sex blog.[122]

According to Kate D'Adamo of Sex Workers Outreach Project NYC and Sex Workers Action New York, "Paypal has for several years made the decision that if they assume someone is involved in the sex trade, they will shut down that account and, in every case that I've heard, keep the money."[123] The war on sexual expression has been going on inside PayPal for at least a decade, but the passage of FOSTA has emboldened PayPal and helped spread its disposition to other online financial service providers.

WePay famously deleted a crowdfunding campaign to raise money for porn performer Eden Alexander's medical bills when she was dying of an infection that caused multiple organ failures because the campaign was linked to sites that sold pornography.[124] Square refused to work with Searah Deysach, the owner of a Chicago-based indie, education-focused, woman-owned sex toy store.[125] After giving a TED Talk titled "Make Love Not Porn," Cindy Gallup launched a crowdsourced porn site based on her ideas from the talk. According to the site, "MakeLoveNotPorn is Pro-sex. Pro-porn. Pro-knowing the difference. We're the world's first user-generated, human-curated social sex video-sharing platform, celebrating #realworldsex as a counterpoint to porn, with the aim of socializing sex—making it easier for everyone to talk about, in order to promote good sexual values and good sexual behavior."[126] PayPal, Amazon, Google Checkout, and Chase all refused their services to Gallup's site.[127] Companies like these are regularly denying financial services based on loosely defined conceptions of sex work and pornography. These are essential financial services for small businesses and self-employed content producers, and thus for the majority of LGBTQIA+, feminist, pro-sex, disabled, working-class, POC, and non-native English-speaking sex workers, adult entertainers, and erotic artists.

In the wake of these denials of service, a number have turned to maintaining Amazon wish lists in lieu of currency and have faced similar discrimination from Amazon, which has begun deleting their wish lists without warning. When contacted about their policies on deleting wish lists, Amazon told the Daily Dot that they would delete any wish list that contained "evidence" that it was being used for "bartering." Amazon made these determinations in any instance where a wish list was directly connected to an adult site as an option for "gifting," regardless of whether this gifting was transactional. Amazon further noted that wish lists would be deleted if they were set to "public" and contained "certain" adult items. When prompted for more information, Amazon revealed that a wish list that contains phallic-shaped vibrators would be deleted but one that contained a compact vibrating personal massager would not, based on the former's "more suggestive shape."[128]

This is in spite of the fact that sex toys are available for purchase *on* Amazon and in great abundance. These determinations yet again mobilize an ambiguous set of criteria that can be leveraged on an ad hoc basis to systematically deny services, and thus revenue, to already marginalized sex workers and adult content creators.

Perhaps the best exemplar of these ambiguous and ad hoc policies wreaking havoc on the financial livelihoods and everyday lives of small business and self-employed sex workers and adult content creators is Patreon. Patreon is an online platform that helps content creators gain and manage revenue from their online content and has become central to many small and niche content creators' livelihoods. On its home page, Patreon promises to allow content creators "to have a direct relationship with [their] biggest fans, get recurring revenue from [their] work, and create on [their] own terms."[129] The site boasts two million patrons, one hundred thousand monthly active content creators, and an estimated $300 million in creator earnings for 2018.[130] In 2016, PayPal put pressure on Patreon to stop facilitating adult entertainment and sex work platform-wide, which Patreon resisted, agreeing only to remove PayPal donation links from sexual content. At the same time, Patreon actively courted adult entertainers and sex workers and reportedly promised them via private email that their accounts were safe on the site.[131] In September of 2017, the company accepted a new round of investment capital and shortly thereafter made changes to its terms of service.[132] These new terms of service banned the use of the platform to generate revenue from any and all pornographic material, though the definition of what exactly constitutes pornography for Patreon is left purposefully ambiguous.[133]

Users were immediately skeptical about these changes, but they were told the following by Patreon: "The TL;DR is that if what you were doing before was okay, then probably what you're continuing to do is okay. And if what you're doing is in too much of a gray area, then we'll be reaching out."[134] However, just a half year later, FOSTA was passed and Patreon began suspending and reporting many users for "implied nudity." These suspensions were most notably doled out to a number of cam models and adult entertainers who used the site to sell adult content, charge for private webcam sessions, or maintain adults-only websites.[135] A number of artists have also had their content censored. Take, for example, Kate Victoria, a photographer whose account was suspended without warning for "public nudity" despite containing no images that exposed genitalia. According to Victoria, the only image that did contain nudity was censored by text.[136] In contrast, Engadget interviewed a Patreon representative and presented them with potentially adult pages to see which they might censor. The representative was shown the Patreon page of an adult performer who created "sexy content for her fans." She offered "personalized sexy pictures," "access to a secret Instagram account," and even "10 minute live webcam session[s], through Skype, once ·per month" to higher-tiered patrons. The representative noted that this content would *not* violate the new terms of service.[137]

Patreon has for years provided a frustratingly vague definition of what constitutes pornography and whether or not pornography violates their terms of service.[138] As Liara Roux notes in her open letter to Patreon, the company's definition is similar to Supreme Court Justice Potter Stewart's—"I know it when I see it"—in its ambiguity and ad hoc nature. She writes, "This is an outdated, legally unclear, and importantly, *extremely problematic* view of adult media."[139] The problems that arise here are multifaceted. First, as we have seen, vague definitions and case-by-case determinations inevitably lead to biased content moderation, often skewing toward the heteronormative. Second, the frequent changes of policy combined with conflicting messaging leaves sex workers, adult entertainers, and erotic artists unable to make stable financial plans or formulate long-term business strategies. These are already extremely precarious sources of income and the lack of stability Patreon is introducing is a catalyst for life crises like homelessness or physical and mental health complications. Lastly, as Roux also notes, this new policy inordinately affects queer, trans, disabled, POC, and people whose first language is not English.[140] In particular, porn versus art distinctions are mobilizations of class warfare, as only those adult content producers with the discursive fluency and educational background to successfully situate their content as artistic stand a chance to escape censorship. Lower socioeconomic status correlates strongly with content creators who are queer, trans, disabled, POC, and who do not speak English as their first language. This class status only gets reinforced by cutting primarily these content creators off from sources of revenue.

Prior to the post-FOSTA ramp-up in suspensions, Patreon CEO Jack Conte published an email sent to adult content creators in response to Roux's open letter. In his response, Conte both notes that it breaks his heart that content creators are afraid for their pages and doubles down on the argument that Patreon "never allowed pornography or sexual services."[141] After reading it over, Roux noted that Conte only exemplified more clearly that Patreon is more committed to its own image in the eyes of investors and banking partners than to maintaining the well-being and safety of its legal content creators.[142] By banning sex workers and adult entertainers, Patreon forces the production of erotica, pornography, and sexual expression into the mainstream market so heavily dominated by mainstream heteroporn. Content producers are forced to implement their own web services, seek the few financial services left available to them, and market individual pieces of their content through platforms already dominated by mainstream heteroporn. This essentially shuts down the economy of patronage in which alt-porn and queer content can be produced and disseminated for free, with creators being supported by those in the community who have the means to donate funds to their cause.

It is hard to isolate a discrete cause or responsible party for this system-wide denial of financial services to small businesses and self-employed people whose work focuses on sex toys, sex work, adult content creation, and erotic art. Every financial service provider involved tends to invoke "high-risk" profiles and argue that the next person higher up in the chain prevents them from servicing these "high-risk" customers. WePay, Square, Patreon, and PayPal not only blame each other, but they also blame credit card companies like Visa and Mastercard and banks like JPMorgan Chase particularly. Visa and Mastercard have both denied all responsibility, claiming they had nothing to do with the decisions made by companies like PayPal to refuse service. This is all despite the fact that both a federal appeals court and the Federal Deposit Insurance Corporation have declared that it is against federal financial regulations to refuse business or close accounts based on a "high-risk" assessment determined solely on the customer's work being related to human sexuality.[143]

Some of the pressure is coming from the US Department of Justice under what it calls "Operation Choke Point," which requires banks to identify any customers engaging in what the government defines as "risky" activity and "choke off" those customers' access to financial services. According to Frank Keating, CEO of the American Bankers Association, "Justice is pressuring banks to shut down accounts without pressing charges against a merchant or even establishing that the merchant broke the law."[144] If banks refuse, they are penalized by the government, regardless of whether the bank committed any wrongdoing or whether the customer was engaged in illegal activity. While

Operation Choke Point primarily targets payday lenders, evidence has been surfacing since 2014 that it has also targeted those in adult industries and may be connected to the glut of adult film stars whose Chase accounts were closed around the same time.[145] In short, the only thing that is clear is that there is a system-wide felt sense of urgency to not only avoid any transactional relationship with but also to punish any person whose work is connected to sex, sexuality, or sexual expression. As I—and others—have demonstrated repeatedly, this inordinately impacts financially disadvantaged and marginalized groups, who for that very reason do not have strong enough advocacy to alter this trend of systemic discrimination. It is this cultural context that helped incubate a law like FOSTA, which has in turn only amplified this felt sense of urgency among financial service providers.

The result of this legislation is to make financial services less available to smaller market and independent sex workers and adult content creators. As we have seen repeatedly, this inordinately impacts LGBTQIA+ content creators, making that content less available to those who might benefit from it and forcing its creators to enter marketplaces already dominated by mainstream heteroporn. Additionally, this new internet-wide impetus to police sexual expression more heavily offers opportunities for alt-right misogynist trolls to wage campaigns of harassment and oppression on sex workers and adult entertainers. As we will see below, these opportunities were quickly recognized and taken advantage of, as the alt-right mobilized on 8chan and Reddit to develop new strategies and tactics for waging their anti-sex war on porn.

THE #THOTAUDIT AND ALT-RIGHT EXPLOITATION OF FOSTA-SESTA
The impact of FOSTA was immediately felt across the internet as sex workers and adult entertainers found themselves under systematic attack, being banned from online platforms, having their content removed, being denied financial services, having their accounts and funds frozen or seized, and being doxed by digital misogynists and thus receiving a glut of hate mail and death threats. This was in addition to facing real-world consequences like losing their jobs. The long-standing efforts of anti-porn grassroots activists to use standard governmental and financial channels to disrupt the political economy of adult entertainment and sex work have been coupled with a campaign by alt-right internet trolls to punish "e-whores." It is worth noting that this very term belies the penetration of NCOSE's "intersectional"

articulation of sexual exploitation. The lines between prostitution and digitally mediated dissemination are blurred such that cam models are considered prostitutes. This campaign is nowhere more visible than in the response to David Wu's November 2018 Facebook post calling for a campaign to report self-admitted sex workers to the Internal Revenue Service (IRS) in an attempt to get them audited. At the time, Wu's Facebook page contained a depiction of him as Jason Voorhees, the murderer from the Friday the 13th movie franchise, dismembering a sex worker.[146] Wu's call quickly spread to Reddit, 4chan, 8chan, and Twitter and went viral after subsequently being dubbed "thot audit."

The word "thot" is an acronym that means "that ho over there" and was most often used in Black communities. It has been prevalent in hip-hop lyrics for many years, for instance.[147] The word has obvious misogynistic overtones. It near universally refers to women and analyzes them purely as sexual objects. Thots are women who are easy to sexually possess and thus can be dismissed as worthless. Just like the term "slut," thot is wielded with obvious class antagonism as well.[148] Thot status is primarily an aesthetic designation based not on any real information about a woman's sexual history but on her consumption habits (i.e., style, tastes). As Amanda Hess writes, "If women are products, then thots are cheap goods. More than that, they're knockoffs: low-quality merchandise that attempts to masquerade as luxury items."[149] As with most alt-right memes, thot also contains a racial component, as it is a term from Black communities primarily used to designate Black women as cheap imposters of high-class, hard-to-sleep-with, white women.

As I have mentioned, the original strategy behind the campaign was to report "thots" to the IRS in hopes of getting them audited. Roosh V championed this effort early on, arguing that anyone who managed to get a thot audited would be awarded 30 percent of any taxes recouped by the IRS after the audit. Roosh wrote, "There is actual financial incentive to defeating thottery."[150] In his YouTube video on the "thot audit," Roosh gave voice to what he described as the "righteous anger" of online male communities, like gamers on Twitch, who were enraged by the "boobie streamers" taking over their digital communities—women who have nothing to offer to society but their bodies—and the "paypigs" that support them.[151] Increasingly prone to blending religious rhetoric with his outbursts, Roosh argued, "God is gonna judge these hoes" with his "cleansing fire."[152] In the same video, Roosh echoes complaints that video games are incorporating homosexual and transgender propaganda, thus showing queer materials to young people, demonstrating concretely the intersection between the biologization of gender roles and the reification of heteronormativity. He argues that sexualizing people at younger ages turns them into homosexuals, that sex education is meant to turn people gay, and notes that he would be on the verge of murderous violence if people were trying to "homosexualize" his children. Roosh argues, "Giving the women the right to vote, the right to choose their careers, everything, was such a mistake. It goes against the natural order. Women were never designed to have choice in anything, except what color clothes her baby gets to wear."[153] Roosh borders on viewing the situation as a conspiracy to "disconnect the sexes," lower the population, and turn all men into homosexuals and all women into sluts. His response is right out of the alt-right playbook, as he reiterates throughout the 150-minute video that he is not telling men to do anything, but he won't blame them if they report sex workers to the IRS. The entire video is an effective endorsement and catalyst of this sort of behavior despite these lines intentionally placed to offer plausible deniability of inciting it.

Men's rights activists like Roosh's followers and members of the incel community—incited by tweets from the official Twitter account for incels. is—quickly organized to begin reporting sex workers to the IRS. The trolls found out that using the IRS's whistleblower program is extremely tedious. You have to submit, in paper via physical mail, a person's physical address, full legal name, date of birth, taxpayer identification number, and specific information about the alleged fraud being committed.[154] The organizers of these "Right Wing Tax Squads" worked largely via 8chan and the r/ThotAudit subreddit, which had nearly two thousand followers before it was banned on November 27, 2018.[155] One Reddit user responded to the problems with IRS reporting by posting, "Find the thots paypal email, send them money, and then report them for selling goods against paypals services. . . . It's against Paypal's rules to solicit digital sexual content. All of their funds will be locked pretty quickly."[156] The dissatisfied trolls quickly turned from reporting sex workers to the IRS to abusing the content moderation policies of online platforms to damage the livelihoods of sex workers, a tactic that has been used by foreign governments and partisan groups to, for example, silence the Syrian resistance movement and the Catalonian independence movement.[157] On one thread of the subreddit users described a way to expedite the reporting process, "including spamming webforms with multiple reports, including links to illustrate the breach of the company's terms of service, and threatening to report the breach to the media if the company did not immediately ban the sex worker."[158]

To further streamline this process, these digital misogynists organized via 8chan the construction of what they termed the "ThotBot," a web crawler that would automatically crawl the web to capture the screen names, full names, locations, links to wish lists, individuals' payment processors, and bios of online sex workers, which it would then compile into a spreadsheet to make reporting them for violations of terms of use easier. By December, ThotBot had already captured the information of more than 166,000 sex workers.[159] An 8chan poster wrote, "Find every piece of law breaking action that the left does. It's fucking easy since they broadcast it all on social media for the public to find. Get their dox, use it to report their illegal activities to the authorities, rinse and repeat."[160] The creator of the ThotBot told *WIRED* via direct message that the intention behind the crawler was the "total excommunication or extermination of whores in society" and noted that they ought to face the death penalty.[161]

Where the first leg of the ThotAudit campaign of reporting sex workers to the IRS was an abject failure, this second leg has led to serious consequences for sex workers and adult entertainers online. Take, for example, Lily Adams, who makes and sells pornographic photos and videos online. In the wake of the thot audit, Adams took to Twitter describing the campaign as a witch hunt. Within a minute, her account was flagged and added to a review list. On the same morning that her account was reviewed by thot auditors, Adams's PayPal account was frozen indefinitely with $256 left in it. By the end of the day, she was banned by every cash app she was using.[162] Porn performer Ela Darling was doxed, and her family received calls from internet trolls at their workplaces to harass them about her vocation.[163] Stories like these are increasingly becoming the norm among online sex workers and adult entertainers. They find themselves in a renewed state of precarity that is culturally invisible because so many of us have bought into the Pandora's box of porn myth, assuming that sexual speech and content flows freely across the internet. Instead, the internet has been canalized to facilitate the flow of heteronormative content at the expense of queer communities. And this new heteronormative infrastructure is being viciously exploited by digital misogynists to renew their violent crusade against queer and female bodies.

On March 5, 2020, as the COVID-19 pandemic was dominating news head-lines, South Carolina Senator Lindsey Graham introduced the Eliminating Abusive and Rampant Neglect of Interactive Technologies Act—known as the EARN IT Act—to Congress. The EARN IT Act intends to radically expand the surveillance of sexual speech online, calling for the formation of a nineteen-person commission to develop vaguely defined "best practices" that ISPs and content platforms like social media sites will be strongly incen-tivized to institute—facing hefty fines and potential criminal charges if they refuse.[1] As the ACLU noted in their opposition letter to the Senate, the pro-posed commission developing these best practices will be constituted solely of Department of Justice officials, elected officials, and industry representa-tives, with no representation of LGBTQIA+ communities, sex workers, or other marginalized communities that will be impacted by the bill.[2] As the ACLU noted,

> After SESTA/FOSTA, platforms censored a great deal of legal sex-related speech, disproportionately harming the LGBTQ community, and the speech of sex workers, generally, harming their ability to organize and engage online. The EARN IT Act will incentivize similar censorship efforts by platforms. Platforms will again ban and censor sex-related speech, especially if it relates to youth. These sex-related speech censorship regimes are particularly harmful to LGBTQ com-munities and to sex worker communities because their advocacy often discusses or relates to matters involving sex and sex education. Furthermore, censoring the online speech of the LGBTQ community also harms LGBTQ youth, who often first explore their identities by seeking information and building community online, before engaging with their identities offline, especially if their friends or family may not accept who they are.[3]

Beyond the further expansion of censorship of LGBTQIA+ communities, the EARN IT Act also threatens to enact backdoors through encryption protocols in digital communications technologies. Riana Pfefferkorn, a research scholar at the Stanford Internet Observatory, described EARN IT as a "bait and switch" that attempts to mobilize people's anger at "Big Tech" toward a long-standing governmental desire to ban strong encryption.[4] The ACLU has identified strong encryption as essential not only to the political protests demanding racial justice in the United States but also to less visible efforts to organize the LGBTQIA+ community, institute HIV prevention, deliver public health resources to marginalized communities, and safeguard domestic violence victims.[5] These impacts will reverberate internationally. As has been seen time and again, social media companies and ISPs that are either (1) headquartered in the United States or (2) are dependent on doing business in the United States tend to implement rather uniform content moderation procedures across their entire platforms. The standards set here will impact people across the world. And further, as Ruane notes, offering a backdoor to encryption for the US government will make it difficult for these companies to resist similar requests from foreign governments, including those that actively criminalize or persecute the LGBTQIA+ community.[6]

Myriad institutions, including the ACLU, the Electronic Freedom Foundation, Human Rights Watch, Wikimedia Foundation, and Freedom Works, have submitted open letters to Congress outlining the dangers of the EARN IT Act, similarly as was done in the case of FOSTA-SESTA in 2018. Sex workers have also been organizing against the act creatively because of social distancing measures. For instance, Veil Machine, a sex worker–led art collective, put on a twelve-hour virtual variety show/peepshow called "E-Viction" that was meant to highlight the ways in which sex workers and marginalized people are being evicted from digital spaces.[7] These actions are eerily similar to those that unfolded prior to FOSTA—briefs and letters filed from free speech–oriented nonprofits and tech platforms and small-scale activism from feminist, LGBTQIA+ communities, and sex workers. While these efforts are truly admirable, and I want to find hope in them, the signs that I have been piecing together in my research for this book point toward a trend in the opposite direction. The EARN IT Act is just another bulwark to further solidify and entrench the social conservative position. If it passes, it will be wielded with lethal force against marginalized communities. If it doesn't, another will soon take its place, leveraging the rhetorical force of child sex trafficking to distract from its more malignant intentions.

The theorist Michel Foucault once argued that, contrary to popular opinion that the Victorian Era was a sexually repressive era, beneath the surface, people could not stop talking about sex. Today, we are experiencing the opposite. In an era popularly conceived to be sexually liberated, heterogeneous, and with all forms and representations of sex readily available at the stroke of a key, beneath the surface, sex is being ignored by most and targeted for repression by a small but influential subset of the population. As we've seen throughout this book, there is a growing sentiment in online discourse that sexual expression needs to be combated. While this opinion may be held by a minority of internet users, it is given an atypical amount of power in shaping our online discourse and thus the future of the internet. As I've shown, this is largely due to two primary factors. First, the privileges this heteronormative, white, bourgeois minority enjoys—ranging from technical literacy to strong organizational structures, strategies, and tactics to the media coverage their taboo transgressions generate—allows them to exert a disproportionate amount of power on the internet. Second, they have formed strong alliances and become the unlikely bedfellows of evangelical Christians and anti-porn feminists, allowing them to form a multifaceted discourse that shifts emphases from scientific rationality to feminist critique to Christian conservative family values to violent misogyny based on what is convenient given the context in and audience for which their message is disseminated.

The influence of this growing sentiment against sexual expression can be seen everywhere, from the coders developing digital tools and technologies to the underlying code for major internet platforms to the "human algorithms" that oversee content moderation online to the way the US government understands, legislates for, and regulates the internet. As we've seen, many coders hold misogynistic and anti-LGBTQIA+ sentiments, a problem exacerbated by the lack of diversity in the tech sector. Whether intentional or not, these biases get embedded into the structure of the algorithms they produce in the form of biased data inputs or biased parameters for machine learning. As they say, garbage in, garbage out. The result is algorithms that reinforce cultural biases and prejudices in a way that is largely opaque to the public and at a worrisome new scale. Once these systems are trained and embedded into our digital infrastructures, they are very costly to change. In line with the hacker ethic of continually patching bugs in a product like bailing water from a sinking ship, the most frequent solution is to suggest ad hoc readjustments and the addition of human review to edge cases. However, this will always lead to two problems. First, the human review process is produced by the same companies that built the biased system in the first place, and their normative viewpoints tend to inflect their protocols for human review just as much as their code for algorithmic review. Second, because of capitalist incentives to maximize profits—and, in fact, the legal obligation of publicly traded companies to do so—this content moderation labor will always be farmed out to contract laborers; in the case of sexual expression, it will be outsourced to undertrained and overworked Indian and Filipino laborers. Reviewers will have mere seconds to make determinations about the content being reviewed and rather than reflecting the contextual and localized community standards in which the content was produced and circulated, these judgments will be made according to the most conservative global standards to protect platform brand integrity and advertiser revenues. This isn't likely to change unless the public relations expenditures internet platforms incur when they have to apologize for overblocking LGBTQIA+ content become more expensive than it would be for them to reconstruct their algorithms, retrain their moderators, and hire more moderators who are better trained and given more time to review sexually expressive content.

Further, it is difficult to trust that these companies could achieve such a change even if they were well-intentioned. For example, while tech companies are at least paying lip service to feminism and LGBTQIA+ civil rights and in some instances installing people dedicated to progress when it comes to these issues in positions within middle management, too frequently, these measures are rendered moot by the coders who work in isolation from them and the top executives who flout them in an attempt to buy their high school fantasies of unlimited heterosexual and misogynistic access to female bodies. The limitations of these progressive midlevel employees were demonstrated all too clearly in Google's firing of Timnit Gebru in December 2020. Even if there were well-intentioned tech executives, they would still be subject to US law and regulations, which, as we've seen particularly in the case of FOSTA, are increasingly oriented toward combating sexual expression on the internet, none more so than LGBTQIA+ and feminist sexual expression.

The impact that this curtailing of sexual expression has is always disproportionately borne by those already structurally positioned for disempowerment and marginalization, most notably women and LGBTQIA+ communities, but also communities marginalized by race, nationality, and ability. This is most noticeable when we examine who bears the burden of "overblocking," the phenomena in which unintended pieces of content are blocked because content filters are designed to be overbroad—any "catch-all" filter will also catch a lot of nonpornographic content in the process. In the instance of art, we can clearly see that while canonical, Western (re: white, male, Eurocentric, colonial, and the like) art *can* trigger content filters, it is considered embarrassing when it does so. This art is indexed to prevent this from happening, and there are specific "carve-outs" in the content moderation review procedures meant to protect it from being censored. This is not the case for other forms of art, whether it is lesser indexed art from decolonial communities or the amateur art produced by online communities—a particularly salient practice in online LGBTQIA+ communities.

For additional evidence of the undue burden borne by these communities one only needs to look at which sex educational and nonpornographic sexually expressive content gets censored on the internet. As I've shown, it is inordinately LGBTQIA+ community resources, activist groups, and sex educators that are getting censored by the overbroad content moderation algorithms and human reviewers. This occurs for a number of reasons, including (1) their identities are at least partially tethered to sexual expression, and thus LGBTQIA+ discourse requires freedom of sexual expression to exist; (2) they don't have the institutional support or financial resources to seek redress from internet platforms and ISPs when their content gets blocked as if it were pornography; and (3) the cultural pornographication of LGBTQIA+ identity is exacerbated by the frequency of LGBTQIA+ terms being used in descriptions of mainstream heteroporn—e.g., "bisexual girl in MFF threesome," "lesbian dominatrix uses strap-on"—which floods algorithms with signals that words like "bisexual" or "lesbian" are *dirty* words. This was never about simply blocking hard-core pornography but about the pornographication of a large group of people's everyday lives, identities, and forms of self-expression.

These effects are felt particularly acutely by LGBTQIA+ children. By positioning children as naturally "pure" with no inner sexual drives, children find themselves increasingly dependent on adult "protection" and evacuated of all agency and autonomy.[8] As Henry Giroux argues,

> Unable to understand childhood as a historical, social, and political construction enmeshed in relations of power, many adults shroud children in an aura of innocence and protectedness that erases any viable notion of adult responsibility even as it evokes it. In fact, the ascription of innocence largely permits adults to not assume responsibility for their role in setting children up for failure, for

abandoning them to the dictates of marketplace mentalities that remove the supportive and nurturing networks that provide young people with adequate healthcare, food, housing, and educational opportunities.[9]

For our purposes, we can expressly view these educational opportunities through the lens of *sex* education. By asserting that children and adolescents are pure, sexless beings, parents and other authority figures at the same time deny their responsibility for educating children about sex and sexuality. Instead, children are left to learn about sex and sexuality from the pornographic marketplace, which is misrepresentative enough of sex and sexuality for heterosexual children and wildly nonrepresentative for LGBTQIA+ children and adolescents looking to learn about and explore their sexuality.

What makes all of this even harder to swallow is that this entire system of porn censorship is not really slowing down the production, distribution, and consumption of pornography. Mainstream heteroporn proliferates as do the structurally produced ills of sex work within this largely heteropatriarchal mode of production. Sure, content moderation does a rather good job of keeping nudity off Facebook, YouTube, and Google Images, but technology companies celebrate themselves for putting pornography out of sight and thus out of mind. What these systems actually do is make it more difficult to accidentally stumble upon porn. However, they don't make it much more difficult at all to find porn if you are looking for it, even if you are not supposed to be able to find it (as in the instance of many adolescents). This focus on preventing exposure to porn at *some* times while facilitating access to it at *other* times has had very problematic effects on the range of sexual expression that can be readily found in pornography. By setting themselves up as gatekeepers and trying to determine the exact instances when a person may want to view pornography, they play into the hands of the mainstream heteroporn industry. The mainstream heteroporn industry alone is capitalized, horizontally integrated, and vertically integrated enough to force its product through this gauntlet of censorship. By a combination of SEO, sophisticated hub-and-spokes affiliate networks, and legal representation, mainstream heteroporn producers make sure their content is always available and nearly exclusively so. Barred from revenue by undue censorship, deprioritization in search, shadow bans, and content demonetizations that can't be adjudicated because of their small size and lack of capital, niche producers of feminist and LGBTQIA+ pornography at best become largely invisible and at worst cease to exist.

In essence, we increasingly find ourselves in a digital world where sexual expression is considered to be a private matter, not meant to take place on social networks but only to be consumed or enacted in private. I imagine here an archetypical person who holes up in a room with the door closed, wakes up their screen, and signals that now is the time they'd like to engage with mainstream heteroporn. If this engagement with heteronormative porn is confined to the privacy of the bedroom, then the engagement with queer porn can be understood as once again confined to the silence and invisibility of the closet. This increasing tendency to bracket pornography to a digital bedroom, safely distant from the social media we increasingly understand as our digital public sphere, privileges heteronormativity. As we've seen, LGBTQIA+ discourse requires some level of tolerance for sexual speech in the public sphere—as does much of feminist discourse (e.g., marital rape requires that the private become public for just and democratic solutions to be found). As if it weren't enough that the bulk of sexual expression is filtered out of public discourse, nonpornographic LGBTQIA+ discourse is over-blocked, and LGBTQIA+ pornography is rendered invisible or nonexistent.

The result of all of this is what I have called "the digital closet." The digital personae of LGBTQIA+ people are forcibly stripped of all sexual expressivity after having been pornographied, and they are forced to digitally segregate that aspect of themselves from their everyday online existence. To not have your account banned, to not have your content censored, to not find yourself demonetized, or, in short, to participate in this new internet-mediated world of ours, you must relegate a certain part of your identity to a digital closet—usually one with a gym bag containing the few odd bits of pornography that push the boundaries of the "abnormal" sexual desires that you've been able to scrape out from the homogenous glut of mainstream heteroporn (with little help from tube sites or Google Search). As Michele Barrett and Mary McIntosh note, this can lead to "a prison whose walls and bars are constructed of the ideas of domestic privacy and autonomy."[10]

Taken individually, each instance of heteronormative bias I've examined throughout the book and recapitulated above is rather easily dismissed by technology companies' public relations departments as simply being a mistake made by enormously complex systems operating at web scale on billions of pieces of content or the rogue misogyny and homophobia of a few bad actors. Perhaps even more unfortunately, these arguments are convincing to a sizable portion of their users. Lisa Nakamura has found similar explanations for racism online, which is often positioned as "a 'glitch' or malfunction of a network designed to broadcast a signal, a signal that is hijacked or polluted by the pirate racist."[11] Following Nakamura, I hope to have shown that heteronormativity is not a glitch online but a *feature* of the internet writ large. By connecting a broad overview of misogynist and heteronormative discourse online (chapter 1) to the coding practices and content moderation policies at technology companies (chapter 2) and demonstrating their broad, enduring, and consistent negative impact on LGBTQIA+ communities over time (chapters 3 and 4), my hope is that in aggregate these many cases and examples might serve as a convincing gestalt from which we can begin to see the growing heteronormativity of the internet.

For some, this will likely still be an ersatz argument, lacking the smoking gun of direct admission of guilt or the empirical evidence of a heteronormative module embedded in every algorithm on the internet, as some people are still wont to give the benefit of the doubt to technology companies. Unfortunately, with blackboxed proprietary algorithms dominating the internet and a scattered and ephemeral archive of overzealous censorship, it will be difficult to ever convince these people. Further, the fact that cultural, political, and economic victories are never securely won but must continually be refought can inspire cynicism, apathy, and, in the worst cases, nihilism. However, this is the harsh reality that we must face. Just as the door to the closet seemed to have been pried open with the blood, sweat, and tears of millions of people, its logic is being rearticulated in our digital world and embedded in the infrastructure of the internet. This battlefront has been reopened, and like a hydra, heteronormativity has reared another head.

In light of this, critique is not enough. In my opinion, ending the book here would be dodging the key question implicit in any such critique; namely, *what can be done?* For those willing to see the whole that emerges from these many parts, there are some steps we might take, ranging from revisionist actions that might make the argument more convincing and ameliorate some of the worst heteronormative abuses of power to the revolutionary that might reshape the internet and society for the next generation. While I will outline the beginnings of some potential strategies and tactics that might be useful in the battle at hand, I would like to offer some caveats. My ideas here will be partial, perspectival, and quite possibly wrong. There can be no singular answer to this most difficult of questions, and someone who enjoys my privileges is perhaps least qualified to respond. As such, I'd invite you to correct my response, to critique my critique, even if it means tearing down everything I've pieced together here to start anew or exposing the normativity in my own analysis. It is my hope that smarter and more qualified people than me will be determining the course of action necessitated in response to the digital closet.

THE REVISIONIST RESPONSE TO THE DIGITAL CLOSET

The revisionist response to the digital closet includes collective actions that we might all engage in to strengthen our case against the increasing heteronormativity of the internet and to ameliorate some of the harms that it inflicts, unduly borne by the most marginalized in our communities. The revisionist response is meant to provide some framework for what can be done immediately or in the short term while more expansive responses are formulated and implemented. This is a culture war of many fronts and will take a steadfast, diverse, and distributed set of actors committed to many different strategies and tactics over different time frames to make significant progress. Toward that end, here are a few of the action items that I think are readily achievable and can be articulated within the preexisting framework and discourse on the internet, free speech, and civil rights that are prominent in Silicon Valley.

1. Vigilance and Accountability through Data Collection

We—and by this I mean the alliance of people willing to work toward queering our internet architecture—need more, better, and longer duration data on internet censorship. While we could demand this from companies themselves—or we could demand that our governments demand it on our behalf—it is unlikely that they will provide it. The possibility of spammers reverse engineering their filtration systems from this data will endanger their ad revenue too greatly for them to provide this information willingly. If it cannot be obtained by demand, it ought to be collected independently by research centers, universities, and community members. Some initial efforts have been made in this direction, but they are not well funded or robust enough. Ideally, everyone on social media would know where to go and how to submit a report of the overzealous censorship of sexual speech. With a large enough dataset, we can make much more convincing arguments; we can demonstrate that heteronormativity is not a glitch but a feature of the internet.

2. Initiate a Public Discourse on Sexual Speech

We need to be having a much more robust conversation about what constitutes pornography, in which contexts, when it is actually in the best interests of children and adolescents to censor it, and how best to do so. This conversation needs to better reflect LGBTQIA+, sex-positive, and sex-critical voices. We need to figure out what values we actually share and examine how they intersect with civic justice. We need to consider the evidence we have about sexual speech and pornography in particular in doing so.

3. More and Better Evidence on the Impact of Sexual Speech

Throughout my research for this book, it was a struggle to connect the incredibly heterogeneous and siloed empirical evidence that came to bear on sexual speech online. This is no wonder, as disciplinary boundaries often prevent the very confluences of ideas necessary to address a problem like this. This is only exacerbated by the difficulty of getting funding for and internal review board (IRB) approval for studies on the impact of sexual speech, especially when they examine people under eighteen years old. It would be helpful if we advocated for more, better, and reproducible studies of the impact that sexual speech has on people that are then confirmed through multiple repeat trials. This same energy ought to be applied as well to researching the material impacts of online sex work so that we can better understand the needs of digital sex workers. The social sciences are particularly well equipped to do this if we make it a priority.

4. Anti-Censorship Commitment

In 2007, Google shareholders voted down a sweeping anti-censorship initiative.[12] Similar initiatives have been introduced at or suggested to other internet platforms to no avail. We ought to press these companies to reconsider anti-censorship commitments and press our governments to put similar commitments into legislation and bureaucratic regulations as well. While anathema to shareholders, these commitments easily fit within the techno-libertarian, free speech–oriented ethos of the technology sector and can be argued for on grounds that are thus familiar to tech executives. Extracting a specific commitment to protecting LGBTQIA+ discourse online would be particularly beneficial, as they can be brought to bear as pressure on companies to redress grievances more quickly and thoroughly.

5. Better Adjudication Mechanisms

One of the more opaque aspects of content moderation online is the adjudication mechanisms available to people who believe their content was blocked unjustly or in error. The accounts that I came across repeatedly showed tech companies sending out mixed messages, repeatedly sending vague form letters in response to each complaint, or ignoring requests for adjudication altogether. We ought to advocate for more carve-outs for LGBTQIA+ discourse and sexual speech and specific channels of adjudication for content that may have been blocked due to heteronormativity and/or homophobia. This is a rather low-cost solution and fits within the content moderation workflow that already exists at most tech companies—it is a simple matter of prioritizing and escalating LGBTQIA+ content to the more senior and better trained moderators and/or instating targeted carve-outs to preserve LGBTQIA+ discourse. These costs, it could be argued, would easily be offset by the benefits of avoiding the embarrassing public relations nightmares of censoring clearly nonpornographic LGBTQIA+ content.

6. Demand AI Explicability

Big data and AI ethics are rapidly growing discourses that increasingly stress the need for neural network explicability and interpretability. Some computer scientists argue that this will unnecessarily handcuff the development of AI systems.[13] However, it is the only means for having a public discourse on such systems. Recent trends in neural network research have begun to demonstrate methods for feature visualization and attribution in neural network applications.[14] We ought to demand that companies applying machine learning and neural networks to content moderation institute more robust feature visualization and attribution and make these outputs publicly available so that we might better understand how their algorithms are working and offer constructive criticism for improving them.

7. Demand "Human Algorithm" Explicability

In the wake of the content moderation scandals that surrounded the 2016 US presidential election, Facebook introduced transparency measures to its content moderation policy making. This first step is applaudable and ought to be replicated industry-wide. It needs to be taken further though, and further transparency ought to be granted to the public or nonprofit industry watchdogs who can keep track of who is making content moderation

policies, who is influencing these policy makers, and who is enacting
these policies and making decisions about individual pieces of content.
Moderation of sexual content ought to be further prioritized, with more
care and consideration given to policy making and more training being
given to content moderation laborers. Ideally, this would also include lo-
cation or cultural context being factored into decision-making. Further
use also ought to be made of the click-to-reveal dynamics implemented at
companies like Facebook for potentially gory photos, allowing borderline
sexual content to persist on the site behind a click-through barrier or even
behind age verification, though this latter is rife with its own problems.

8. Reinstate the Off Button

Google SafeSearch and other companies that host but mask pornography
on their platforms need to reinstate a full opt-out option. All content on
these platforms should be indexed and searchable with the same ease, and
the decision of when to show or not show "pornographic" results ought to
be left to users rather than keyword and behavior-based predictive analytics.
Gating pornography behind a select few keywords puts mainstream heteroporn producers at an undue advantage, as they can leverage their technological prowess, access to corporate lawyers, and advertising capital to make
sure their content is "optimized" to show up first in any content search.
This seems like a relatively simple to implement and cost-effective solution
and thus is a demand worth making. Similar demands ought to be made if
other platforms can be convinced to host sexual speech behind click-
through or age verification barriers, though, as of now, this demand per-
tains mostly to Google.

THE REVOLUTIONARY RESPONSE TO THE DIGITAL CLOSET

The revolutionary response to the digital closet encompasses those strategies that aim for changes that are much more difficult to achieve or need to
occur over a longer time frame. The revolutionary response needs to remain
flexible and responsive to social contexts and the needs of the marginalized.
It is particularly difficult to imagine because we are all fed a narrative of the
inevitability of our current technologies and the impossibility of thinking
outside the frameworks of the nation-state and capitalism. That said, it is
worth staking out some initial thoughts on what such a response might look

like, even though it will inevitably fall short. Toward that end, here are some action items that might help us orient a revolutionary response to the digital closet, each of which requires a more or less radical break from our current ideology and the current state of affairs.

1. Defund the Police

Following the calls of the Black Lives Matter movement and other social justice organizers, we ought to make defunding the police a core strategy. The particular focus ought to be on defunding vice squads that enforce prostitution laws and criminalize sex work, as well as the branches of the Justice Department now focused on the overbroad enforcement of FOSTA. Where police departments continue to exist, we might also follow New Zealand's model and train police officers to be more accountable and available to LGBTQIA+ and sex worker communities so that they can have equal access to protection under the law. Extending that concept, police also ought to be better equipped to handle the types of online harassment that digital sex workers might face, including things like trolls and stalkers.

2. Legalize Sex Work Online and Offline

A tightly coupled second aim ought to be to legalize sex work, both online and offline, in recognition that the criminal justice system is not the appropriate apparatus to address the material ills of sex work. This has the added benefit of creating a loophole in FOSTA, which notably *does not apply* in Nevada because of state legislation on prostitution there. While a more revolutionary approach would be to demand this at the federal level, it also works as a revisionist approach, as the same idea can be applied at local and state levels perhaps more immediately.

3. Make Sex a Concern for the Welfare State

Again, following the trends in the current progressive movement of demanding an expansion to the welfare state—including universal health care, sweeping environmental regulations, unemployment insurance, and so on—we might add to that list that sex be treated as a public health concern and an important prong of the welfare state. I mean this both in a rehabilitative sense—offering social services like housing, health care, food, job training, education, and so on, to sex workers (regardless of whether they agree or intend to exit sex work)—and in a more proactive and positive sense. By the latter, we might begin to think about fulfilling, enjoyable, diverse sex as part of what it means to live a healthy and happy life. We might radically expand and diversify sex education, not only in public schools but also in public discourse through public service announcements and other informational campaigns. We might aim to become the society we already imagine ourselves to be that can openly talk about sex and sexuality in a productive, informative, transformative sense. Needless to say, I imagine this in an anti-heteronormative and feminist sense that would highlight increasingly things like consent and mutual pleasure.

4. Direct Action through Community Organizing

While this is less difficult to imagine as many LGBTQIA+ and sex worker communities are already engaging in the practice, we might imagine radically expanding our communal capacities to address our concerns directly without the need to appeal to state or corporate powers. I am thinking here of the sex worker activist groups AIDS Myanmar Association, Durbar Mahila Samanwaya Committee, Veshya Anyay Mukti Parishad, and the Thai group Empower or trans and queer community groups looking to address violence without recourse to police like Safe Outside the System Collective of the Audre Lorde Project in New York City; For Crying Out Loud!, Communities Against Rape and Abuse, and the Northwest Network of Bisexual, Trans, Lesbian and Gay Survivors of Abuse in Seattle; Creative Interventions and Generative Somatics in Oakland; Community United Against Violence in San Francisco; and Philly Stands Up![15] In particular, we can look to *The Revolution Starts at Home* and the Creative Interventions Tool Kit as inspiration for how community problems can be solved by committed community members engaging in direct action.[16] I think this is a model we might look to expand on and develop.

5. Make Communications Infrastructures and/or Social Media Platforms into Public Utilities

It has always struck me as odd that among the demands made by progressive organizers that turning phone and ISPs and now social media platforms into public utilities was not a more prominent demand. It is nearly impossible to access state services or maintain gainful employment without maintaining perpetual internet and mobile phone connectedness, and it has become increasingly difficult to navigate higher education and the workplace without using social media. Internet and telephone services definitely present themselves as public utilities, as increasingly do social media platforms and other technologies, such as Google Search. We might take that model to rethink technology's place in our society and either demand public ownership or an extremely restrictive private licensing agreement where companies are allowed to provide the service for limited profit but under tight constraints aimed at the public good. This goal would subsume similar but smaller-scale goals like reinstituting net neutrality or extending net neutrality to mobile communications. The result may be universal and free access to phone and internet communications and tighter regulations on content moderation policies—making them responsive to our needs rather than advertisers' brand images.

6. Fully Automated Luxury Gay Space Communism

In the end, many of the strategies here are interconnected with and dependent on a much larger revolutionary movement toward the overthrow of global capitalism and its attendant imperialist nation-states. With power concentrated in the hands of either, we're left to fend for ourselves and take what moderate revisions we can get. While it may be a yet to be imagined -ism that gives shape to an allied intersectional revolutionary movement like this, to me, it looks like for now the closest concept we have to imagine a society that can meet these demands of radical democracy, robust social welfare, and freedom of self-expression is communism—particularly of the variety often memed about in earnest on the internet, Fully Automated Luxury Gay Space Communism. Let's all blast off together.

ACKNOWLEDGMENTS

There is no one I could possibly thank more than my wife and partner Bethany Monea, who listened to me talk about this book incessantly, gave feedback on multiple drafts, and encouraged me to keep going even when I felt like procrastinating. Without her, this book would certainly not exist. I'd also like to thank my family for providing me with the love, support, and distraction of life outside academia that made writing a book like this possible, including Paul Monea, Christian Monea, Heidi Bradshaw, Ben Bradshaw, Brooke Monea, Blake Monea, Bubba Douglas, Paul Monea (Sr.), Michele Reber, Robb Reber, Sean Reber, Brandon Reber, Ben Rudick, Sarah Fink, and Jim Rudick. I'd like to particularly thank Cindi Rudick who helped keep me grounded and gave me the confidence to keep going, even when I doubted my ability to complete this project.

This project would have long ago stalled out were it not for Benjamin Peters, whose sage advice and selfless willingness to help me shape the initial ideas and structure the book proposal made this book possible. He is a continued inspiration for me and the regulative ideal that I try to meet as a scholar. I cannot thank him enough. I'd also like to thank David Weinberger for going through countless iterations of the proposal with me until I had finally figured out exactly what I was writing and how to (with any luck) make it interesting and accessible to broader audiences. Gita Manaktala has been all that I could ask for in an editor: open, kind, supportive, and encouraging. All of this was greatly appreciated as a scholar working on my first manuscript who had very little idea of how things worked going into this process. Lastly, from MIT, I'd like to thank my wonderful reviewers, who hopefully will read this, as it's my only chance to tell them how generous, insightful, and inspiring their feedback was on my manuscript. They helped to make this book better and to make me a better writer.

I'd like to thank George Mason University, including the College for Humanities and Social Sciences, the English Department, and the Cultural Studies Program for giving me the time and freedom to pursue this book project. I cannot imagine a better environment in which to write my first book. Deb Shutika and Denise Albanese selflessly protected my time as a junior faculty member and made sure I had time to complete this project. Paul Smith, Jessica Scarlata, and Hatim El-Hibri have all been close confidants throughout the process and provided invaluable insight into the project and the publication process. I'd also like to thank my PhD seminar students for agreeing to read and give me illuminating feedback on the manuscript, including Muna Al Taweel, Angela Barajas, Terilee Edwards-Hewitt, Jason Grant, Travis Lamken, Luma Mousa, Kylie Musolf, Mark Peterson, Maillim Santiago, Ian Sinnett, Srishti Sood, Pavithra Suresh, Chelsea Triggs, Mariah Wakefield, and Wenzhu Xu. Kylie Musolf's detailed feedback in particular helped shape my revision plan for the book.

I'd also like to thank my friends and colleagues who listened to me talk about the book, attended my presentations, and helped me work out some of the ideas that initiated the project, including Charlie Strong, Scott Sundvall, Josh Coleman, Chris Drain, Jessa Lingel, Ezekiel Dixon-Román, Ken Pinion, David Parisi, Mel Gregg, Sarah Sharma, Jeremy Packer, Kyle Stein, and Hollis Griffin. Last, but certainly not least, I'd like to thank the journalists and community activists who tirelessly archived and wrote stories about the censorship of LGBTQIA+ content online. Violet Blue's and Samantha Cole's work were both invaluable for me, and I cannot thank them enough for it.

INTRODUCTION

1. Nicholas Carlson, "Well, These New Zuckerberg IMs Won't Help Facebook's Privacy Problems," Business Insider, May 13, 2010, accessed January 25, 2020, https://www.businessinsider.com/well-these-new-zuckerberg-ims-wont-help-facebooks-privacy-problems-2010-5.

2. Shoshana Zuboff, *The Age of Surveillance Capitalism: The Fight for a Human Future at the New Frontier of Power* (New York: PublicAffairs, 2019); Cal Newport, *Digital Minimalism: Choosing a Focused Life in a Noisy World* (New York: Portfolio/Penguin, 2019).

3. Bruce Schneier, *Data and Goliath: The Hidden Battles to Collect Your Data and Control Your World* (New York: W. W. Norton, 2016).

4. Sarah Banet-Weiser, *Empowered: Popular Feminism and Popular Misogyny* (Durham, NC: Duke University Press, 2018); Herman Gray, "Subject (ed) to Recognition," *American Quarterly* 65, no. 4 (2013): 771–798; Inderpal Grewal, *Transnational America; Feminisms, Diasporas, Neoliberalisms* (Durham, NC: Duke University Press, 2005); Larry Gross, *Up from Invisibility: Lesbians, Gay Men, and the Media in America* (New York: Columbia University Press, 2001); Radha S. Hedge, *Circuits of Visibility: Gender and Transnational Media Cultures* (New York: NYU Press, 2011).

5. Zuboff, *The Age of Surveillance Capitalism.*

6. "Accelerating Acceptance 2019: Executive Summary," GLAAD, accessed February 4, 2020, https://www.glaad.org/publications/accelerating-acceptance-2019.

7. Throughout the book I have used the term "alt-right," which was in vogue during the years it was written and partially structuring political commentary at key points during the implementation of FOSTA-SESTA in the United States. While I recognize that the term has been deconstructed and now is perhaps better replaced with simpler and more enduring concepts like White Supremacy or White Nationalism, I use it here to capture a broader range of discourse, including what scholars have identified as the "alt-light": interlocutors positioning themselves somewhere between explicit White Supremacists and far-right public news outlets. These interlocutors surely maintain their own versions of racism and in my research have been

unanimously misogynist, but might not sufficiently qualify for membership with the White Supremacist or White Nationalist crowds. As such, I've maintained "alt-right," the problematic term of the times, for its broader descriptive power in this conjuncture.

8. Violet Blue, "The Internet War on Sex Is Here," Engadget, December 7, 2018, accessed February 14, 2019, https://www.engadget.com/2018/12/07/the-internet-war-on-sex-is-here.

9. Tim Alberta, "How the GOP Gave Up on Porn," Politico, November/December 2018, accessed February 17, 2019, https://www.politico.com/magazine/story/2018/11/11/republican-party-anti-pornography-politics-222096.

10. Alberta, "How the GOP Gave Up on Porn."

11. Alberta, "How the GOP Gave Up on Porn."

12. Caitlin Dewey, "Is Rule 34 Actually True? An Investigation into the Internet's Most Risqué Law," *Washington Post*, April 6, 2016, accessed February 17, 2019, https://www.washingtonpost.com/news/the-intersect/wp/2016/04/06/is-rule-34-actually-true-an-investigation-into-the-internets-most-risque-law.

13. "Things Are Looking Up in America's Porn Industry," NBC News, January 20, 2015, accessed February 17, 2019, https://www.nbcnews.com/business/business-news/things-are-looking-americas-porn-industry-n289431.

14. "2018 Year in Review," Pornhub, December 11, 2018, accessed February 17, 2019, https://www.pornhub.com/insights/2018-year-in-review.

15. "The Top 500 Sites on the Web," Alexa, accessed February 17, 2019, https://www.alexa.com/topsites.

16. Newport, *Digital Minimalism*.

17. Mark Andrejevic, *Infoglut: How Too Much Information Is Changing the Way We Think and Know* (New York: Routledge, 2013).

18. Jonathan Jones, "Are These Shakespeare's Dirty Pictures?," *Guardian*, December 10, 2010, accessed February 17, 2019, https://www.theguardian.com/artanddesign/jonathanjonesblog/2010/dec/10/shakespeare-dirty-pictures; Jonathan Jones, "Marcantonio Raimondi: The Renaissance Printer Who Brought Porn to Europe," *Guardian*, October 13, 2016, accessed February 17, 2019, https://www.theguardian.com/artanddesign/jonathanjonesblog/2016/oct/13/marcantonio-raimondi-renaissance-printer-i-modi-the-positions-porn-europe.

19. Alberta, "How the GOP Gave Up on Porn."

20. Patchen Barrs, *The Erotic Engine: How Pornography Has Powered Mass Communication, from Gutenberg to Google* (Toronto: Doubleday Canada, 2010); Jonathan Coopersmith, "Pornography, Technology and Progress," *Icon* 4 (1998): 94–125; Jonathan Coopersmith, "Pornography, Videotape and the Internet," *IEEE Technology and Society Magazine* 19, no. 1 (2000): 27–34; Jonathan Coopersmith, "Does Your Mother

Know What You Really Do? The Changing Nature and Image of Computer-Based Pornography," *History and Technology* 22, no. 1 (2006): 1–25.

21. Kaveh Waddell, "How Porn Leads People to Upgrade Their Tech," *Atlantic*, June 7, 2016, accessed February 17, 2019, https://www.theatlantic.com/technology /archive/2016/06/how-porn-leads-people-to-upgrade-their-tech/486032.

22. The Radicalesbians, "The Woman-Identified Woman," in *Out of the Closets: Voices of Gay Liberation*, ed. Karla Jay and Allen Young (New York: NYU Press, 1972), 172–176; Gloria Anzaldúa, *Borderlands/La Frontera: The New Mestiza* (San Francisco: Aunt Lute Books, 1987); Cherríe Moraga, *Loving in the War Years* (Boston: South End, 1983); Michelle Wallace, *Black Macho and the Myth of the Super Woman* (New York: Verso, 2015); Adrienne Rich, "Compulsory Heterosexuality and Lesbian Existence," *Signs* 5, no. 4 (1980): 631–660.

23. Jane Ward, *The Tragedy of Heterosexuality* (New York: NYU Press, 2020), 1.

24. Ward, *The Tragedy of Heterosexuality*, 125–153.

25. Jonathan Ned Katz, *The Invention of Heterosexuality* (New York: Dutton, 1995).

26. Katz, *The Invention of Heterosexuality*, 39.

27. Katz, *The Invention of Heterosexuality*, 37–40. It is interesting to note that this still led to interesting gender dynamics, as female-female sex acts were *not* considered disruptive of procreative potential and thus not equated with male-male, male-animal, or masturbatory sex acts.

28. Katz, *The Invention of Heterosexuality*, 19–32.

29. Peter Gay, *The Bourgeois Experience, Victoria to Freud (3 Volumes)* (Chicago: University of Chicago Press, 1986); Sheila Rothman, *Woman's Proper Place: A History of Changing Ideals and Practices, 1870 to the Present* (New York: Basic Books, 1978).

30. John D'Emilio and Estelle B. Freedman, *Intimate Matters: A History of Sexuality in America*, 3rd ed. (Chicago: University of Chicago Press, 2012), 108.

31. Katz, *The Invention of Heterosexuality*, 50.

32. D'Emilio and Freedman, *Intimate Matters*, 415–416.

33. D'Emilio and Freedman, *Intimate Matters*, 50–51.

34. Kristen Schilt and Laurel Westbrook, "Doing Gender, Doing Heteronormativity: 'Gender Normals,' Transgender People, and the Social Maintenance of Heterosexuality," *Gender and Society* 23, no. 4 (August 2009): 440–464.

35. Michele Barrett and Mary McIntosh, *The Anti-Social Family*, 2nd ed. (New York: Verso, 2015).

36. Michael Anderson, *Approaches to the History of the Western Family, 1500–1914* (New York: Cambridge University Press, 1980), 14.

37. Barrett and McIntosh, *The Anti-Social Family*; Jean-Louis Flandrin, *Families in Former Times: Kinship, Household and Sexuality* (New York: Cambridge University

Press, 1979); C. C. Harris, "The Changing Relation between Family and Societal Form in Western Society," in *Sociology of the Family*, 2nd ed., ed. Michael Anderson (New York: Penguin, 1980); Gayle Rubin, "The Traffic in Women: Notes on the 'Political Economy of Sex,'" in *Toward an Anthropology of Women*, ed. Rayna R. Reiter (New York: Monthly Review Press, 1975): 157–210.

38. Jacques Donzelot, *The Policing of Families*, trans. Robert Hurley (Baltimore: Johns Hopkins University Press, 1997).

39. Barrett and McIntosh, *The Anti-Social Family*, 56.

40. Friedrich Engels, "The Origin of the Family, Private Property and the State," in *The Marx-Engels Reader*, 2nd ed., ed. Robert C. Tucker (New York: W. W. Norton, 1978), 734–759.

41. Barrett and McIntosh, *The Anti-Social Family*, 76.

42. Eve Kosofsky Sedgwick, *Epistemology of the Closet* (Berkeley: University of California Press, 2008), 3.

43. Michael Warner and Lauren Berlant, "Sex in Public," *Critical Inquiry* 24, no. 2 (1998): 547–566.

44. Nancy Fraser, "Rethinking the Public Sphere: A Contribution to the Critique of Actually Existing Democracy," *Social Text*, no. 25/26 (1990): 56–80.

45. Gayle Rubin, "Thinking Sex: Notes for a Radical Theory of the Politics of Sexuality," in *Pleasure and Danger: Exploring Female Sexuality*, ed. Carole S. Vance (New York: Routledge, 1984), 278.

46. Melissa Gira Grant, *Playing Whore* (London: Verso, 2014).

47. Juno Mac and Molly Smith, *Revolting Prostitutes: The Fight for Sex Workers' Rights* (New York: Verso, 2020), 23.

48. Leo Bersani, "Is the Rectum a Grave?" *October* 43 (Winter 1987): 197–222.

49. Mac and Smith, *Revolting Prostitutes*, 27–29.

50. Jo Doezema, *Sex Slaves and Discourse Masters: The Construction of Trafficking* (New York: Zed Books, 2010).

51. See Aya Gruber, Amy J. Cohen, and Kate Mogulescu, "Penal Welfare and the New Human Trafficking Intervention Courts," *Florida Law Review* 68 (2016): 1333–1402; Forrest Stuart, *Down, Out, and under Arrest: Policing and Everyday Life in Skid Row* (Chicago: University of Chicago Press, 2016).

52. Rosalind Gill, "Postfeminist Media Culture: Elements of a Sensibility," *European Journal of Cultural Studies* 10, no. 2 (2007): 147–166; Angela McRobbie, *The Aftermath of Feminism: Gender, Culture, and Social Change* (London: SAGE Publications, 2009); Diane Negra and Yvonne Tasker, eds., *Interrogating postfeminism: Gender and the Politics of Popular Culture* (Durham, NC: Duke University Press, 2007); Banet-Weiser, *Empowered*.

53. Banet-Weiser, *Empowered*, 19–21.

54. Mac and Smith, *Revolting Prostitutes*, 31–34.

55. Mac and Smith, *Revolting Prostitutes*, 35.

56. See Alexander Monea, "Race and Computer Vision," in *The Democratization of Artificial Intelligence: Net Politics in the Era of Learning Algorithms*, ed. Andreas Sudmann (Bielefeld, Germany: Transcript, 2019), 189–208.

57. See Charlton D. McIlwain, *Black Software: The Internet and Racial Justice, from the AfroNet to Black Lives Matter* (New York: Oxford University Press, 2019); André Brock, *Distributed Blackness: African American Cybercultures* (New York: NYU Press, 2020).

58. Janet Abbate, *Recoding Gender: Women's Changing Participation in Computing* (Cambridge, MA: MIT Press, 2012); Mar Hicks, *Programmed Inequality: How Britain Discarded Women Technologists and Lost Its Edge in Computing* (Cambridge, MA: MIT Press, 2018); Walter Isaacson, *The Innovators: How a Group of Hackers, Geniuses, and Geeks Created the Digital Revolution* (New York: Simon & Schuster, 2014).

59. Joy Buolamwini and Timnit Gebru, "Gender Shades: Intersectional Accuracy Disparities in Commercial Gender Classification," in *Proceedings of Machine Learning Research: Conference on Fairness, Accountability and Transparency*, ed. Sorelle A. Friedler and Christo Wilson (PMLR, 2018), 77–91.

60. Ruha Benjamin, *Race after Technology: Abolitionist Tools for the New Jim Code* (Medford, MA: Polity, 2019).

61. Safiya U. Noble, *Algorithms of Oppression: How Search Engines Reinforce Racism* (New York: NYU Press, 2018), 1.

62. See Elizabeth Ellcessor, *Restricted Access: Media, Disability, and the Politics of Participation* (New York: 2016); Elizabeth Ellcessor and Benjamin Kirkpatrick, ed., *Disability Media Studies* (New York: NYU Press, 2017).

CHAPTER 1

1. Richard Nixon, "Statement about the Report of the Commission on Obscenity and Pornography," The American Presidency Project, October 24, 1970, accessed July 10, 2019, https://www.presidency.ucsb.edu/documents/statement-about-the -report-the-commission-obscenity-and-pornography.

2. "Playboy Interview: Jimmy Carter," *Playboy*, November 1976, 63–86.

3. Tim Alberta, "How the GOP Gave Up on Porn," Politico, November 11, 2018, accessed February 17, 2019, https://www.politico.com/magazine/story/2018 /11/11/republican-party-anti-pornography-politics-222096.

4. Whitney Strub, *Perversion for Profit: The Politics of Pornography and the Rise of the New Right* (New York: Columbia University Press, 2013), 7.

5. *Attorney General's Commission on Pornography, Final Report, July 1986* (Washington, DC: Government Printing Office, 1986); Cf. Robert H. Burger, "The Meese Report on Pornography and Its Respondents: A Review Article," *The Library Quarterly: Information, Community, Policy* 57, no. 4 (1987): 436–447.

6. Catharine A. MacKinnon, *Feminism Unmodified: Discourses on Life and Law* (Cambridge, MA: Harvard University Press, 1987), 176.

7. Catharine A. MacKinnon, *Toward a Feminist Theory of the State* (Cambridge, MA: Harvard University Press, 1989), 196.

8. Andrea Dworkin and Catharine A. MacKinnon, *Pornography and Civil Rights: A New Day for Women's Equality* (Minneapolis: Organizing Against Pornography, 1988); Andrea Dworkin, *Pornography Is a Civil Rights Issue for Women* (Minneapolis: Organizing Against Pornography, 1986); Catharine A. MacKinnon, *Feminism Unmodified*.

9. Andrea Dworkin, *Right-Wing Women: The Politics of Domesticated Females* (London: Women's Press, 1983).

10. For example, Carole S. Vance (ed.), *Pleasure and Danger: Exploring Female Sexuality* (New York: Routledge, 1984); Mariana Valverde, *Sex, Power and Pleasure* (Toronto: Women's Press, 1985); Gayle Rubin, "Misguided, Dangerous and Wrong: An Analysis of Antipornography Politics," in *Bad Girls and Dirty Pictures: The Challenge to Reclaim Feminism*, ed. Alison Assister and Avedon Carol (London: Pluto), 18–40; Eithne Johnson, "Appearing Live on Your Campus!: Porn-Education Roadshows," *Jump Cut* 41 (1997): 27–35; Lynne Segal, "Only the Literal: The Contradictions of Anti-Pornography Feminism," *Sexualities* 1, no. 1 (1998): 43–62.

11. Strub, *Perversion for Profit*. See chapters 7 and 8.

12. Gayle Rubin, "Thinking Sex: Notes for a Radical Theory of the Politics of Sexuality," in *Pleasure and Danger: Exploring Female Sexuality*, ed. Carole S. Vance (New York: Routledge, 1984), 267–319.

13. Jay Daniel Thompson, "Invisible and Everywhere: Heterosexuality in Anti-Pornography Feminism," *Sexualities* 18, no. 5/6 (2015): 750–764.

14. A conclusion shared by Angel Nagle, *Kill All Normies: Online Culture Wars From 4Chan And Tumblr to Trump and the Alt-Right* (Washington, DC: Zero Books, 2017).

15. Thomas McBee, "A Sociological Investigation of #NoWanks," *New York Magazine*, December 14, 2018, accessed June 16, 2019, https://www.thecut.com/2018/12/a-sociological-investigation-of-nowanks.html.

16. Sarah Banet-Weiser, *Empowered: Popular Feminism and Popular Misogyny* (Durham, NC: Duke University Press, 2018), 116–117.

17. Adrienne Massanari, "#Gamergate and the Fappening: How Reddit's Algorithm, Governance, and Culture Support Toxic Technocultures," *New Media & Society* 19, no. 3 (March 2017): 329–346.

18. Mancel Horta Ribeiro, Jeremy Blackburn, Barry Bradlyn, Emiliano De Cristofaro, Gianluca Stringhini, Summer Long, Stephanie Greenberg, and Savvas Zannettou, "From Pick-Up Artists to Incels: A Data-Driven Sketch of the Manosphere," arXiv preprint arXiv:2001.07600 (2020).

19. Jack Bratich, "Affective Convergence in Reality Television: A Case Study in Divergence," in *Flow TV: Television in the Age of Media Convergence*, eds. Michael Kackman, Marnie Binfield, Matthew Thomas Payne, Allison Perlman, and Bryan Sebok (New York: Routledge, 2011): 529–549.

20. Matthew N. Lyons, "Alt-Right: More Misogynistic than Many Neonazis." *Threewayfight*, December 3, 2016, accessed January 30, 2021, http://threewayfight .blogspot.com/2016/12/alt-right-more-misogynistic-than-many.html.

21. Danielle Keats Citron, *Hate Crimes in Cyberspace* (Cambridge, MA: Harvard University Press, 2016); Laura Portwood-Stacer, "Media Refusal and Conspicuous Non-consumption: The Performative and Political Dimensions of Facebook Abstention," *New Media & Society* 15, no. 7 (2013): 1041–1057.

22. For example, Tracie Farrell, Miriam Fernandez, Jakub Novotny, and Harith Alani, "Exploring Misogyny across the Manosphere in Reddit," in *Proceedings of the 10th ACM Conference on Web Science* (New York: ACM, 2019), 87–96.; Debbie Ging, "Alphas, Betas, and Incels: Theorizing the Masculinities of the Manosphere," *Men and Masculinities* 22, no. 4 (2019): 638–657; Lise Gotell and Emily Dutton, "Sexual Violence in the 'Manosphere': Antifeminist Men's Rights Discourses on Rape," *International Journal for Crime, Justice and Social Democracy* 5, no. 2 (2016): 65; Alice E. Marwick and Robyn Caplan, "Drinking Male Tears: Language, the Manosphere, and Networked Harassment," *Feminist Media Studies* 18, no. 4 (2018): 543–559; Shawn P. Van Valkenburgh, "Digesting the Red Pill: Masculinity and Neoliberalism in the Manosphere," *Men and Masculinities* 24, no. 1 (December 2018): 84–103.

23. Gail Dines, *Pornland: How Porn Has Hijacked Our Sexuality* (Boston: Beacon Press, 2011).

24. Banet-Weiser, *Empowered*, 118; Sarah Banet-Weiser and Kate M. Miltner, "#MasculinitySoFragile: Culture, Structure, and Networked Misogyny," *Feminist Media Studies* 16, no. 1 (2015): 171–174.

25. "Daryush 'Roosh' Valizadeh," Southern Poverty Law Center, accessed February 9, 2019, https://www.splcenter.org/fighting-hate/extremist-files/individual/ daryush-roosh-valizadeh.

26. Roosh V, "Return of Kings Is Going on Hiatus," Return of Kings, October 1, 2018, accessed February 9, 2019, http://www.returnofkings.com/195790/return -of-kings-is-going-on-hiatus.

27. For instance, his guides to "banging" in various countries are often in the top fifty to one hundred bestsellers for English-language books about those countries.

28. Calla Wahlquist and Josh Halliday, "Daryush 'Roosh V' Valizadeh Cancels Neomasculinist Meetings over Safety," *Guardian*, February 4, 2016, accessed February 9, 2019, https://www.theguardian.com/australia-news/2016/feb/04/daryush -roosh-v-valizadeh-cancels-neo-masculinist-meetings-over-safety.

29. Lindy West, "Now Roosh V and His Band of Sad Men in Dark Rooms Know How It Feels to Be Bombarded with Bile," *Guardian*, February 7, 2016, accessed February 9, 2019, https://www.theguardian.com/commentisfree/2016/feb/07/ daryush-roosh-v-valizadeh-and-his-acolytes-pilloried.

30. Roosh V, "Everything You Wanted to Know about Daryush 'Roosh' Valizadeh but Were Afraid to Ask," Rooshv.com, February 4, 2016, accessed February 9, 2019. https://www.rooshv.com/everything-you-wanted-to-know-about-daryush -valizadeh-but-were-afraid-to-ask.

31. Ginger Gorman, *Troll Hunting: Inside the World of Online Hate and Its Human Fallout* (Prahan, Australia: Hardie Grant Publishing, 2019); Whitney Phillips, *This Is Why We Can't Have Nice Things: Mapping the Relationship between Online Trolling and Mainstream Culture* (Cambridge, MA: MIT Press, 2016).

32. Roosh V, "Neomasculinity," Rooshv.com, March 4, 2015, accessed February 9, 2019, https://www.rooshv.com/neomasculinity.

33. Quintus Curtius, "The Origins of Neomasculinity," Return of Kings, March 9, 2015, accessed February 9, 2019, http://www.returnofkings.com/58237/the -origins-of-neomasculinity. N.B., for Quintus Curtius, the promise of the '80s was exemplified by fantasy-laden epics like *Back to the Future*, Sylvester Stallone's action films, Bruce Springsteen's music, and hair metal, and its loss was equally visible in the appearance in the '90s and '00s of bands like Nirvana and Alice in Chains and films like *The Matrix, Fight Club*, and *Being John Malkovich*.

34. Curtius, "The Origins."

35. Roosh V, "Neomasculinity" (emphases mine).

36. Roosh V, "What Is Neomasculinity?" Rooshv.com, May 6, 2015, accessed February 9, 2019, https://www.rooshv.com/what-is-neomasculinity.

37. Roosh V, "What Is Neomasculinity?"

38. Roosh V, "What Is Neomasculinity?"

39. Roosh V, "What Is Neomasculinity?"

40. Roosh V, "What Is Neomasculinity?"

41. Roosh V, "What Is Neomasculinity?" It is both amusing and distressing to note that a group of people so deeply influenced by Friedrich Nietzsche can so plainly express *ressentiment* and bad conscience. As Nietzsche wrote, "But thus I counsel you my friends: mistrust all in whom the drive to punish is strong!" Friedrich Nietzsche, *Thus Spoke Zarathustra,* eds. Adrian del Caro and Robert B. Pippin, trans. Adrian del Caro (New York: Cambridge University Press, 2006), p. 77.

42. Roosh does cite some evidence that single-parent homes lead to increased crime rates and attention deficit hyperactivity disorder diagnoses but interprets the evidence deterministically, refusing to examine the correlations between class and income in single-parent households with these behaviors. His faith in the nuclear family is just that. Roosh V, "What Is Neomasculinity?"

43. Roosh V, "What Is Neomasculinity?"

44. Roosh V, "What Is Neomasculinity?"

45. Roosh V, "What Is Neomasculinity?" For evidence, Roosh links to an overview of a University of Pennsylvania Medicine study that found neurological differences between men and women that were theorized to be connected to men's superior performance at learning and performing single tasks and women's superior performance at memory and social cognition. It is worth noting that this was a preliminary, not a conclusive, study, and that the differences were much more pronounced in people over the age of fourteen and thus are potentially due in part to nurture. Given our knowledge of neural plasticity, it is reading against the grain of contemporary neurology to so brashly assume that these neurological differences are due solely to genetic factors rather than the internalization of gender roles through nurture. See Madhura Ingalhalikar, Alex Smith, Drew Parker, Theodore D. Satterthwaite, Mark A. Elliott, Kosha Ruparel, Hakon Hakonarson, Raquel E. Gur, Ruben C. Gur, and Ragini Verma, "Sex Differences in the Structural Connectome of the Human Brain," *Proceedings of the National Academy of Sciences* 111, no. 2 (January 14, 2014): 823–828.

46. Roosh V, "What Is Neomasculinity?"

47. Roosh V, "What Is Neomasculinity?" Further, Roosh is extremely concerned about environmental pollution and dystopian regulation that might reduce the amount of testosterone in society, an idea that belies the close connection between the alt-right and conspiratorial or paranoid thinking.

48. See, for example, David C. Geary, *Male, Female: The Evolution of Human Sex Differences* (Washington, DC: American Psychological Association, 2009); Linda Mealey, *Sex Differences: Developmental and Evolutionary Strategies* (New York: Academic Press, 2000).

49. Melanie Blackless, Anthony Charuvastra, Amanda Derryck, Anne Fausto-Sterling, Karl Lauzanne, and Ellen Lee, "How Sexually Dimorphic Are We? Review and Synthesis," *American Journal of Human Biology* 12, no. 2 (March 2000): 151–166.

50. Anatomical sex correlates to things like height, weight, distribution of fat cells, metabolism, and so on, but not perfectly. An anatomical man with all five markers of the sex will not necessarily manifest all or any of these traits. All of this has little necessary connection with gender roles (socially prescribed norms based on sexual dimorphism) and gender identity (how one interprets and lives one's life according to those roles, some of which one may accept, reject, invert, and so on). The biggest takeaway here is that people ought to check their essentialism at the door and

express a bit more humility about the limits of their personal knowledge when it comes to sex, gender, and sexuality, especially when they are not trained experts in genetics, neurology, or any other field they are cherry-picking their supporting evidence from.

51. Roosh V, "What Is Neomasculinity?"

52. Eric Vilain, John C. Achermann, Erica Eugster, Vincent R. Harley, Yves Morel, Jean D. Wilson, and Olaf Hiort, "We Used to Call Them Hermaphrodites," *Genetics in Medicine* 9, no. 2 (2007): 65–66.

53. Here Roosh links to two news article write-ups of scientific studies linking transgender identity to drug use and suicide and one (outdated) survey of studies of postoperative studies of "transsexual" life satisfaction. See, respectively, Jerome Hunt, "Why the Gay and Transgender Population Experiences Higher Rates of Substance Use," Center for American Progress, March 9, 2012, accessed February 9, 2019, https://www.americanprogress.org/issues/lgbt/reports/2012/03/09/11228 /why-the-gay-and-transgender-population-experiences-higher-rates-of-substance -use/; Emily Alpert Reyes, "Transgender Study Looks at 'Exceptionally High' Suicide-Attempt Rate," *Los Angeles Times*, January 28, 2014, accessed February 9, 2019, http://articles.latimes.com/2014/jan/28/local/la-me-ln-suicide-attempts -alarming-transgender-20140127; David Batty, "Sex Changes Are not Effective, Say Researchers," *Guardian*, July 30, 2004, accessed February 9, 2019, https://www .theguardian.com/society/2004/jul/30/health.mentalhealth.

54. See Dean Spade, *Normal Life: Administrative Violence, Critical Trans Politics, and the Limits of Law* (Durham: Duke University Press, 2015).

55. He cites no comparable data to the studies on trans populations for other LGBTQIA+ populations.

56. Roosh cites evidence that marriages fail if women have had more than two sex partners, that female promiscuity leads to substance abuse, and that birth control impairs fertility. There are no corresponding negative outcomes for men outside of them having less time and energy to pursue other tasks.

57. See Roosh V, "Amazon Has Banned 9 of My Books without Explanation," Rooshv.com, September 10, 2018, accessed February 9, 2019, http://www.rooshv .com/amazon-has-banned-9-of-my-books-without-explanation; Roosh V, "Return of Kings Is Going on Hiatus."

58. "r/NoFap," Reddit, accessed June 14, 2019, https://www.reddit.com/r/ NoFap.

59. Anisa Subedar, "The Online Groups of Men Who Avoid Masturbation," BBC News, June 24, 2017, accessed February 17, 2019, https://www.bbc.com/news/ blogs-trending-40382766.

60. David J. Lee, "The NoFap Phenomenon: There's Nothing New about This Fight against Self-Love," *Psychology Today*, March 3, 2015, accessed June 14, 2019,

https://www.psychologytoday.com/us/blog/women-who-stray/201503/the
-nofap-phenomenon.

61. American Medical Association, *Human Sexuality* (Chicago: American Medical Association, 1972).

62. Planned Parenthood, "Masturbation," Planned Parenthood, accessed June 14, 2019, https://www.plannedparenthood.org/learn/sex-and-relationships/masturbation; Cf. Jon Knowles, "Masturbation—From Stigma to Sexual Health," Planned Parenthood, November 2002, accessed June 14, 2019, https://www.plannedparenthood.org/files/5513/9611/7867/masturbation_11-02.pdf.

63. Aniruddha Das, "Masturbation in the United States," *Journal of Sex & Marital Therapy* 33, no. 4 (2007): 301–317.

64. Brian Y. Park, Gary Wilson, Jonathan Berger, Matthew Christman, Bryn Reina, Frank Bishop, Warren P. Klam, and Andrew P. Doan, "Is Internet Pornography Causing Sexual Dysfunctions? A Review with Clinical Reports," *Behavioral Sciences* 6, no. 3 (2016): 17.

65. Nicole Prause and James Pfaus, "Viewing Sexual Stimuli Associated with Greater Sexual Responsiveness, not Erectile Dysfunction." *Sexual Medicine* 3, no. 2 (2015): 90–98; Nicole Prause, Vaughn R. Steele, Cameron Staley, Dean Sabatinelli, and Greg Hajcak, "Modulation of Late Positive Potentials by Sexual Images in Problem Users and Controls Inconsistent with 'Porn Addiction,'" *Biological Psychology* 109 (2015): 192–199.

66. Michael S. Exton, Tillmann H. C. Krüger, Norbert Bursch, Philip Haake, Wolfram Knapp, Manfred Schedlowski, and Uwe Hartmann, "Endocrine Response to Masturbation-Induced Orgasm in Healthy Men following a 3-Week Sexual Abstinence," *World Journal of Urology* 19, no. 5 (2001): 377–382.

67. Kris Taylor and Sue Jackson, "'I Want That Power Back': Discourses of Masculinity within an Online Pornography Abstinence Forum," *Sexualities* 21, no. 4 (2018): 621–639.

68. Gary Wilson, *Your Brain on Porn: Internet Pornography and the Emerging Science of Addiction* (Kent: Commonwealth Publishing, 2014).

69. Gary Wilson, "The Great Porn Experiment," May 16, 2012, TEDx Talks video, accessed June 16, 2019, https://www.youtube.com/watch?v=wSF82AwSDiU.

70. Wilson, "The Great Porn Experiment.

71. Taylor and Jackson, "'I Want That Power Back.'"

72. Thomas W. Laqueur, *Solitary Sex: A Cultural History of Masturbation* (Brooklyn: Zone Books, 2004).

73. *Onania: Or, the Heinous Sin of Self-Pollution, and All Its Frightful Consequences (in Both Sexes) Considered* (London: Printed for H. Cooke, 1712).

74. Stephen Greenblatt, "My, Myself, and I," *New York Review of Books*, April 8, 2004, accessed February 17, 2019, https://www.nybooks.com/articles/2004/04/08/me-myself-and-i.

75. Michael Stolberg, "Self-Pollution, Moral Reform, and the Venereal Trade: Notes on the Sources and Historical Context of *Onania* (1716)," *Journal of the History of Sexuality* 9, no. 1–2 (January/April 2000): 37–61.

76. John D'Emilio and Estelle B. Freedman, *Intimate Matters: A History of Sexuality in America*, 3rd ed. (Chicago: University of Chicago Press, 2012/1988).

77. Edward L. Rowan, *The Joy of Self-Pleasuring: Why Feel Guilty about Feeling Good?* (New York: Prometheus Books, 2000), 117.

78. Michael S. Patton, "Twentieth-Century Attitudes toward Masturbation," *Journal of Religion and Health* 25, no. 4 (1986): 291–302.

79. Robert T. Michael, John H. Gagnon, Edward O. Laumann, and Gina Kolata, *Sex in America: A Definitive Survey* (Boston: Little, Brown and Co., 1994), 161.

80. Knowles, "Masturbation—From Stigma to Sexual Health." Cf. William H. Masters, Virginia E. Johnson, and Robert C. Kolodny, *Masters and Johnson on Sex and Human Loving* (Boston: Little, Brown and Co., 1986); Warren McNab, "Masturbation: The Neglected Topic in Sexuality Education," *Family Life Education* 12, no. 2 (1993): 10–15.

81. Thomas McBee, "A Sociological Investigation of #NoWanks," *New York Magazine*, December 14, 2018, accessed June 16, 2019, https://www.thecut.com/2018/12/a-sociological-investigation-of-nowanks.html.

82. Stanley G. Hall, *Adolescence: Its Psychology and Its Relations to Physiology, Anthropology, Sociology, Sex, Crime, Religion, and Education*, Vol. 1 (New York: D. Appleton and Co., 1908), 445.

83. Jeffrey Jensen Arnett, "G. Stanley Hall's *Adolescence*: Brilliance and Nonsense," *History of Psychology* 9, no. 3 (2006): 186–197.

84. Edward L. Rowan, "Editorial: Masturbation According to the Boy Scout *Handbook*," *Journal of Sex Education & Therapy* 15, no. 2 (1989): 77–81.

85. Jesse Singal, "Why We're Scared of Masturbation," *New York Magazine*, August 4, 2014, accessed February 17, 2019, https://www.thecut.com/2014/08/why-were-scared-of-masturbation.html.

86. Singal, "Why We're Scared."

87. Robert Weiss, "Is 'No Fap' Movement Start of Tech Backlash?," *Huffington Post*, May 19, 2013, accessed February 17, 2019, https://www.huffingtonpost.com/robert-weiss/no-fap-movement_b_3302874.html.

88. Sarah Sharma, "Going to Work in Mommy's Basement," *Boston Review*, June 19, 2018, accessed June 15, 2019, http://bostonreview.net/gender-sexuality/sarah-sharma-going-work-mommys-basement.

89. Gavin McInnes, "Introducing: The Proud Boys," *Taki's Magazine*, September 15, 2016, June 19, 2019, https://www.takimag.com/article/introducing_the_proud_boys_gavin_mcinnes.

90. Gavin McInnes, "We Are Not Alt-Right," OfficialProudBoys.com, August 21, 2017, accessed February 28, 2019, https://officialproudboys.com/proud-boys/we-are-not-alt-right.

91. Robert Culkin, "Proud Boys: Who Are They?" OfficialProudBoys.com, August 24, 2017, accessed February 28, 2019, https://officialproudboys.com/proud-boys/whoaretheproudboys.

92. Gavin McInnes, "Introducing: The Proud Boys," *Taki's Magazine*, September 15, 2016, accessed June 19, 2019, https://www.takimag.com/article/introducing_the_proud_boys_gavin_mcinnes.

93. Jason Wilson, "Who Are the Proud Boys, 'Western Chauvinists' involved in Political Violence?" *Guardian*, July 14, 2018, accessed February 28, 2019, https://www.theguardian.com/world/2018/jul/14/proud-boys-far-right-portland-oregon.

94. Simon Houpt, "Everything Inside Gavin McInnes," *Globe and Mail*, August 18, 2017, accessed June 19, 2019, https://www.theglobeandmail.com/arts/television/gavin-mcinnes-path-to-the-far-rightfrontier/article36024918.

95. "Proud Boys," Southern Poverty Law Center, accessed February 28, 2019, https://www.splcenter.org/fighting-hate/extremist-files/group/proud-boys; John Paul Tasker, "Canada Labels the Proud Boys, Neo-Nazi Groups as Terrorists," CBC News, February 03, 2021, accessed February 6, 2021, https://www.cbc.ca/news/politics/canada-proud-boys-terrorists-1.5899186.

96. Southern Poverty Law Center, "Proud Boys"; Tasker, "Canada Labels Proud Boys."

97. Vanessa Grigoriadis, "The Edge of Hip: Vice, the Brand," *New York Times*, September 28, 2003, accessed June 16, 2019, https://www.nytimes.com/2003/09/28/style/the-edge-of-hip-vice-the-brand.html.

98. Matt Forney, "10 Signs You Might be a Cuckservative," Return of Kings, July 27, 2015, accessed June 16, 2019, https://www.returnofkings.com/68170/10-signs-you-might-be-a-cuckservative.

99. Gavin McInnes, "'Cuckservatism' Explained: What This New Political Meme Gets Right—and Wrong," Rebel, August 5, 2015, accessed June 16, 2019, https://www.therebel.media/_cuckservatism_explained.

100. Gavin McInnes, "Transphobia Is Perfectly Natural," Thought Catalog, August 8, 2014, accessed June 16, 2019, https://thoughtcatalog.com/gavin-mcinnes/2014/08/transphobia-is-perfectly-natural.

101. I spent some time deliberating on how to approach using this quote and have opted to keep it in because of its importance for demonstrating the depth of Proud

Boydom's hatred and cisnormativity but used asterisks to avoid putting the racial slur into print. Source: "Proud Boys," Southern Poverty Law Center, accessed February 28, 2019, https://www.splcenter.org/fighting-hate/extremist-files/group/proud-boys.

102. Gavin McInnes, "The Gavin McInnes Show 375," Compound Media, June 28, 2017, accessed June 16, 2019, https://www.compoundmedia.com/shows/the-gavin-mcinnes-show/954.

103. McInnes, "The Gavin McInnes Show."

104. McInnes, "The Gavin McInnes Show." N.B., the distance from a woman required for watching pornography and masturbating seems pliable. In an interview for *This American Life*, Franklin Wright, digital media strategist and staff writer for the official *Proud Boy Magazine* described the rule as requiring Proud Boys to only be within ten yards of a woman, "White Haze," *This American Life*, September 22, 2017, accessed June 16, 2019, https://www.thisamericanlife.org/626/white-haze.

105. McInnes, "The Gavin McInnes Show."

106. John D'Emilio and Estelle B. Freedman, *Intimate Matters: A History of Sexuality in America,* 3rd ed. (Chicago: University of Chicago Press, 2009).

107. Thomas McBee, "A Sociological Investigation of #NoWanks," *New York Magazine*, December 14, 2018, accessed June 16, 2019, https://www.thecut.com/2018/12/a-sociological-investigation-of-nowanks.html.

108. McBee, "A Sociological Investigation." Cf. Lux Alptraum, "Why Are the Proud Boys so Obsessed with Not Masturbating?" Medium, October 19, 2018, accessed June 16, 2019, https://medium.com/s/story/why-are-the-proud-boys-so-obsessed-with-masturbation-c9932364ebe2.

109. Gavin McInnes, "Some Clarification on the 4th Degree," *Proud Boy Magazine*, July 14, 2017, accessed June 19, 2019, https://officialproudboys.com/columns/some-clarification-on-the-4th-degree.

110. McInnes, "Some Clarification on the 4th."

111. McInnes, "We Are Not Alt-Right."

112. Jason Wilson, "FBI Now Classifies Far-Right Proud Boys as 'Extremist Group'," Documents Say," *Guardian*, November 19, 2018, accessed February 26, 2019, https://www.theguardian.com/world/2018/nov/19/proud-boys-fbi-classification-extremist-group-white-nationalism-report.

113. James Wilson, "Proud Boys Founder Gavin McInnes Quits 'Extremist' Far-Right Group," *Guardian*, November 22, 2018, accessed February 26, 2019, https://www.theguardian.com/world/2018/nov/22/proud-boys-founder-gavin-mcinnes-quits-far-right-group.

114. Avery Anapol, "YouTube Bans Proud Boys Founder Gavin McInnes," *The Hill*, December 10, 2018, accessed January 30, 2021, https://thehill.com/policy/technology/420562-youtube-bans-proud-boys-founder-gavin-mcginnes.

115. Sheera Frenkel and Annie Karni, "Proud Boys Celebrate Trump's 'Stand by' Remark about Them at the Debate," *New York Times*, September 29, 2020, accessed January 30, 2021, https://www.nytimes.com/2020/09/29/us/trump-proud-boys -biden.html.

116. "Incel Wiki," Incels.wiki, June 4, 2019, accessed June 12, 2019, https://incels .wiki/w/Incel_Wiki.

117. Incels.wiki, "Incel Wiki."

118. Incels.wiki, "Incel Wiki."

119. Brian Gilmartin, *Shyness & Love: Causes, Consequences, and Treatment* (Lanham: University Press of America, 1987).

120. "Incelosphere," Incels.wiki, May 24, 2019, accessed June 12, 2019, https:// incels.wiki/w/Incelosphere.

121. Denise Donnelly, "Involuntary Celibacy: A Life Course Analysis," *Journal of Sex Research* 38, no. 2 (2001): 159–169.

122. Incels.wiki, "Incel Wiki."

123. Zack Beauchamp, "Our Incel Problem," Vox, April 23, 2019, accessed June 17, 2019, https://www.vox.com/the-highlight/2019/4/16/18287446/incel-definition -reddit.

124. I've intentionally avoided naming the men who committed these crimes so as to avoid perpetuating their legacy while remembering their acts and victims, too many to name. For more information, see Nicky Woolf, "'PUAhate' and 'ForeverAlone': Inside Elliot Rodger's Online Life," *Guardian*, May 30, 2014, accessed June 17, 2019, https://www.theguardian.com/world/2014/may/30/elliot-rodger -puahate-forever-alone-reddit-forums; Nina Burleigh, "Hating Women Was His Disease," *Observer*, May 28, 2024, accessed June 17, 2019, https://observer.com /2014/05/hating-the-players-elliot-rodger.

125. Cf. Keegan Hankes and Alex Amend, "The Alt-Right Is Killing People," Southern Poverty Law Center, February 5, 2018, accessed June 17, 2019, https:// www.splcenter.org/20180205/alt-right-killing-people.

126. "Inceldom Spectrum," Incels.wiki, May 13, 2019, accessed June 12, 2019, https://incels.wiki/w/Inceldom_spectrum.

127. "Blackpill," Incels.wiki, May 21, 2019, accessed June 12, 2019, https://incels .wiki/w/Blackpill.

128. Angus John Bateman, "Intra-sexual Selection in *Drosophila*," *Heredity* 2 (1948): 349–368.

129. Bateman, "Intra-sexual Selection."

130. Patricia Adair Gowaty, Yong-Kyu Kim, and Wyatt W. Anderson, "No Evidence of Sexual Selection in a Repetition of Bateman's Classic Study of Drosophila

Melanogaster," *Proceedings of the National Academy of Sciences* 109, no. 29 (2012): 11740–11745.

131. Zuleyma Tang-Martínez, "Rethinking Bateman's Principles: Challenging Persistent Myths of Sexually Reluctant Females and Promiscuous Males," *Journal of Sex Research* 53, no. 4–5 (2016): 532–559.

132. Patricia Adair Gowaty and Stephen P. Hubbell, "Chance, Time Allocation, and the Evolution of Adaptively Flexible Sex Role Behavior," *Integrative and Comparative Biology* 45, no. 5 (2005): 931–944; Rufus A. Johnstone, John D. Reynolds, and James C. Deutsch, "Mutual Mate Choice and Sex Differences in Choosiness," *Evolution* 50, no. 4 (1996): 1382–1391.

133. Christine M. Drea, "Bateman Revisited: The Reproductive Tactics of Female Primates." *Integrative and Comparative Biology* 45, no. 5 (2005): 915–923.

134. Sarah Blaffer Hrdy, *The Woman That Never Evolved,* rev. ed. (Cambridge: Harvard University Press, 1999).

135. Gillian R. Brown, Kevin N. Laland, and Monique Borgerhoff Mulder, "Bateman's Principles and Human Sex Roles," *Trends in Ecology & Evolution* 24, no. 6–14 (2009): 297–304.

136. Stevan J. Arnold, "Bateman's Principles and the Measurement of Sexual Selection in Plants and Animals," *American Naturalist* 144 (1994): S126–S149.

137. "Blackpill," Incels.wiki, May 21, 2019, accessed June 12, 2019, https://incels .wiki/w/Blackpill.

138. NCOSE, "About," National Center on Sexual Exploitation, accessed February 16, 2019, https://endsexualexploitation.org/about.

139. NCOSE, "Pornography & Public Health: Research Summary," National Center on Sexual Exploitation, August 2, 2017, accessed February 14, 2019, 1, https://endsexualexploitation.org/download/pornography-public-health-research -summary.

140. NCOSE, "Pornography & Public Health," 1–2.

141. NCOSE, "Pornography & Public Health," 2–3.

142. NCOSE, "Pornography & Public Health," 7–10.

143. NCOSE, "Pornography & Public Health, 8.

144. Elizabeth Nolan Brown, "Anti-Porn Summit on Capitol Hill Mixes Moralist, Feminist, and Public Health Rhetoric with Insane Results," Reason, July 14, 2015, accessed February 15, 2019, http://reason.com/blog/2015/07/14/congress-holds -anti-porn-summit; Reason Staff, "Sen. Orrin Hatch Demands More Porn Prosecutions," Reason, April 7, 2011, accessed February 15, 2019, http://reason.com/blog /2011/04/07/sen-orrin-hatch-demands-more-p. Cf. Anthony D'Amato, "Porn Up, Rape Down," Northwestern Public Law Research Paper No. 913013, June 23, 2006, https://dx.doi.org/10.2139/ssrn.913013.

145. NCOSE, "Pornography & Public Health," 14

146. NCOSE, "Pornography & Public Health," 21–24.

147. NCOSE, "Pornography & Public Health," 22.

148. For example, Lynne Segal, *Straight Sex: Rethinking the Politics of Pleasure* (Brooklyn: Verso, 2015/1994); Michèle Barrett and Mary McIntosh, *The Anti-Social Family* (Brooklyn: Verso, 2015/1982).

149. NCOSE, "Pornography & Public Health," 4–7.

150. NCOSE, "Pornography & Public Health," 10.

151. NCOSE, "Pornography & Public Health," 4.

152. NCOSE, "Pornography & Public Health." 4.

153. Kimberlé Crenshaw, "Demarginalizing the Intersection of Race and Sex: A Black Feminist Critique of Antidiscrimination Doctrine, Feminist Theory and Antiracist Politics," *University of Chicago Legal Forum* 139 (1989): 139–167; Kimberlé Crenshaw, "The Urgency of Intersectionality," October 2016, TED video, accessed June 21, 2019. https://www.ted.com/talks/kimberle_crenshaw_the_urgency_of _intersectionality.

154. NCOSE, "Defending Dignity: 2016 Review of the National Center on Sexual Exploitation's Efforts to Promote Sexual Justice," National Center on Sexual Exploitation, 2016, 23, accessed February 16, 2019, https://endsexualexploitation .org/wp-content/uploads/NCOSE-2016-Newsletter-Final-1.pdf.

155. NCOSE, "2018 Impact Report," National Center on Sexual Exploitation, 2018, 24, accessed February 16, 2019, https://endsexualexploitation.org/articles /ncose-2018-impact-report.

156. According to their 990 tax forms, during the 2015 election year, Morality in Media took in just under $1.1 million, and in 2016, the company only brought in about $600,000, small amounts for the oversized impact the organization claims to have, "Return of Organization Exempt from Income Tax: Morality in Media, Inc.," Foundation Center, accessed June 18, 2019, http://990s.foundationcenter.org/990 _pdf_archive/132/132608326/132608326_201606_990.pdf.

157. Josh Israel, "This is the Way the War on Pornography Ends," Think Progress, October 8, 2014, accessed February 15, 2019, https://thinkprogress.org/this-is-the -way-the-war-on-pornography-ends-466fc4b53109.

158. NCOSE, "Educating & Engaging the Public," National Center on Sexual Exploitation, accessed February 16, 2019, https://endsexualexploitation.org/ educating.

159. Brown, "Anti-Porn Summit on Capitol Hill."

160. Israel, "This Is the Way the War on Pornography Ends."

161. Republican National Committee, "Republican Platform 2016," GOP, 2016, accessed February 16, 2019, https://www.gop.com/the-2016-republican-party -platform.

162. "Victory! FL House Declares Pornography a Public Health Risk," NCOSE, February 21, 2018, accessed February 16, 2019, https://endsexualexploitation .org/articles/victory-fl-house-declares-pornography-public-health-risk/; "Kansas Resolution Continues Societal Awakening about the Negative Impacts of Pornography," NCOSE, February 7, 2018, accessed February 16, 2019, https:// endsexualexploitation.org/articles/kansas-resolution-harms-of-pornography/; "Louisiana Is the 5th State to Formally Recognize Public Health Harms of Pornography," NCOSE, November 30, 2017, accessed February 16, 2019, https:// endsexualexploitation.org/articles/louisiana-5th-state-formally-recognize-public -health-harms-pornography/; "The Governor of Tennessee Just Officially Declared Pornography a Public Health Crisis," NCOSE, June 21, 2017, accessed February 16, 2019, https://endsexualexploitation.org/articles/the-governor-of-tennessee-just -officially-declared-pornography-a-public-health-crisis/; "Arkansas Just Declared Pornography a Public Health Crisis," NCOSE, March 29, 2017, accessed February 16, 2019, https://endsexualexploitation.org/articles/arkansas-just-declared -pornography-public-health-crisis/; "Virginia Resolution Recognizing Harms of Pornography Moves Forward!" NCOSE, February 2, 2017, accessed February 16, 2019, https://endsexualexploitation.org/articles/virginia-resolution-recognizing -harms-pornography-moves-forward/; "South Dakota Unanimously Declared Pornography a Public Health Crisis," NCOSE, February 2, 2017, accessed February 16, 2019, https://endsexualexploitation.org/articles/south-dakota-unanimously -declared-pornography-public-health-crisis/; "Utah Recognizes Pornography as a Public Health Crisis: Ceremonial Signing with Governor Herbert," NCOSE, April 20, 2016, accessed February 16, 2019, https://endsexualexploitation.org/articles/ south-dakota-unanimously-declared-pornography-public-health-crisis.

163. NCOSE, "2018 Impact Report," 8.

164. NCOSE, "2018 Impact Report," 13.

165. NCOSE, "Defending Dignity," 6.

166. NCOSE, "Three Recent Victories We Almost Missed: Snapchat, Google, U.S. Navy," National Center on Sexual Exploitation, January 17, 2019, accessed February 16, 2019, https://endsexualexploitation.org/articles/three-victories.

CHAPTER 2

1. Jamie Hutchinson, "Culture, Communication, and an Information Age Madonna," *IEEE Professional Communication Society Newsletter* 45, no. 3 (May/June 2001): 1–7, 1.

2. Emily Chang, *Brotopia: Breaking Up the Boy's Club of Silicon Valley* (New York: Portfolio/Penguin, 2018), 1.

3. Hutchinson, "Culture, Communication."

4. Linda Kinstler, "Finding Lena, the Patron Saint of JPEGs," *WIRED*, January 31, 2019, accessed February 13, 2019, https://www.wired.com/story/finding-lena-the -patron-saint-of-jpegs.

5. Sunny Bains, "Nude Image Creates Feelings of Exclusion," *Electronic Engineering Times* 955 (May 26, 1997): 45.

6. Maddie Zug, "A Centerfold Does Not Belong in the Classroom," *Washington Post*, April 24, 2015, accessed June 8, 2019, https://www.washingtonpost.com/opinions /a-playboy-centerfold-does-not-belong-in-tj-classrooms/2015/04/24/76e87fa4 -e47a-11e4-81ea-0649268f729e_story.html.

7. Deanna Needell and Rachel Ward, "Stable Image Reconstruction Using Total Variation Minimization," *SIAM Journal on Imaging Sciences* 6, no. 2 (2013): 1035– 1058.

8. Corinne Iozzio, "The *Playboy* Centerfold That Helped Create the JPEG," *Atlantic*, February 9, 2016, accessed July 7, 2019, https://www.theatlantic.com/technology/ archive/2016/02/lena-image-processing-playboy/461970.

9. Lorna Roth, "Looking at Shirley, the Ultimate Norm: Colour Balance, Image Technologies, and Cognitive Equity," *Canadian Journal of Communication* 34, no. 1 (2009): 111–136; Jonathan Sterne, *MP3: The Meaning of a Format* (Durham, NC: Duke University Press, 2017); Suzanne Vega, "Tom's Essay," *New York Times*, September 23, 2008, accessed June 8, 2019, https://opinionator.blogs.nytimes.com /2008/09/23/toms-essay.

10. Sarah Sharma, "Going to Work in Mommy's Basement," *Boston Review*, June 19, 2018, accessed June 15, 2019, http://bostonreview.net/gender-sexuality/sarah -sharma-going-work-mommys-basement.

11. Emily Chang, *Brotopia*.

12. Banet-Weiser, *Empowered*, 131.

13. Nathan Ensmenger, "Beards, Sandals, and Other Signs of Rugged Individualism: Masculine Culture within the Computing Professions," *Osiris* 30, no. 1 (2015): 38–65.

14. Kristina Bell, Christopher Kampe, and Nicholas Taylor, "Of Headshots and Hugs: Challenging Hypermasculinity through 'The Walking Dead' Play," *Ada: A Journal of Gender, New Media, and Technology* 7, accessed January 30, 2021, https:// adanewmedia.org/2015/04/issue7-bellkampetaylor.

15. Adrienne Masanari, "# Gamergate and the Fappening: How Reddit's Algorithm, Governance, and Culture Support Toxic Technocultures," *New Media & Society* 19, no. 3 (2017): 329–346.

16. Banet-Weiser, *Empowered*, 156.

17. Sue Decker, "A Fish Is the Last to Discover Water: Impressions from the Ellen Pao Trial," Recode, March 26, 2015, accessed July 5, 2019, https://www.vox.com/2015/3/26/11560742/a-fish-is-the-last-to-discover-water-impressions-from-the-ellen-pao.

18. Trae Vassallo, Ellen Levy, Michele Madansky, Hillary Mickell, Bennett Porter, Monica Leas, and Julie Oberweis, "Elephant in the Valley," Elephant in the Valley, 2017, accessed July 5, 2019, https://www.elephantinthevalley.com.

19. Chang, *Brotopia*, 216.

20. Chang, *Brotopia*, 207.

21. Chang, *Brotopia*, 198.

22. Chang, *Brotopia*, 184.

23. Chang, *Brotopia*, 192.

24. Chang, *Brotopia*, 186.

25. Janet Abbate, *Recoding Gender: Women's Changing Participation in Computing* (Cambridge, MA: MIT Press, 2012); Mar Hicks, *Programmed Inequality: How Britain Discarded Women Technologists and Lost Its Edge in Computing* (Cambridge, MA: MIT Press, 2018); Walter Isaacson, *The Innovators: How a Group of Hackers, Geniuses, and Geeks Created the Digital Revolution* (New York: Simon & Schuster, 2014).

26. Chang, *Brotopia*, 6–7.

27. Sarah Myers West, Meredith Whittaker, and Kate Crawford, "Discriminating Systems: Gender, Race, and Power in AI," AI Now, April 2019, accessed February 26, 2020, https://ainowinstitute.org/discriminatingsystems.pdf.

28. Adam Bryant, "In Head-Hunting, Big Data May Not Be Such a Big Deal," *New York Times*, June 19, 2013, accessed July 9, 2019, https://www.nytimes.com/2013/06/20/business/in-head-hunting-big-data-may-not-be-such-a-big-deal.html.

29. Chang, *Brotopia*, 80–83.

30. Chang, *Brotopia*, 76–79.

31. Sarah-Jane Leslie, Andrei Cimpian, Meredith Meyer, and Edward Freeland, "Expectations of Brilliance Underlie Gender Distributions across Academic Disciplines," *Science* 347, no. 6219 (2015): 262–265.

32. Emilio J. Castilla and Stephen Benard, "The Paradox of Meritocracy in Organizations," *Administrative Science Quarterly* 55, no. 4 (2010): 543–676.

33. Michael Young, *The Rise of the Meritocracy* (New York: Routledge, 2017/1958).

34. Michelle M. Duguid and Melissa C. Thomas-Hunt, "Condoning Stereotyping? How Awareness of Stereotyping Prevalence Impacts Expression of Stereotypes," *Journal of Applied Psychology* 100, no. 2 (2015): 343–359.

35. Liza Mundy, "Why Is Silicon Valley So Awful to Women?" *Atlantic*, April 2017, accessed July 5, 2019, https://www.theatlantic.com/magazine/archive/2017/04/why-is-silicon-valley-so-awful-to-women/517788.

36. James Damore, "Google's Ideological Echo Chamber: How Bias Clouds Our Thinking about Diversity and Inclusion," Internet Archive Wayback Machine, July 2017, accessed February 16, 2019, https://web.archive.org/web/20170809220001/https://diversitymemo-static.s3-us-west-2.amazonaws.com/Googles-Ideological-Echo-Chamber.pdf.

37. Damore, "Google's Ideological Echo Chamber."

38. Damore, "Google's Ideological Echo Chamber."

39. Damore, "Google's Ideological Echo Chamber."

40. Damore, "Google's Ideological Echo Chamber."

41. Damore, "Google's Ideological Echo Chamber."

42. Sarah Emerson, Louise Matsakis, and Jason Koebler, "Internal Reactions to Google Employee's Manifesto Show Anti-Diversity Views Have Support," Motherboard, August 5, 2017, accessed February 16, 2019. https://motherboard.vice.com/en_us/article/ywpamw/internal-reaction-to-google-employees-manifesto-show-anti-diversity-views-have-support; Ashley Feinberg, "Internal Messages Show Some Googlers Supported Fired Engineer's Manifesto," *WIRED*, August 8, 2017, accessed February 16, 2019, https://www.wired.com/story/internal-messages-james-damore-google-memo.

43. Louise Matsakis, "Google Employee's Anti-Diversity Manifesto Goes 'Internally Viral,'" Motherboard, August 5, 2017, accessed February 16, 2019, https://motherboard.vice.com/en_us/article/kzbm4a/employees-anti-diversity-manifesto-goes-internally-viral-at-google.

44. Ethan Varian and Samantha Masunaga, "Here's What Google Workers Are Saying about an Employee's Controversial Diversity Memo," *Los Angeles Times*, August 7, 2017, accessed February 16, 2019, https://www.latimes.com/business/technology/la-fi-tn-google-diversity-reaction-20170807-story.html.

45. Feinberg, "Internal Messages Show."

46. Emerson, Matsakis, and Koebler, "Internal Reactions to Google Employee's Manifesto."

47. Matsakis, "Google Employee's Anti-Diversity Manifesto."

48. Daisuke Wakabayashi, "Contentious Memo Strikes Nerve Inside Google and Out," *New York Times*, August 8, 2017, accessed February 26, 2019, https://www.nytimes.com/2017/08/08/technology/google-engineer-fired-gender-memo.html.

49. Office of Federal Contract Compliance Programs, *United States Department of Labor v. Google, Inc.* OFCCP No. R00197955 (2017), accessed June 10, 2019,

https://www.dol.gov/sites/dolgov/files/legacy-files/newsroom/newsreleases/
OFCCP20162406_0.pdf.

50. Sam Levin, "Google Accused of 'Extreme' Gender Pay Discrimination by US
Labor Department," *Guardian*, April 7, 2017, accessed February 16, 2019, https://
www.theguardian.com/technology/2017/apr/07/google-pay-disparities-women
-labor-department-lawsuit.

51. Levin, "Google Accused of 'Extreme.'"

52. "Presidential Executive Order on the Revocation of Federal Contracting Executive Orders," White House, March 27, 2017, accessed June 10, 2019, https://www
.whitehouse.gov/presidential-actions/presidential-executive-order-revocation
-federal-contracting-executive-orders.

53. Carrie Mihalcik, "Department of Labor Drops Appeal Fight for Google Salary
Data," CNET, February 4, 2019, accessed June 10, 2019, https://www.cnet.com/
news/department-of-labor-drops-appeal-in-fight-for-google-pay-data.

54. Jonathan Easley, "Poll: Google Was Wrong to Fire Engineer Over Diversity
Memo," *The Hill*. August 28, 2017, accessed June 6, 2019, https://thehill.com
/policy/technology/348246-poll-google-was-wrong-to-fire-engineer-over
-diversity-memo.

55. James Damore, "Why I Was Fired by Google," *Wall Street Journal*, August 11,
2017, accessed February 16, 2019, https://www.wsj.com/articles/why-i-was-fired
-by-google-1502481290.

56. Sundar Pichai, "Note to Employees from CEO Sundar Pichai," *Google: The Keyword*, August 8, 2017, accessed June 6, 2019, https://www.blog.google/outreach
-initiatives/diversity/note-employees-ceo-sundar-pichai.

57. Amrita Khalid, "Google: Employees Can Protest YouTube, Just Not Near Its
Pride Float," Engadget, June 25, 2019, accessed June 26, 2019, https://www.engadget
.com/2019/06/25/google-employees-can-protest-youtube-just-not-near-its-pride-f.

58. Christine Fisher, "Google Employees Petition to Ban the Company from SF
Pride," Engadget, June 26, 2019, accessed June 26, 2019, https://www.engadget
.com/2019/06/26/google-employees-protest-san-francisco-pride-parade.

59. James Damore, "I'm James Damore, AMA," Reddit, 2017, accessed June 6,
2019, https://www.reddit.com/r/JamesDamore/comments/6thcy3/im_james
_damore_ama; Feinberg, "Internal Messages Show."

60. See Abby Olheiser, "How James Damore Went from Google Employee to
Right-Wing Internet Hero," *Washington Post*, August 12, 2017, accessed February
16, 2019, https://www.washingtonpost.com/news/the-intersect/wp/2017/08/12
/how-james-damore-went-from-google-employee-to-right-wing-internet-hero.

61. Matthew Kassel, "The Annie Leibovitz of the Alt-Right," *New York Times*,
July 20, 2017, accessed June 10, 2019, https://www.nytimes.com/2017/07/20/
magazine/the-annie-leibovitz-of-the-alt-right.html.

62. Shona Ghosh, "Fired Google Engineer James Damore Spent Hours Answering Questions on Reddit," Business Insider, August 14, 2017 accessed February 16, 2019, https://www.businessinsider.com/fired-google-engineer-james-damore -defended-himself-on-reddit-2017-8.

63. Feinberg, "Internal Messages Show."

64. Jordan B. Peterson, "James Damore and His Google Memo on Diversity," August 8, 2017, accessed February 18, 2019, https://youtu.be/SEDuVF7kiPU.

65. For example, Adam Grant, "The Differences between Men and Women Are Vastly Exaggerated," Time, August 8, 2017, accessed February 15, 2019, http://time .com/4892151/adam-grant-google-memo-gender-differences.

66. Janet Shibley Hyde, "The Gender Similarities Hypothesis," American Psychologist 60, no. 6 (2005): 581–592; Samantha C. Paustian-Underdahl, Lisa Slattery Walker, and David J. Woehr, "Gender and Perceptions of Leadership Effectiveness: A Meta-Analysis of Contextual Moderators," Journal of Applied Psychology 99, no. 6 (2014): 1129–1145.

67. Nicole M. Else-Quest, Janet Shibley Hyde, and Marcia C. Linn, "Cross-National Patterns of Gender Differences in Mathematics: A Meta-Analysis," Psychological Bulletin 136, no. 1 (2010): 103–127; Zahra Hazari, Geoff Potvin, Robynne M. Lock, Florin Lung, Gerhard Sonnert, and Philip M. Sadler, "Factors That Affect the Physical Science Career Interest of Female Students: Testing Five Common Hypotheses," Physical Review Special Topics, Physics Education Research 9, no. 2 (2013): 1–8; Janet S. Hyde, Elizabeth Fennema, and Susan J. Lamon, "Gender Differences in Mathematics Performance: A Meta-Analysis," Psychological Bulletin 107, no. 2 (1990): 139–155; William Ickes, Paul R. Gesn, and Tiffany Graham, "Gender Differences in Empathic Accuracy: Differential Ability or Differential Motivation?," Personal Relations 7, no. 1 (2000): 95–109; Michael Johns, Toni Schmader, and Andy Martens, "Knowing Is Half the Battle: Teaching Stereotype Threat as a Means of Improving Women's Math Performance," Psychological Science 16, no. 3 (2005): 175–179; Victor Lavy and Edith Sand, "On the Origins of Gender Gaps in Human Capital: Short- and Long-Term Consequences of Teachers' Biases," Journal of Public Economics 167 (2018): 263–279; Sarah M. Lindberg, Janet Shibley Hyde, Jennifer L. Petersen, and Marcia C. Linn, "New Trends in Gender and Mathematics Performance: A Meta-Analysis," Psychological Bulletin 136, no. 6 (2010): 1123–1135; Brian A. Nosek, Frederick L. Smyth, Natarajan Sriram, and Nicole M. Linder, "National Differences in Gender–Science Stereotypes Predict National Sex Differences in Science and Math Achievement," Proceedings of the National Academy of Sciences 106, no. 26 (June 2009): 10593–10597.

68. Rong Su, James Rounds, and Patrick Ian Armstrong, "Men and Things, Women and People: A Meta-Analysis of Sex Differences in Interests," Psychological Bulletin 135, no. 6 (2009): 859–884.

69. Bernard E. Whitley Jr., "Gender Differences in Computer-Related Attitudes and Behavior: A Meta-Analysis," Computers in Human Behavior 13, no. 1 (1997): 1–22.

70. "Men and Women: No Big Difference," American Psychological Association, October 20, 2005, accessed February 16, 2019, https://www.apa.org/research/action/difference.

71. Diane F. Halpern, *Sex Differences in Cognitive Abilities*, 3rd ed. (Mahwah, NJ: Lawrence Erlbaum, 2000); Diane F. Halpern, "A Cognitive-Process Taxonomy for Sex Differences in Cognitive Abilities," *Current Directions in Psychological Science* 13, no. 4 (2004): 135–139.

72. See Paul Edwards, *The Closed World: Computers and the Politics of Discourse in Cold War America* (Cambridge, MA: MIT Press, 1997).

73. Steven Levy, *Hackers: Heroes of the Computer Revolution* (Sebastopol, CA: O'Reilly, 2010/1984).

74. Dennis Hayes, *Behind the Silicon Curtain: The Seductions of Work in a Lonely Area* (Boston: South End Press, 1999), 82.

75. Noam Cohen, *The Know-It-Alls: The Rise of Silicon Valley as a Political Powerhouse and Social Wrecking Ball* (New York: The New Press, 2017), 156.

76. Levy, *Hackers*, 75.

77. Levy, *Hackers*, 75.

78. Cohen, *The Know-It-Alls*, 29.

79. Levy, *Hackers*, 58.

80. Hayes, *Behind the Silicon Curtain*.

81. Richard Barbrook and Andy Cameron, "The Californian Ideology," *Science as Culture* 26 (1996): 44–72.

82. Christian Fuchs, *Digital Labour and Karl Marx* (New York: Routledge, 2014); Nick Dyer-Witheford, *Cyber-Proletariat: Global Labour in the Digital Vortex* (London: Pluto Press, 2015).

83. Steven Levy, *In the Plex: How Google Thinks, Works, and Shapes Our Lives* (New York: Simon & Schuster, 2011), 54.

84. Finn Brunton, *Spam: A Shadow History of the Internet* (Cambridge, MA: MIT Press, 2013).

85. Matt Cutts, "How Does SafeSearch Work?," August 19, 2011, accessed June 27, 2018, https://www.youtube.com/watch?v=H2EIN24r-3M.

86. Levy, *In the Plex*, 54.

87. Eric Schmidt and Jonathan Rosenberg, *How Google Works* (New York: Grand Central Publishing, 2017), 76–77.

88. "Google Cloud and Autodesk Enable 10x Improvement in Media Rendering Efficiency," *Google Cloud Platform Blog*, April 18, 2016, accessed June 27, 2018, https://cloudplatform.googleblog.com/2016/04/Google-Cloud-and-Autodesk-enable-10x-improvement-in-media-rendering-efficiency.html.

89. "Cloud Vision API," Google, accessed June 27, 2018, https://cloud.google.com /vision (emphasis mine).

90. Google, "Cloud Vision API."

91. "Method: Images.annotate," Google Cloud Vision API: APIs & Reference, January 22, 2018, accessed June 27, 2018, https://cloud.google.com/vision/docs/ reference/rest/v1/images/annotate#safesearchannotation.

92. "Filtering Inappropriate Content with the Cloud Vision API," *Google Cloud Big Data and Machine Learning Blog*, August 17, 2016, accessed June 27, 2018, https:// cloud.google.com/blog/big-data/2016/08/filtering-inappropriate-content-with -the-loud-vision-api.

93. "Safe Search Detection Beta Features," Google Cloud Vision API: Documentation, January 18, 2018, accessed June 27, 2018, https://cloud.google.com/vision /docs/beta-explicit-content.

94. It is interesting to note that these results change over very short time scales, even if analyzing the *exact same* image. An analysis of the same Venus de Milo image days later came back as only possibly "racy" (and one notch more likely to be violent but still unlikely overall). The moral of this story is that if you are doing research on the Cloud Vision API, save all your JSON data for each and every run through!

95. Tarleton Gillespie, *Custodians of the Internet: Platforms, Content Moderation, and the Hidden Decisions That Shape Social Media* (New Haven, CT: Yale University Press, 2018).

96. Courtney Demone, "Do I Have Boobs Yet?" Mashable, September 30, 2015, accessed February 5, 2020, https://mashable.com/2015/09/30/do-i-have-boobs -now.

97. Jia Deng, Wei Dong, Richard Socher, Li-Jia Li, Kai Li, and Li Fei-Fei, "Image-Net: A Large-Scale Hierarchical Image Database," *IEEE Conference on Computer Vision and Pattern Recognition*, June 2009, 248–255.

98. "ImageNet Summary and Statistics," ImageNet, 2016, accessed June 27, 2018, http://image-net.org/about-overview.

99. The ILSVRC was modeled off the PASCAL VOC challenge that was begun in 2005. However, the PASCAL VOC challenge made use of only about twenty thousand images and twenty object classes, whereas the ILSVRC uses 1,000 object classes and many more images. Olga Russakovsky, Jia Deng, Hao Su, Jonathan Krause, Sanjeev Satheesh, Sean Ma, Zhiheng Huang, Andrej Karpathy, Aditya Khosla, Michael Bernstein, Alexander C. Berg, and Li Fei-Fei, "ImageNet Large Scale Visual Recognition Challenge," *International Journal of Computer Vision* 115, no. 3 (2015): 211–252.

100. Christian Szegedy, Wei Liu, Yangqing Jia, Pierre Sermanet, Scott Reed, Dragomir Anguelov, Dumitru Erhan, Vincent Vanhoucke, and Andrew Rabinovich, "Going Deeper with Convolutions," *Proceedings of the IEEE Conference on Computer Vision and Pattern Recognition*, 2015, 1–9.

101. "WordNet: A Lexical Database for English," WordNet, 2018, accessed June 27, 2018, https://wordnet.princeton.edu.

102. WordNet, "WordNet: A Lexical Database."

103. As we'll see in a moment, ImageNet almost exclusively makes use of the noun synsets from WordNet, and thus we will be ignoring the verb synsets for "sex" here.

104. "Sex," WordNet, accessed March 14, 2018, http://wordnetweb.princeton .edu/perl/webwn?o2=&o0=1&o8=1&o1=1&o7=&o5=&o9=&o6=&o3=&o4=&s= sex&i=134&h=11000013000013130020222200013001300002220022130130222213130220213130000002013013022022213130002222130220130130200010011231231231231230200000#c.

105. WordNet, "Sex."

106. WordNet, "Sex."

107. Aylin Caliskan, Joanna J. Bryson, and Arvind Narayanan, "Semantics Derived Automatically from Language Corpora Necessarily Contain Human Biases," *Science* 356, no. 6334 (2017): 183–186, 183.

108. WordNet, "Sex."

109. WordNet, "Sex."

110. Anthony M. Kennedy and Supreme Court of the United States, *U.S. Reports: Lawrence et al. v. Texas, 539 U.S. 558.* (2002) (Antonin Scalia, dissenting), https:// www.loc.gov/item/usrep539558.

111. WordNet, "Sex."

112. WordNet, "Sex."

113. Thomas Gossett, *Race: The History of an Idea in America* , new ed. (New York: Oxford University Press, 1997).

114. "About ImageNet," ImageNet, 2016, accessed June 27, 2018, http://image -net.org/about-overview.

115. Ido Ramati and Amit Pinchevski, "Uniform Multilingualism: A Media Gene-alogy of Google Translate," *New Media & Society* 20, no. 7 (2017): 2550–2565.

116. ImageNet, "About ImageNet."

117. See Alexander Monea, "Graph Force: Rhetorical Machines and the *n*-arization of Knowledge," *Computational Culture* 5 (2016); Alexander Monea, "The Graphing of Difference: Numerical Mediation and the Case of Google's Knowledge Graph," *Cultural Studies ✕ Critical Methodologies* 16, no. 5 (2016): 452–461.

118. On Amazon's Mechanical Turk specifically, see Ali Alkhatib, Michael S. Bern-stein, and Margaret Levi, "Examining Crowd Work and Gig Work through the His-torical Lens of Piecework," in *Proceedings of the 2017 CHI Conference on Human Factors in Computing Systems*, 4599–4616. 2017; Birgitta Bergvall-Kåreborn and Debra Howcroft, "Amazon Mechanical Turk and the Commodification of Labour," *New*

Technology, Work and Employment 29, no. 3 (2014): 213–223; Alice M. Brawley and Cynthia LS Pury, "Work Experiences on MTurk: Job Satisfaction, Turnover, and Information Sharing," *Computers in Human Behavior* 54 (2016): 531–546; Karën Fort, Gilles Adda, and K. Bretonnel Cohen, "Amazon Mechanical Turk: Gold Mine or Coal Mine?," *Computational Linguistics* 37, no. 2 (2011): 413–420; Lilly Irani and M. Six Silberman, "From Critical Design to Critical Infrastructure: Lessons from Turkopticon," *Interactions* 21, no. 4 (2014): 32–35; Lilly Irani, "The Cultural Work of Microwork," *New Media & Society* 17, no. 5 (2015): 720–739; Niloufar Salehi, Lilly C. Irani, Michael S. Bernstein, Ali Alkhatib, Eva Ogbe, and Kristy Milland, "We Are Dynamo: Overcoming Stalling and Friction in Collective Action for Crowd Workers," in *Proceedings of the 33rd Annual ACM Conference on Human Factors in Computing Systems*, 1621–1630. 2015; Siddarth Suri and Mary L. Gray, *Ghost Work: How to Stop Silicon Valley from Building a New Global Underclass* (New York: Houghton Mifflin Harcourt, 2019). On gamification to extract unpaid labor, see Benedikt Morschheuser, Juho Hamari, and Jonna Koivisto, "Gamification in Crowdsourcing: A Review," in *2016 49th Hawaii International Conference on System Sciences (HICSS)*, 4375–4384. IEEE, 2016; Marigo Raftopoulos and Steffen P. Walz, "It's Complicated: The Ethics of Gamified Labour," *CHI 2015* 2015. On the extraction of unpaid labor more broadly, see Nick Dyer-Witheford, *Cyber-Proletariat: Global Labour in the Digital Vortex* (Toronto, ON: Pluto Press, 2015); Henry Jenkins, Sam Ford, and Joshua Green, *Spreadable Media: Creating Value and Meaning in a Networked Culture* (New York: NYU Press, 2018); Trebor Scholz (ed.), *Digital Labor: The Internet as Playground and Factor* (New York: Routledge, 2012); Nick Srnicek, *Platform Capitalism* (New York: John Wiley & Sons, 2017); Rosalind Gill and Andy Pratt, "In the Social Factory? Immaterial Labour, Precariousness and Cultural Work," *Theory, Culture & Society* 25, no. 7–8 (2008): 1–30; Tiziana Terranova, "Free Labor: Producing Culture for the Digital Economy," *Social Text* 18, no. 2 (2000): 33–58.

119. The primary obstacles to progress in machine vision are GPU processing power, the training time we are willing to tolerate, and the size of our visual databases. GPU processing has grown fast enough lately to mitigate the first two problems. The primary obstacle to advancement is aggregating massive amounts of representative and accurately labeled images. See Alex Krizhevsky, Ilya Sutskever, and Geoffrey E. Hinton, "ImageNet Classification with Deep Convolutional Neural Networks," *Advances in Neural Information Processing Systems* 25 (2012): 1097–1105.

120. Krizhevsky, Sutskever, and Hinton, "ImageNet Classification," 1097.

121. Christopher Olah, "ConvNets: A Modular Perspective," *Colah's Blog*, July 8, 2014, accessed June 27, 2018, https://colah.github.io/posts/2014-07-Conv-Nets -Modular.

122. Antonio Torralba and Alexei A. Efros, "An Unbiased Look at Dataset Bias," in *Proceedings of the IEEE Conference on Computer Vision and Pattern Recognition (CVPR)*, Colorado Springs, CO, June 20–25 (Piscataway, NJ: IEEE, 2011), 1521–1528.

123. wzamen01, "HP Computers Are Racist," December 10, 2009, accessed June 27, 2018, https://youtu.be/t4DT3tQqgRM.

124. Joy Buolamwini and Timnit Gebru, "Gender Shades: Intersectional Accuracy Disparities in Commercial Gender Classification," *Proceedings of the 1st Conference on Fairness, Accountability and Transparency*, PMLR 81 (2018), 77–91.

125. Margaret M. Fleck, David A. Forsyth, and Chris Bregler, "Finding Naked People," in *European Conference on Computer Vision*, eds. Bernard F. Buxton and Roberto Cipolla (Berlin: Springer-Verlag, 1996), 593–602.

126. Rehanullah Khan, Allan Hanbury, Julian Stöttinger, and Abdul Bais, "Color Based Skin Classification," *Pattern Recognition Letters* 33, no. 2 (2012): 157–163; Mauricio Perez, Sandra Avila, Daniel Moreira, Daniel Moraes, Vanessa Testoni, Eduardo Valle, Siome Goldenstein, and Anderson Rocha, "Video Pornography Detection through Deep Learning Techniques and Motion Information," *Neurocomputing* 230 (2017): 279–293; C. Prema and D. Manimegalai, "Survey on Skin Tone Detection Using Color Spaces," *International Journal of Applied Information Systems* 2, no. 2 (2012): 18–26; Christian X. Ries and Rainer Lienhart, "A Survey on Visual Adult Image Recognition," *Multimedia Tools and Applications* 69, no. 3 (2014): 661–688; Alaa Y. Taqa and Hamid A. Jalab, "Increasing the Reliability of Skin Detectors," *Scientific Research and Essays* 5, no. 17 (2010): 2480–2490.

127. Mirza Rehenuma Tabassum, Alim Ul Gias, Md Kamal, Hossain Muhammad Muctadir, Muhammad Ibrahim, Asif Khan Shakir, Asif Imran et al., "Comparative Study of Statistical Skin Detection Algorithms for Sub-continental Human Images," arXiv preprint arXiv:1008.4206 (2010).

128. Sam Corbett-Davies, Emma Pierson, Avi Feller, Sharad Goel, and Aziz Huq, "Algorithmic Decision Making and the Cost of Fairness," *Proceedings of the 23rd ACM SIGKDD International Conference on Knowledge Discovery and Data Mining*, 2017, 797–806.

129. Alexander Monea, "Race and Computer Vision," in *The Democratization of Artificial Intelligence: Net Politics in the Era of Learning Algorithms*, ed. Andreas Sudmann (Bielefeld, Germany: Transcript, 2019), 189–208.

130. Shankar, Shreya, Yoni Halpern, Eric Breck, James Atwood, Jimbo Wilson, and D. Sculley, "No Classification without Representation: Assessing Geodiversity Issues in Open Data Sets for the Developing World," arXiv preprint arXiv:1711.08536 (2017).

131. Terrance de Vries, Ishan Misra, Changhan Wang, and Laurens van der Maaten, "Does Object Recognition Work for Everyone?" *Proceedings of the IEEE Conference on Computer Vision and Pattern Recognition Workshops*, 2019, 52–59.

132. Tom Simonite, "Google Turns to Users to Improve Its AI Chops Outside the U.S.," *WIRED*, April 5, 2018, accessed June 26, 2019, https://www.wired.com/story/google-turns-to-users-to-improve-its-ai-chops-outside-the-us.

133. Tulsee Doshi, "Introducing the Inclusive Images Competition," *Google AI Blog*, September 6, 2018, https://ai.googleblog.com/2018/09/introducing-inclusive -images-competition.html.

134. Samantha Cole, Emanuel Maiberg, and Anna Koslerova, "'Frankenstein's Monster': Images of Sexual Abuse Are Fueling Algorithmic Porn," Mother- board, November 10, 2020, accessed January 30, 2021, https://www.vice.com /en/article/akdgnp/sexual-abuse-fueling-ai-porn-deepfake-czech-casting-girls -do-porn.

135. "Closet Queen," ImageNet, accessed June 15, 2018, http://wordnetweb .princeton.edu/perl/webwn?o2=&o0=1&o8=1&o1=1&o7=&o5=&o9=&o6=&o3= &o4=&r=1&s=closet+queen&i=1&h=110#c.

136. Alexander Cho, "Default Publicness: Queer Youth of Color, Social Media, and Being Outed by the Machine," *New Media & Society* 20, no. 9 (2018): 3183–3200.

137. "Advances in AI Are Used to Spot Signs of Sexuality: Machines That Read Faces Are Coming," *Economist*, September 9, 2017, accessed October 15, 2019, https://www.economist.com/science-and-technology/2017/09/09/advances-in -ai-are-used-to-spot-signs-of-sexuality.

138. Yilun Wang and Michael Kosinski, "Deep Neural Networks Are More Accu- rate than Humans at Detecting Sexual Orientation from Facial Images," *Journal of Personality and Social Psychology* 114, no. 2 (February 2018): 246–257.

139. Blaise Agüera y Arcas, Margaret Mitchell, and Alexander Todorov, "Physiog- nomy's New Clothes," Medium, May 6, 2017, accessed October 15, 2018, https:// medium.com/@blaisea/physiognomys-new-clothes-f2d4b59fdd6a; Greggor Mattson, "Artificial Intelligence Discovers Gayface. Sigh." *Scatterplot: The Unruly Darlings of Public Sociology*, September 10, 2017, accessed October 15, 2018, https:// scatter.wordpress.com/2017/09/10/guest-post-artificial-intelligence-discovers -gayface-sigh.

140. Edwin Black, *IBM and the Holocaust: The Strategic Alliance between Nazi Germany and America's Most Powerful Corporation* (New York: Crown, 2012); Matt Kennard, "Business Is Booming for the U.K.'s Spy Tech Industry," Intercept, May 11, 2018, accessed June 27, 2018, https://theintercept.com/2018/05/11/gbhq-surveillance -spying-technology.

141. See Dean Spade, *Normal Life: Administrative Violence, Critical Trans Politics, and the Limits of Law* (Durham, NC: Duke University Press, 2015).

142. John Cheney-Lippold, *We Are Data: Algorithms and the Making of Our Digital Selves* (New York: NYU Press, 2017), 220–221.

143. See, for instance, Gillespie, *Custodians of the Internet*; Sarah T. Roberts, *Behind the Screen: Content Moderation in the Shadows of Social Media* (New Haven, CT: Yale University Press, 2019).

144. "Facebook Publishes Enforcement Numbers for the First Time," Facebook Newsroom, May 15, 2018, accessed June 30, 2019, https://newsroom.fb.com/news/2018/05/enforcement-numbers.

145. "An Update on How We Are Doing at Enforcing Our Community Standards," Facebook Newsroom, May 23, 2019, accessed June 30, 2019, https://newsroom.fb.com/news/2019/05/enforcing-our-community-standards-3.

146. "Community Standards Enforcement Report," Facebook Transparency, May 2019, accessed June 30, 2019, https://transparency.facebook.com/community-standards-enforcement.

147. "Facebook's Community Standards: How and Where We Draw the Line," Facebook Newsroom, May 23, 2017, accessed June 30, 2019, https://newsroom.fb.com/news/2017/05/facebooks-community-standards-how-and-where-we-draw-the-line.

148. Adrian Chen, "Inside Facebook's Outsourced Anti-Porn and Gore Brigade, Where 'Camel Toes' Are More Offensive than 'Crushed Heads,'" *Gawker*, February 16, 2012, accessed February 14, 2019, https://gawker.com/5885714/inside-facebooks-outsourced-anti-porn-and-gore-brigade-where-camel-toes-are-more-offensive-than-crushed-heads.

149. Nick Hopkins, "Facebook Moderators: A Quick Guide to Their Job and Its Challenges," *Guardian*, May 21, 2017, accessed February 13, 2019, https://www.theguardian.com/news/2017/may/21/facebook-moderators-quick-guide-job-challenges.

150. Max Fisher, "Inside Facebook's Secret Rulebook for Global Political Speech," *New York Times*, December 27, 2018, accessed February 11, 2019, https://www.nytimes.com/2018/12/27/world/facebook-moderators.html.

151. Hopkins, "Facebook Moderators."

152. Fisher, "Inside Facebook's Secret Rulebook."

153. Jason Koebler and Joseph Cox, "The Impossible Job: Inside Facebook's Struggle to Moderate Two Billion People," Motherboard, August 23, 2018, accessed February 11, 2019, https://motherboard.vice.com/en_us/article/xwk9zd/how-facebook-content-moderation-works.

154. Fisher, "Inside Facebook's Secret Rulebook."

155. Tarleton Gillespie, "Facebook Can't Moderate in Secret Anymore," Culture Digitally, May 23, 2017, accessed February 13, 2019, http://culturedigitally.org/2017/05/facebook-cant-moderate-in-secret-any-more.

156. Hopkins, "Facebook Moderators."

157. Koebler and Cox, "The Impossible Job."

158. Fisher, "Inside Facebook's Secret Rulebook."

159. Adrian Chen, "Facebook Apologizes for Censoring Gay Kiss Picture," *Gawker*, April 19, 2011, accessed February 14, 2019, https://gawker.com/5793536 /facebook-apologizes-for-censoring-gay-kiss-picture.

160. Ben Sullivan, "You Need to Care about Facebook Censoring an Iconic Vietnam War Photo," Motherboard, September 9, 2016, accessed July 3, 2019, https://www .vice.com/en_us/article/pgkmdn/you-need-to-care-about-facebook-censoring-an -iconic-vietnam-war-photo.

161. Joseph Cox, "Leaked Documents Show Facebook's 'Threshold' for Deleting Pages and Groups," Motherboard, July 18, 2018, accessed February 13, 2019, https://motherboard.vice.com/en_us/article/ne5nxz/leaked-documents-facebook -threshold-delete-pages-groups.

162. "Community Standards," Facebook, accessed June 30, 2019, https://www .facebook.com/communitystandards.

163. Facebook, "Community Standards."

164. Facebook, "Community Standards."

165. Facebook, "Community Standards."

166. Shira Ovide, "Private Messages Aren't Exactly Private at Facebook," Bloomberg, April 5, 2018, accessed July 1, 2019, https://www.bloomberg.com/ opinion/articles/2018-04-05/facebook-private-messages-aren-t-exactly-private.

167. Violet Blue, "The Internet War on Sex Is Here," Engadget, December 7, 2018, accessed February 14, 2019, https://www.engadget.com/2018/12/07/the-internet -war-on-sex-is-here.

168. Elizabeth Nolan Brown, "Facebook Supported 'Sex Trafficking' Law FOSTA to Cozy Up to Republican Critics: Reason Roundup," Reason, November 15, 2018, accessed July 1, 2019, https://reason.com/2018/11/15/how-facebook-sold-out-sex -workers.

169. Facebook, "Community Standards."

170. Facebook, "Community Standards."

171. Gillespie, *Custodians of the Internet*, 148.

172. "Product Policy Forum: April 9, 2019," Facebook Newsroom, April 9, 2019, accessed June 30, 2019, https://fbnewsroomus.files.wordpress.com/2018/11/ppf -final-deck_04.09.2019.pdf.

173. Jessica Blankenship, "The Social and Legal Arguments for Allowing Women to Go Topless in Public," *Atlantic*, September 18, 2013, accessed July 2, 2019, https:// www.theatlantic.com/national/archive/2013/09/the-social-and-legal-arguments -for-allowing-women-to-go-topless-in-public/279755.

174. Facebook Newsroom, "Product Policy Forum."

175. Sarah Begley, "Here's Where It's Legal for Women to Go Topless in the U.S.," *Time*, April 24, 2015, accessed July 2, 2019, https://time.com/3834365/map-topless-laws.

176. Demone, "Do I Have Boobs Now?"

177. "Content Standards Forum: January 15, 2019," Facebook Newsroom, January 15, 2019, accessed June 30, 2019, https://fbnewsroomus.files.wordpress.com/2018/11/csf-final-deck_01.15.19.pdf.

CHAPTER 3

1. Philip Elmer-Dewitt, "On a Screen Near You: Cyberporn," *Time*, August 3, 1995, 146, no. 1, accessed October 15, 2019, http://fortune.com/2015/07/01/cyberporn-time-marty-rimm.

2. Philip Elmer-Dewitt, "Finding Marty Rimm," *Fortune*, July 1, 2015, accessed October 15, 2018, http://fortune.com/2015/07/01/cyberporn-time-marty-rimm.

3. On earlier moral panics, see Whitney Strub, *Obscenity Rules: Roth v. United States and the Long Struggle over Sexual Expression* (Lawrence, KS: University Press of Kansas, 2013).

4. Henry Jenkins, "Empowering Children in the Digital Age: Towards a Radical Media Pedagogy," *Radical Teacher* 50 (1997): 30–35, 31.

5. "Censorship in a Box: Why Blocking Software Is Wrong for Public Libraries," *ACLU*, June 17, 1998, accessed October 15, 2018, https://www.aclu.org/news/new-aclu-report-condemns-mandatory-blocking-software-public-libraries; "Libraries, the Internet, and the Law: Adults Must Have Unfiltered Access," *ACLU*, January 11, 2010, accessed October 15, 2018, https://www.aclu-wa.org/news/libraries-internet-and-law-adults-must-have-unfiltered-access; Ann Beeson, Chris Hansen and Barry Steinhardt, "Farenheit 451.2: Is Cyberspace Burning?" *ACLU*, August 1997, accessed October 15, 2018, https://www.aclu.org/other/fahrenheit-4512-cyberspace-burning?redirect=cpredirect/15145.

6. Victoria Rideout, Caroline Richardson, and Paul Resnick, "See No Evil: How Internet Filters Affect the Search for Online Health Information," Kaiser Family Foundation Study, December 2002, accessed October 15, 2018, https://www.kff.org/other/report/see-no-evil-how-internet-filters-affect.

7. See Strub, *Obscenity Rules*.

8. Linda Greenhouse, "The Supreme Court: Internet Access; Court Upholds Law to Make Libraries Use Internet Filters," *New York Times*, June 24, 2003, accessed October 15, 2018, https://www.nytimes.com/2003/06/24/us/supreme-court-internet-access-court-upholds-law-make-libraries-use-internet.html.

9. Deborah Caldwell-Stone, "Filtering and the First Amendment: When Is It Okay to Block Speech Online?" *American Libraries*, April 2, 2013, accessed October 15,

2018, https://americanlibrariesmagazine.org/2013/04/02/filtering-and-the-first
-amendment.

10. NCOSE, "EBSCO Information Services: A Major Contributor to Sexual
Exploitation," *National Center on Sexual Exploitation*, accessed February 16, 2019,
https://endsexualexploitation.org/ebsco.

11. NCOSE, "EBSCO Information Services."

12. Jackie Zubrzycki, "Do Online Databases Filter Out Enough Material?" *Education Week*, July 14, 2017, accessed February 17, 2019, http://blogs.edweek.org
/edweek/curriculum/2017/07/EBSCO_online_databases_filter_inappropriate
_material.html.

13. NCOSE, "Colorado School District Discontinues Contract with EBSCO for
Providing Sexually Explicit Material in K–12 School Databases," National Center on Sexual Exploitation, https://endsexualexploitation.org/articles/colorado
-school-district-discontinues-contract-with-ebsco-for-providing-sexually-explicit
-material-in-k-12-school-databases.

14. NCOSE, "Starbucks Will Begin Filtering Pornography from WiFi," National
Center on Sexual Exploitation, January 15, 2019, accessed June 19, 2021, https://
endsexualexploitation.org/articles/starbucks-wifi; NCOSE, "Porn Free WiFi Campaign Targets McDonald's and Starbucks," National Center on Sexual Exploitation,
March 17, 2015, accessed June 19, 2021, https://endsexualexploitation.org/articles
/porn-free-wifi-campaign-targets-mcdonalds-and-starbucks.

15. Freedom House, "Freedom on the Net: 2016," *Freedom House*, accessed June 25,
2019, 9, https://freedomhouse.org/sites/default/files/FOTN_2016_BOOKLET
_FINAL.pdf.

16. Freedom House, "Freedom on the Net," 9.

17. Lukasz Szulc, "Banal Nationalism and Queers Online: Enforcing and Resisting
Cultural Meanings of .tr," *New Media & Society* 17, no. 9 (2015): 1530–1546.

18. Freedom House, "Freedom on the Net: 2017," *Freedom House*, accessed June
25, 2019, 7 https://freedomhouse.org/sites/default/files/FOTN_2017_Final.pdf.

19. Andrew K. Pryzkylski and Victoria Nash, "Internet Filtering and Adolescent
Exposure to Online Sexual Material," *Cyberpsychology, Behavior, and Social Networking*
21, no. 7 (2018): 405–410, 405.

20. Benjamin Edelman, "Empirical Analysis of Google SafeSearch," Berkman Center for Internet and Society, 2003, accessed June 27, 2018, https://cyber.harvard.edu
/archived_content/people/edelman/google-safesearch.

21. It would be greatly beneficial if there were more comprehensive and longer
duration data collection procedures put in place to better keep track of what is getting blocked, when, why, and for how long. More ethnographic data cataloguing
web admins' and content creators' responses to censorship and their navigation of

the adjudication process would be a great supplement to this larger database. Without these things in place, it is very difficult to provide a rigorous accounting of the negative effects of content moderation practices online.

22. Aimee Dawson, "Facebook Censors 30,000 Year-Old Venus of Willendorf as 'Pornographic,'" *Art Newspaper*, February 27, 2018, accessed June 27, 2018, https://www.theartnewspaper.com/news/facebook-censors-famous-30-000-year-old-nude-statue-as-pornographic.

23. Victoria Stapley-Brown, "Paris Court Hears Arguments in Facebook Censorship Case Centering on Courbet's *Origin of the World*," *Art Newspaper*, February 2, 2018, accessed June 27, 2018, https://www.theartnewspaper.com/news/paris-court-hears-arguments-in-facebook-censorship-case-centering-on-courbet-s-origin-of-the-world.

24. Tim Schneider, "The Gray Market: Why Art Censorship Is Built Into Facebook's DNA (and Other Insights)," Artnet, March 5, 2018, accessed February 14, 2019, https://news.artnet.com/market/gray-market-facebook-art-censorship-1235822.

25. Michael Stokes, "The (Straight) Male Gaze Rules on Sanitized Social Media," *Advocate*, December 11, 2018, accessed February 11, 2019, https://www.advocate.com/commentary/2018/12/11/straight-male-gaze-rules-sanitized-social-media.

26. Images with broken links were not used for the study, leading to a final number of ninety-six images for each dataset.

27. Tom White, "About," Nips4Creativity, December 8, 2017, accessed July 6, 2019, http://nips4creativity.com/art/tom-white.

28. Tom White, "Synthetic Abstractions," Medium, August 23, 2018, accessed July 6, 2019, https://medium.com/@tom_25234/synthetic-abstractions-8f0e8f69f390; Tom White, "Perception Engines," Medium, April 4, 2018, accessed July 6, 2019, https://medium.com/artists-and-machine-intelligence/perception-engines-8a46bc598d57

29. "eroGANous," Tumblr, accessed July 6, 2019, https://eroganous.tumblr.com.

30. Jason Bailey, "AI Artists Expose 'Kinks' in Algorithmic Censorship," *Artnome*, December 11, 2018, accessed August 25, 2020, https://www.artnome.com/news/2018/12/6/ai-artists-expose-kinks-in-algorithmic-censorship.

31. Jake Elwes, "Machine Learning Porn," JakeElwes.com, 2016, accessed August 25, 2020, https://www.jakeelwes.com/project-MLPorn.html.

32. Jason Bailey, "AI Art Just Got Awesome," *Artnome*, April 5, 2018, accessed August 25, 2020, https://www.artnome.com/news/2018/3/29/ai-art-just-got-awesome.

33. Jason Bailey, "AI Artists Expose 'Kinks.'"

34. Chris Brickell, "Sexuality, Power and the Sociology of the Internet." *Current Sociology* 60, no. 1 (2011): 28–44.

35. Jane D. Brown and Kelly L. L'Engle, "X-Rated: Sexual Attitudes and Behaviors Associated with U.S. Early Adolescents' Exposure to Sexually Explicit Media," *Communication Research* 36, no. 1 (February 2009): 129–151.

36. Roger Lancaster, *Sex Panic and the Punitive State* (Berkeley: University of California Press, 2011).

37. Feona Attwood, Clarissa Smith and Martin Barker, "'I'm Just Curious and Still Exploring Myself': Young People and Pornography," *New Media & Society* 20, no. 10 (October 2018): 3738–3759; Azy Barak and William A. Fisher, "The Future of Internet Sexuality," in *Sex and the Internet: A Guidebook for Clinicians*, ed. Al Cooper (New York: Brunner-Routledge, 2002), 263–280; Sylvain C. Boies, Gail Knudson, and Julian Young, "The Internet, Sex, and Youths: Implications for Sexual Development," *Sexual Addiction & Compulsivity* 11, no. 4 (October 1, 2004): 343–363; Al Cooper, Sylvain Boies, Marlene Maheu, and David Greenfield, "Internet Sexuality: The Next Sexual Revolution," in *Psychological Perspectives on Human Sexuality*, ed. Lenore T. Szuchman and Frank Muscarella (New York: John Wiley & Sons, 2000), 519–545. Kristian Daneback, Sven-Axel Månsson, Michael W. Ross, and Christine M. Markham, "The Internet as a Source of Information about Sexuality," *Sex Education: Sexuality, Society and Learning* 12, no. 5 (2012): 583–598; Kristian Daneback, Michael W. Ross and Sven-Axel Månsson, "Characteristics and Behaviours of Sexual Compulsives Who Use the Internet for Sexual Purposes," *Sexual Addiction & Compulsivity* 13, no. 1 (2006): 53–67; Nicola M. Döring, "The Internet's Impact on Sexuality: A Critical Review of 15 Years of Research," *Computers in Human Behavior* 25, no. 5 (2009): 1089–1101; Eric W. Owens, Richard J. Behun, Jill C. Manning, and Rory C. Reid, "The Impact of Internet Pornography on Adolescents: A Review of the Research," *Sexual Addiction & Compulsivity* 19, no. 1–2 (January 1, 2012): 99–122.

38. Daneback, Månsson, Ross, and Markham, "The Internet as a Source of Information about Sexuality"; Daneback, Ross, and Månsson, "Characteristics and Behaviours of Sexual Compulsives."

39. Amber Madison, "When Social-Media Companies Censor Sex Education," *Atlantic*, March 4, 2015, accessed February 14, 2019, https://www.theatlantic.com /health/archive/2015/03/when-social-media-censors-sex-education/385576.

40. Amber Madison, "When Social-Media Companies Censor."

41. See Melissa White, "Condom Love: Find Out How Amazing Safer Sex Can Be," Bedsider, April 28, 2014, accessed June 25, 2019, https://www.bedsider.org/ features/332-condom-love-find-out-how-amazing-safer-sex-can-be.

42. Amber Madison, "When Social-Media Companies Censor."

43. Jillian C. York, "Adult Content Policies: A Textbook Case of Private Censorship," Electronic Frontier Foundation, December 7, 2017, accessed January 30,

2021, https://www.eff.org/deeplinks/2017/12/adult-content-policies-textbook
-private-censorship-fail.

44. Jillian C. York, "Adult Content Policies."

45. Violet Blue, "Timeline: Google's Role in Global Sex Censorship," ZDNet.
February 24, 2015, accessed February 14, 2019, https://www.zdnet.com/article/
timeline-googles-role-in-global-sex-censorship.

46. Susannah Fox and Maeve Duggan, "Health Online 2013," Pew Research Center, January 15, 2013, accessed January 30, 2021, https://www.pewresearch.org/
internet/2013/01/15/health-online-2013.

47. Amber Madison, "When Social-Media Companies Censor."

48. Sirin Kale, "Sex Ed Vloggers Say YouTube Is Censoring Their Videos," VICE,
May 15, 2018, accessed June 25, 2019, https://www.vice.com/en_us/article
/9k89wv/sex-ed-vloggers-say-youtube-is-censoring-their-videos.

49. It is worth noting that the term *bisexual* is *not* used to describe MMF threesomes
or larger group sex scenes in mainstream porn and only begins to appear in LGBTQI+
porn when men penetrate one another in these scenes.

50. Michelle Garcia, "Google Removes 'Bisexual' from Its List of Dirty Words,"
Advocate, September 11, 2012, accessed June 27, 2018, https://www.advocate.com
/society/technology/2012/09/11/google-removes-bisexual-its-list-dirty-words.
Cf. Faith Cheltenham, "Google's Bisexual Problem," *Huffington Post*, July 18, 2012,
accessed June 27, 2018, https://www.huffingtonpost.com/faith-cheltenham/
google-instant-search-bisexual_b_1682654.html; "Google Unlocks 'Bisexual' from
Auto Complete and Instant Search Functions: Report," *Huffington Post*, September
11, 2012, accessed June 27, 2019, https://www.huffingtonpost.com/2012/09/11/
google-bisexual-auto-complete-instant-search_n_1872252.html.

51. John Cheney-Lippold, *We Are Data: Algorithms and the Making of Our Digital
Selves* (New York: NYU Press, 2017), 52.

52. Attwood, Smith, and Barker, "'I'm Just Curious and Still Exploring Myself'";
Daneback, Månsson, Ross, and Markham, "The Internet as a Source of Informa-
tion about Sexuality"; Daneback, Kristian, Bente Træen, and Sven-Axel Månsson,
"Use of Pornography in a Random Sample of Norwegian Heterosexual Couples,"
Archives of Sexual Behavior 38, no. 5 (2009): 746–753; Jonathan James McCreadie
Lillie, "Cyberporn, Sexuality, and the Net Apparatus," *Convergence: The International
Journal of Research into New Media Technologies* 10, no. 1 (2004): 43–54.

53. Sylvain C. Boies, "University Students' Uses of and Reactions to Online Sexual
Information and Entertainment: Links to Online and Offline Sexual Behavior," *The
Canadian Journal of Human Sexuality* 11, no. 2 (2002): 77–89; Boies, Knudson, and
Young, "The Internet, Sex, and Youths"; Daneback, Månsson, Ross, and Markham,
"The Internet as a Source of Information about Sexuality," 594.

54. Attwood, Smith, and Barker, "'I'm Just Curious and Still Exploring Myself'"; Boies, "University Students' Uses of and Reactions to Online Sexual Information"; Boies, Knudson, and Young, "The Internet, Sex, and Youths"; Alvain Cooper, Dana E. Putnam, Lynn A. Planchon, and Sylvain C. Boies, "Online Sexual Compulsivity: Getting Tangled in the Net," *Sexual Addiction & Compulsivity* 6, no. 2 (April 1, 1999): 79–104; Daneback, Månsson, Ross, and Markham, "The Internet as a Source of Information about Sexuality"; Kristian Daneback and Cecilia Löfberg, "Youth, Sexuality and the Internet: Young People's Use of the Internet to Learn about Sexuality," in *Youth Culture and Net Culture: Online Social Practices*, ed. Elza Dunkels, Gun-Marie Franberg, and Camilla Hallgren (Hershey, PA: IGI Global, 2011), 190–206; Döring, "The Internet's Impact on Sexuality"; Lynne Hillier and Lyn Harrison, "Building Realities Less Limited Than Their Own: Young People Practising Same-Sex Attraction on the Internet," *Sexualities* 10, no. 1 (February 2007): 82–100; Lillie, "Cyberporn, Sexuality, and the Net Apparatus"; Katelyn Y. A. McKenna, and John A. Bargh, "Coming Out in the Age of the Internet: Identity 'Demarginalization' through Virtual Group Participation," *Journal of Personality and Social Psychology* 75, no. 3 (1998): 681–694; Mark McLelland, *Queer Japan from the Pacific War to the Internet Age* (Lanham, MD: Rowman and Littlefield), 187; Michael W. Ross and Michael R. Kauth, "Men Who Have Sex with Men, and the Internet: Emerging Clinical Issues and their Management," in *Sex and the Internet: A Guide Book for Clinicians*, ed. Al Cooper (New York: Brunner-Routledge, 2002) 47–71.

55. Döring, "The Internet's Impact on Sexuality," 1097.

56. Attwood, Smith, and Barker, "'I'm Just Curious and Still Exploring Myself'," 3747.

57. It might be worth noting that studies of this sort on adolescent web use are relatively rare, even though researchers have found that conducting them doesn't seem to increase adolescent pornography consumption. See Goran Koletić, Nicole Cohen, Aleksandar Štulhofer, and Taylor Kohut, "Does Asking Adolescents about Pornography Make Them Use It? A Test of the Question-Behavior Effect," *Journal of Sex Research* 56 (2018): 1–5.

58. Allow States and Victims to Fight Online Sex Trafficking Act of 2017, H.R.1865.

59. Ann Wagner, "Wagner: FOSTA Delivers Real Results for the American People," July 25, 2018, accessed February 20, 2019, https://youtu.be/pT8fDASTI4I.

60. Violet Blue, "Congress Just Legalized Sex Censorship: What to Know," Engadget, March 30, 2018, accessed February 14, 2019, https://www.engadget.com/2018/03/30/congress-just-legalized-sex-censorship-what-to-know.

61. "ACLU Vote Recommendation to Congress: Oppose H. R. 1865—The 'Allow States and Victims to Fight Online Sex Trafficking Act' (FOSTA)," ACLU, February 26, 2018, accessed February 20, 2019, https://www.aclu.org/letter/aclu-vote-recommendation-congress-oppose-h-r-1865-allow-states-and-victims-fight

-online-sex; Stephen E. Boyd, Assistant Attorney General, United States Department of Justice, Letter to Robert W. Goodlatte, Chairman of the Committee on the Judiciary, U.S. House of Representatives, February 27, 2018, accessed February 20, 2019, https://assets.documentcloud.org/documents/4390361/Views-Ltr-Re-H-R -1865-Allow-States-and-Victims.pdf.

62. Blue, "Congress Just Legalized Sex Censorship."

63. CompTIA, Computer and Communications Industry Association, Interactive Advertising Bureau, Internet Association, Internet Commerce Coalition, Internet Infrastructure Coalition, NetChoice, Software & Information Industry Association, Tech: NYC and the Internet Society, Letter to Rob Portman, Chairman of the Senate Permanent Subcommittee on Investigations, U.S. Senate and Richard Blumenthal, U.S. Senate, August 2, 2017, accessed February 20, 2019, https://cdn1.internetassociation .org/wp-content/uploads/2017/08/S1693-Association-Letter-08-02-2017.pdf.

64. "Statement in Support of the Bipartisan Compromise to the Stop Enabling Sex Traffickers Act," Internet Association, November 3, 2017, accessed February 20, 2019, https://internetassociation.org/statement-in-support-of-the-bipartisan -compromise-to-stop-enabling-sex-trafficking-act-sesta.

65. Elizabeth Nolan Brown, "Facebook Supported 'Sex Trafficking' Law FOSTA to Cozy Up to Republican Critics: Reason Roundup," Reason, November 15, 2019, accessed February 14, 2019, https://reason.com/blog/2018/11/15/how-facebook -sold-out-sex-workers; Sheera Frenkel, Nicholas Confessore, Cecilia Kang, Matthew Rosenberg, and Jack Nicas, "Delay, Deny and Deflect: How Facebook's Leaders Fought through the Crisis," *New York Times*, November 14, 2018, accessed February 14, 2019, https://www.nytimes.com/2018/11/14/technology/facebook -data-russia-election-racism.html.

66. "Power of FOSTA-SESTA Felt within 48 Hours of Senate Passage: Websites Move Swiftly to Shutter Prostitution Ads," NCOSE, March 3, 2018, accessed February 16, 2019, https://endsexualexploitation.org/articles/power-fosta-sesta-felt -within-48-hours-senate-passage-websites-move-swiftly-shutter-prostitution -ads.

67. Elizabeth Nolan Brown, "The New Law That Killed Craigslist's Personals Could End the Web as We've Known It," Daily Beast, March 23, 2018, accessed February 14, 2019, https://www.thedailybeast.com/the-new-law-that-killed -craigslists-personals-could-end-the-web-as-weve-known-it.

68. Elliot Harmon, "Sex Trafficking Experts Say SESTA Is the Wrong Solution," EFF, October 3, 2017, accessed February 20, 2019, https://www.eff.org/deeplinks /2017/10/sex-trafficking-experts-say-sesta-wrong-solution.

69. M. G. Siegler, "Steve Jobs Reiterates: 'Folks Who Want Porn Can Buy an Android Phone," TechCrunch, 2010, accessed February 14, 2019, https:// techcrunch.com/2010/04/19/steve-jobs-android-porn.

70. Violet Blue, "How Sex Censorship Killed the Internet We Love," Engadget, January 31, 2019, accessed February 14, 2019, https://www.engadget.com/2019 /01/31/sex-censorship-killed-internet-fosta-sesta.

71. Michael Keller, "The Apple 'Kill List': What Your iPhone Doesn't Want You to Type," Daily Beast, July 16, 2013, accessed February 14, 2019, https://www .thedailybeast.com/the-apple-kill-list-what-your-iphone-doesnt-want-you-to-type.

72. Keller, "The Apple 'Kill List.'"

73. Megan Carpentier, "10 Things the iPhone Siri Will Help You Get Instead of an Abortion," RawStory, November 29, 2011, accessed June 27, 2019, https://www .rawstory.com/2011/11/10-things-the-iphone-siri-will-help-you-get-instead-of -an-abortion.

74. Nick Wilson, E. Jane MacDonald, Osman David Mansoor, and Jane Morgan, "In Bed with Siri and Google Assistant: A Comparison of Sexual Health Advice," BMJ (2017): 1–7.

75. Adam S. Miner, Arnold Milstein, Stephen Schueller, Roshini Hedge, Christina Mangurian, and Eleni Linos, "Smartphone-Based Conversational Agents and Responses to Questions about Mental Health, Interpersonal Violence, and Physical Health," JAMA Internal Medicine 176, no. 5 (2016): 619–624.

76. Emily Chang, Brotopia: Breaking Up the Boy's Club of Silicon Valley (New York: Penguin, 2018), 8–9.

77. Keller, "The Apple 'Kill List.'"

78. Mariella Moon, "Instagram Blames Apple for Strict Anti-Nudity Stance," Engadget, October 4, 2015, accessed February 14, 2019, https://www.engadget .com/2015/10/04/instagram-apple-freethenipple.

79. Nick Drewe, "The Hilarious List of Hashtags Instagram Won't Let You Search," Data Pack, May 10, 2016, accessed February 13, 2019, http://thedatapack.com/ banned-instagram-hashtags-update.

80. Drewe, "The Hilarious List of Hashtags."

81. Drewe, "The Hilarious List of Hashtags."

82. Leila Ettachfini, "Users Accuse Instagram of Censoring Hashtags about Sex Work and Women," VICE, May 29, 2018, accessed February 14, 2019, https:// broadly.vice.com/en_us/article/xwmg3j/instagram-sesta-fosta-censorship-hashtag -woman.

83. @SexSchoolHub, Sex School, Twitter , January 26, 2019, 7:01 a.m., https:// twitter.com/SexSchoolHub/status/1089176609792376834.

84. Stefanie Duguay, Jean Burgess, and Nicolas Suzor, "Queer Women's Experiences of Patchwork Platform Governance on Tinder, Instagram, and Vine," Convergence 26, no. 2 (April 2020): 237–252.

85. Alexander Cheves, "The Dangerous Trend of LGBTQ censorship on the Internet," *Out*, December 6, 2018, accessed January 30, 2021, https://www.out.com/out-exclusives/2018/12/06/dangerous-trend-lgbtq-censorship-internet.

86. Daniel Villarreal, "Instagram Just Banned Longtime Gay Historian Tom Bianchi, & It's Part of a Troubling Anti-Gay Trend," *LGBTQ Nation*, February 2, 2019, accessed January 30, 2021, https://www.lgbtqnation.com/2019/02/instagram-just-banned-longtime-gay-historian-tom-bianchi-part-troubling-anti-gay-trend.

87. Quoted in Villarreal, "Instagram Just Banned Longtime Gay Historian."

88. David Grant, "Instagram Deleted These Pics of Antoni for Neing 'pornographic'; Photographer Speaks Out," *QUEERTY**, December 17, 2018, accessed January 30, 2021, https://www.queerty.com/instagram-deleted-pics-antoni-pornographic-photographer-speaks-20181217.

89. Graham Gremore, "The Warwick Rowers Are Pissed about Having These Images Censored from Their Instagram Page," *QUEERTY**, December 18, 2018, accessed January 30, 2021, https://www.queerty.com/warwick-rowers-pissed-images-censored-instagram-page-20181218.

90. Jeff Taylor, "This Lesbian Couple Is Fighting Back after Instagram Deleted a Post Celebrating Their Love," *LGBTQ Nation*, December 1, 2017, accessed January 30, 2021, https://www.lgbtqnation.com/2017/12/lesbian-couple-fighting-back-instagram-deleted-post-celebrating-love.

91. Jim Milliot, "Nook Terminating Accounts of Erotica Writers," *Publishers Weekly*, August 23, 2017, accessed February 20, 2019, https://www.publishersweekly.com/pw/by-topic/digital/content-and-e-books/article/74561-nook-terminating-accounts-of-erotica-authors.html.

92. Samantha Cole, "Amazon Is Burying Sexy Books, Sending Erotic Novel Authors to the 'No-Rank Dungeon,'" Motherboard, May 29, 2018, accessed February 14, 2019, https://motherboard.vice.com/en_us/article/bjpjn4/amazon-erotica-best-seller-rankings-removed

93. Nate Hoffelder, "Amazon Has Shadow-Banned Romance Titles from the Kindle Store," The Digital Reader, March 29, 2018, accessed February 14, 2019, https://the-digital-reader.com/2018/03/29/amazon-has-shadow-banned-romance-titles-from-the-kindle-store.

94. Nicholas Deleon, "Apple Is Cracking Down on NSFW Content Inside Reddit Apps," VICE, April 12, 2016, accessed July 5, 2019, https://www.vice.com/en_us/article/78k8yb/reddit-ios-apps-disappear-nsfw-content.

95. Simon Sharwood, "What the @#$%&!? Microsoft Bans Nudity, Swearing in Skype, Emails, Office 365 Docs," The Register, March 28, 2018, accessed July 6, 2019, https://www.theregister.co.uk/2018/03/28/microsoft_services_agreement_bars_offensive_language.

96. "Mobile Operating System Market Share Worldwide," Statcounter, accessed July 6, 2019, http://gs.statcounter.com/os-market-share/mobile/worldwide.

97. Samantha Cole, "Facebook and Patreon Are Making It Harder to Find Sex Educators," Motherboard, July 24, 2018, accessed January 30, 2021, https://www .vice.com/en/article/ev8pg4/facebook-and-patreon-sex-educators-community -guidelines.

98. Cole, "Facebook and Patreon Are Making It Harder to Find Sex Educators."

99. Eli Rosenberg, "Facebook Blocked Many Gay-Themed Ads as Part of Its New Advertising Policy, Angering LGBT Groups," *Washington Post*, October 3, 2018, accessed January 30, 2021, https://www.washingtonpost.com/technology/2018 /10/03/facebook-blocked-many-gay-themed-ads-part-its-new-advertising-policy -angering-lgbt-groups.

100. Jon Christian, "From 'Preggers' to 'Pizzle': Android's Bizarre List of Banned Words," *WIRED*, December 2, 2013, accessed February 14, 2019, https://www .wired.com/2013/12/banned-android-words.

101. Blue, "Timeline."

102. Samantha Cole, "Sex Workers Say Porn on Google Drive Is Suddenly Disappearing," Motherboard, March 21, 2018, accessed June 27, 2019, https://www.vice .com/en_us/article/9kgwnp/porn-on-google-drive-error.

103. Blue, "How Sex Censorship Killed the Internet."

104. Samantha Cole, "Google AdSense Banned a Random Web Page about a 32-Year-Old Bill because It Was about Sexual Abuse," Motherboard, July 6, 2018, accessed January 30, 2021, https://www.vice.com/en/article/ne5j3z/google -adsense-banned-a-random-web-page-about-a-32-year-old-bill-because-it-was -about-sexual-abuse.

105. "About Family Wi-Fi," Google, accessed June 27, 2019, https://support .google.com/wifi/answer/7506043?hl=en.

106. Violet Blue, "Google's Blogger to Delete All 'Adult' Blogs with Ads in Three Days," ZDNet, June 28, 2019, accessed February 14, 2019, https://www.zdnet.com /article/googles-blogger-to-delete-all-adult-blogs-with-ads-in-three-days.

107. Violet Blue, "Google Bans 'Explicit' Adult Content from Blogger Blogs," ZDNet, February 24, 2015, accessed February 14, 2019, https://www.zdnet.com/ article/google-bans-explicit-adult-content-from-blogger-blogs.

108. Jean Burgess and Joshua Green, *YouTube: Online Video and Participatory Culture*, 2nd ed. (Medford, MA: Polity, 2018), 152.

109. Rachel Dunphy, "Can YouTube Survive the Adpocalypse?" *New York Magazine*, December 28, 2017, accessed February 14, 2019, http://nymag.com/ intelligencer/2017/12/can-youtube-survive-the-adpocalypse.html.

110. "Advertiser-Friendly Content Guidelines," YouTube Help, June 2019, accessed June 27, 2019, https://support.google.com/youtube/answer/6162278.

111. "Request Human Review of Videos Marked 'Not Suitable for Most Advertisers,'" YouTube Help, accessed June 27, 2019, https://support.google.com/youtube/answer/7083671?hl=en.

112. Erik Kain, "YouTube Wants Content Creators to Appeal Demonetization, But It's Not Always That Easy," Forbes, September 18, 2017, accessed February 27, 2019, https://www.forbes.com/sites/erikkain/2017/09/18/adpocalypse-2017-heres-what-you-need-to-know-about-youtubes-demonetization-troubles/#57c5e6c26705.

113. David Teich, "How YouTuve Handled Its Brand-Safety Crisis," Digiday, June 14, 2017, accessed February 16, 2019, https://digiday.com/marketing/youtube-handled-brand-safety-crisis.

114. Samantha Cole, "YouTube Banned an Erotic Film Production Company After It Posted Interviews with Sex Workers," VICE, July 13, 2018, accessed June 27, 2019, https://www.vice.com/en_us/article/gy3gdb/youtube-banned-erica-lust-in-conversation-with-sex-workers.

115. Cole, "YouTube Banned an Erotic Film Production Company." Motherboard, July 13, 2018, accessed January 30, 2021, https://www.vice.com/en/article/gy3gdb/youtube-banned-erica-lust-in-conversation-with-sex-workers.

116. Cheves, "The Dangerous Trend of LGBTQ Censorship."

117. Sal Bardo, "YouTube Continues to Restrict LGBTQ Content," Huffington Post, January 17, 2018, accessed February 14, 2019, https://www.huffingtonpost.com/entry/youtube-continues-to-restrict-lgbtq-content_us_5a5e6628e4b03ed177016e90.

118. Stevie Boebi, Twitter, September 19, 2018, 5:16 p.m., https://twitter.com/stevieboebi/status/910296593852596224.

119. Gaby Dunn, Twitter, September 14, 2017, 8:41 p.m., https://twitter.com/gabydunn/status/908536129065967616.

120. Cheves, "The Dangerous Trend of LGBTQ Censorship."

121. Emma Grey Ellis, "YouTube Continues to Fail Its Queer Creators," WIRED, June 5, 2019, accessed February 27, 2019, https://www.wired.com/story/youtube-carlos-maza.

122. @YouTube, Twitter, June 30, 2018, 9:59 a.m., https://twitter.com/YouTube/status/1013104846428344320.

123. "Your Content & Restricted Mode," YouTube, accessed June 25, 2019, https://support.google.com/youtube/answer/7354993?hl=en.

124. YouTube, "Your Content & Restricted Mode."

125. YouTube, "Your Content & Restricted Mode."

126. Elle Hunt, "LGBT Community Anger Over YouTube Restrictions Which Make Their Videos Invisible," *Guardian*, March 19, 2017, accessed February 14, 2019, https://www.theguardian.com/technology/2017/mar/20/lgbt-community -anger-over-youtube-restrictions-which-make-their-videos-invisible.

127. Rowan Ellis, "YouTube Is Anti-LGBT? (Restricted Content Mode)," YouTube, March 16, 2017, accessed June 25, 2019, https://youtu.be/Zr6pS07mbJc.

128. Calum McSwiggan, "This Video Is Too Gay for Kids," March 18, 2017, accessed June 25, 2019, https://youtu.be/woilZ9mU2-U.

129. Tyler Oakley, Twitter, March 19, 2017, 12:28 p.m., https://twitter.com/ tyleroakley/status/843544801916010496.

130. Bardo, "YouTube Continues to Restrict LGBTQ Content."

131. @Neonfiona, Twitter, March 16, 2017, 8:06 a.m., https://twitter.com/neon fiona/status/842390135257874432.

132. @melaniietweets, Twitter, March 19, 2017, 3:37 p.m., https://twitter.com/ melaniietweets/status/843592387922477059.

133. Gigi Gorgeous, "#ProudToBeRestricted," March 19, 2017, accessed June 25, 2019, https://youtu.be/7nXtLQERSGk.

134. @SeaineLove, Twitter, March 16, 2017, 7:44 p.m., https://twitter.com/ SeaineLove/status/842567309323468802.

135. @YouTube Creators, Twitter, March 19, 2017, 5:01 p.m., https://twitter.com /YTCreators/status/843613347367079937.

136. Barbara Ortutay, "YouTube Reverses Some Restrictions on Gay-Themed Content," *Chicago Tribune*, March 20, 2017, accessed February 14, 2019, https:// www.chicagotribune.com/bluesky/technology/ct-youtube-lgbt-censorship-wp -bsi-20170320-story.html.

137. "An Update on Restricted Mode," *YouTube Creator Blog*, April 21, 2017, accessed June 26, 2019, https://youtube-creators.googleblog.com/2017/04/an -update-on-restricted-mode.html.

138. Megan Farokhmanesh, "YouTube Is Still Restricting and Demonetizing LGBT Videos—and Adding Anti-LGBT Ads to Some." The Verge, June 4, 2018, accessed January 30, 2021, https://www.theverge.com/2018/6/4/17424472/youtube-lgbt -demonetization-ads-algorithm.

139. Farokhmanesh, "YouTube Is Still Restricting and Demonetizing LGBT Videos."

140. Samantha Cole, "YouTube Removed a Sex Tech Conference for No Reason," Motherboard, May 7, 2020, accessed January 30, 2021, https://www.vice.com/en/ article/9359zy/youtube-removed-a-sex-tech-conference-for-no-reason.

141. Emma L. Barratt and Nick J. Davis, "Autonomous Sensory Meridian Response (ASMR): A Flow-Like Mental State," *PeerJ* 3 (2015): e851.

142. Giulia Lara Poerio, Emma Blakey, Thomas J. Hostler, and Theresa Veltri, "More than a Feeling: Autonomous Sensory Meridian Response (ASMR) Is Characterized by Reliable Changes in Affect and Physiology," *PLoS ONE* 13, no. 6: e0196645.

143. Barratt and Davis, "Autonomous Sensory Meridian Response (ASMR)."

144. Barratt and Davis, "Autonomous Sensory Meridian Response (ASMR)."

145. Elena Cresci, "YouTube ASMR Videos Are under Attack," Medium, November 15, 2018, accessed June 25, 2019, https://medium.com/s/story/youtube-asmr -videos-are-under-attack-651a0c57aca0.

146. Michelob ULTRA, "The Pure Experience | Michelob ULTRA Pure Gold Super Bowl 2019," January 28, 2019, accessed June 26, 2019, https://youtu.be/ LXmlN9BAddg

147. Melanie Ehrenkranz, "China's Anti-Porn Task Force Is Banning ASMR Videos," Gizmodo, June 19, 2018, accessed June 25, 2019, https://gizmodo.com/chinas -anti-porn-task-force-is-banning-asmr-videos-1826952470.

148. Cresci, "YouTube ASMR Videos Are under Attack."

149. Rchadwick52, "YouTube Censorship for ASMR Is Getting Out of Hand!" *Reddit,* 2018, accessed June 25, 2019, https://www.reddit.com/r/asmr/comments /6ucf2v/youtube_censorship_for_asmr_is_getting_out_of.

150. Violet Blue, "Why PayPal's Crackdown on ASMR Creators Should Worry You," Engadget, September 14, 2018, accessed February 14, 2019, https://www .engadget.com/2018/09/14/paypal-ban-asmr-sound-art-therapy.

151. Blue, "Why PayPal's Crackdown on ASMR Creators."

152. Arielle Pardes, "Small Sounds, Big Money: The Commercialization of ASMR," *WIRED,* June 20, 2019, accessed June 26, 2019, https://www.wired.com /story/commercialization-of-asmr.

153. "Frequently Asked Questions," Tingles, accessed June 26, 2019, https://www .gettingles.com/faq.

154. /the0nethatismany, "Looking for an Alternative to the Tingles App (IOS) [Discussion]," Reddit, 2018, accessed June 26, 2019, https://www.reddit.com/r/asmr/ comments/7ill1i/looking_for_an_alternative_to_the_tingles_app_ios.

155. Pardes, "Small Sounds, Big Money."

CHAPTER 4

1. Chris Isidore, "Yahoo Buys Tumblr, Promises to Not 'Screw It Up,'" CNN, May 20, 2013, accessed July 5, 2019, https://money.cnn.com/2013/05/20/technology/ yahoo-buys-tumblr/index.html.

2. Violet Blue, "Adult Tumblr Blogs Now Removed from Every Form of Search Possible," ZDNet, July 19, 2013, accessed February 14, 2019, https://www.zdnet.com/article/adult-tumblr-blogs-now-removed-from-every-form-of-search-possible.

3. Violet Blue, "After Backlash Yahoo's Tumblr Quietly Restores Adult, NSFW Blogs," ZDNet, July 21, 2013, accessed July 5, 2019, https://www.zdnet.com/article/after-backlash-yahoos-tumblr-quietly-restores-adult-nsfw-blogs.

4. Blue, "After Backlash."

5. Yuyu Chen, "'Nobody at Yahoo Understood Tumblr': Why Marissa Mayer's Big Bet on Tumblr Never Panned Out," Digiday, June 12, 2017, accessed July 5, 2019, https://digiday.com/marketing/tumblr-is-neglected-by-marketers.

6. Ingrid Lunden, "Verizon Closes $4.5B Acquisition of Yahoo, Marissa Mayer Resigns," TechCrunch, 2017, accessed July 5, 2019, https://techcrunch.com/2017/06/13/verizon-closes-4-5b-acquisition-of-yahoo-marissa-mayer-resigns-memo.

7. Hanna Kozlowska, "Tumblr Is Banning Porn and Other Adult Content," Quartz, December 3, 2018, accessed July 5, 2019, https://qz.com/1482821/tumblr-is-banning-porn-and-other-adult-content.

8. Sarah Perez, "Tumblr Rolls Out New Content Filtering Tools with Launch of 'Safe Mode,'" TechCrunch, June 20, 2017, accessed February 14, 2019, https://techcrunch.com/2017/06/20/tumblr-rolls-out-new-content-filtering-tools-with-launch-of-safe-mode.

9. Lance Whitney, "The Reason Tumblr Vanished from the Apple App Store: Child Pornography That Slipped through the Filters," CNET, November 20, 2018, accessed July 5, 2019, https://download.cnet.com/news/the-reason-tumblr-vanished-from-the-app-store-child-pornography-that-slipped-through-the-filters.

10. Luke Barnes, "One Month After Controversial Adult-Content Purge, Far-Right Pages Are Thriving on Tumblr," ThinkProgress, January 17, 2019, accessed February 13, 2019, https://thinkprogress.org/far-right-content-survived-tumblr-purge-36635e6aba4b/

11. "Adult Content," Tumblr, accessed July 5, 2019, https://tumblr.zendesk.com/hc/en-us/articles/231885248-Sensitive-content.

12. "A Better, More Positive Tumblr," Tumblr, December 3, 2018, accessed July 5, 2019, https://staff.tumblr.com/post/180758987165/a-better-more-positive-tumblr.

13. RJ Palmer, Twitter, December 3, 2018, 12:20 p.m., https://twitter.com/arvalis/status/1069687959014625282; @JojoMakes, Twitter, December 5, 2018, 4:55 a.m., https://twitter.com/JojoMakes/status/1070300738503483392; Naomi Edelgard, Twitter, December 5, 2018, 6:29 a.m., https://twitter.com/lucinalu219/status/1070324350115504128; Erika Moen, Twitter, December 3, 2018, 12:50

p.m., https://twitter.com/ErikaMoen/status/1069695308253212672; Rebecca Speas, Twitter, December 4, 2018, 10:37 a.m., https://twitter.com/SpeasySpice/status/1070024415524646913; @aidosaur, Twitter, December 5, 2018, 6:36 a.m., https://twitter.com/aidosaur/status/1070325925085089792; @CitrusFoam, Twitter, December 3, 2018, 12:48 p.m., https://twitter.com/CitrusFoam/status /1069694800868331521; @ruemxu, Twitter, December 3, 2018, 12:35 p.m., https://twitter.com/ruemxu/status/1069691515965005824.

14. Michael Kan, "Tumblr's Child Porn Crackdown Ensnares Legit Blogs in Purge," *PC Magazine*, November 19, 2018, accessed February 19, 2019, https://www.pcmag .com/news/365036/tumblr-purges-blogs-after-getting-delisted-from-app-store.

15. 2stopisshets, Twitter, December 3, 2018, 1:16 p.m., https://twitter.com/ stopcishets/status/1069702002484101120.

16. Paris Martineau, "Tumblr's Porn Ban Reveals Who Controls What We See Online," *WIRED*, December 4, 2018, accessed July 5, 2019, https://www.wired .com/story/tumblrs-porn-ban-reveals-controls-we-see-online.

17. "Why the Tumblr Ban on 'Adult Content' Is Bad for LGBTQ Youth," CBC Radio, January 11, 2018, accessed February 13, 2019, https://www.cbc.ca/radio/ spark/tumblr-ban-on-adult-content-bad-for-lgbtq-youth-1.4973385.

18. CBC Radio, "Why the Tumblr Ban."

19. John Paul Brammer, "'I Fear the Loss of Community': Tumblr's New 'Adult Content' Rules Worry LGBTQ Users," NBC News, December 5, 2018, accessed February 14, 2019, https://www.nbcnews.com/feature/nbc-out/i-fear-loss -community-tumblr-s-new-adult-content-rules-n944196.

20. Tim Highfield and Stefanie Duguay, "'Like a Monkey with a Miniature Cymbal': Cultural Practices of Repetition in Visual Social Media," *AoIR Selected Papers of Internet Research* 5 (2015).

21. Stefanie Duguay, "Why Tumblr's Ban on Adult Content Is Bad for LGBTQ Youth," The Conversation, December 6, 2018, accessed February 13, 2019, https:// theconversation.com/why-tumblrs-ban-on-adult-content-is-bad-for-lgbtq-youth -108215.

22. Avery Dame, "Making a Name for Yourself: Tagging as Transgender Ontological Practice on Tumblr," *Critical Studies in Media Communication* 33, no. 1 (2016): 23–37.

23. Shannon Liao, "Tumblr's Adult Content Ban Means the Death of Unique Blogs That Explore Sexuality," The Verge, December 6, 2018, accessed February 14, 2019, https://www.theverge.com/2018/12/6/18124260/tumblr-porn-ban -sexuality-blogs-unique.

24. Ana Valens, "NSFW Artists Speak Out as Their Accounts Are Suddenly 'Purged' on Tumblr," The Daily Dot, November 20, 2018, accessed July 5, 2019, https://www.dailydot.com/irl/tumblr-nsfw-artists-purged-child-porn.

25. As a refresher, mainstream heteroporn is the term I use to denote the normative version of pornography produced in San Fernando Valley by professionalized production companies that increasingly focuses on gonzo and POV pornography. It is what is most often referenced in mainstream discourse as pornography writ large and the frequent subject of criticism because of its representations of misogyny, heteronormativity, and for its labor relations. Oddly, while it is taken as representative of pornography writ large in most of our public discourse, it is rarely the focus of academic porn studies.

26. Vex Ashley, "Porn on Tumblr—a Eulogy/Love Letter," Medium, December 6, 2018, accessed January 27, 2020, https://medium.com/@vexashley/porn-on -tumblr-a-eulogy-love-letter-6d45e70fefff [emphasis in original].

27. Martineau, "Tumblr's Porn Ban."

28. Martineau, "Tumblr's Porn Ban."

29. Matt Blake, "UK Porn Is about to Change in a Way You're Not Going to Like," VICE, November 24, 2017, accessed February 12, 2019, https://www.vice.com /en_uk/article/9kqp43/uk-porn-is-about-to-change-in-a-way-youre-not-going -to-like.

30. Christopher Hooton, "A Long List of Sex Acts Just Got Banned in UK Porn," *Independent*, December 2, 2014, accessed February 11, 2019, https://www .independent.co.uk/news/uk/a-long-list-of-sex-acts-just-got-banned-in-uk-porn -9897174.html.

31. Hooton, "A Long List of Sex Acts Just Got Banned."

32. "Everything We Know about the UK's Path to Block Online Porn," *WIRED*, January 10, 2019, accessed February 28, 2019, https://www.wired.co.uk/article/ porn-block-ban-in-the-uk-age-verifcation-law.

33. Erika Lust, "The New UK Porn Legislation Will Turn Erotic Film into Boring, Unrealistic Male Fantasy," *Independent*, December 2, 2014, accessed February 11, 2019, https://www.independent.co.uk/voices/comment/the-new-uk-porn-legislation -will-turn-erotic-film-into-boring-unrealistic-male-fantasy-9898052.html.

34. Matt Blake, "UK Porn Is about to Change."

35. "Government Error Delays Online Pornography Age-Check Scheme," BBC News, June 20, 2019, accessed June 26, 2019, https://www.bbc.com/news/ technology-48700906.

36. "UK's Controversial 'Porn Blocker' Plan Dropped," BBC News, October 16, 2019, accessed January 30, 2021, https://www.bbc.com/news/technology -50073102.

37. *WIRED*, "Everything We Know about the UK's Path."

38. Jim Killock, Pamela Cowburn, Alex Haydock, Ed Johnson-Williams, and Simon Migliano, "Collateral Damage in the War against Online Harms: How

Charities, Schools, and Social Support Websites Are Blocked by UK ISP Adult Content Filters," TOP10VPN/Open Rights Group, April 2019, accessed January 30, 2021, https://www.top10vpn.com/assets/2019/04/Top10VPN-and-ORG -Report-Collateral-Damage-in-the-War-Against-Online-Harms.pdf.

39. Matt Blake, "UK Porn Is about to Change."

40. "Who Lasts the Longest?" *Pornhub Insights*, December 10, 2014, accessed June 26, 2019, https://www.pornhub.com/insights/who-lasts-longest.

41. Andy, "Why Are Porn Performers Scared to Talk about Internet Piracy?" *TorrentFreak*, April 13, 2014, accessed February 16, 2019, https://torrentfreak.com/ why-are-porn-perfomers-scared-to-talk-about-internet-piracy-140413.

42. David Auerbach, "Vampire Porn," *Slate*, October 23, 2014, accessed February 16, 2019, https://slate.com/technology/2014/10/mindgeek-porn-monopoly-its -dominance-is-a-cautionary-tale-for-other-industries.html.

43. Joe Pinsker, "The Hidden Economics of Porn," *Atlantic*, April 4, 2016, accessed February 16, 2019, https://www.theatlantic.com/business/archive/2016/04/ pornography-industry-economics-tarrant/476580; cf. Shira Tarrant, *The Pornography Industry: What Everyone Needs to Know* (New York: Oxford University Press, 2016).

44. E. J. Dickson, "#PayForYourPorn Is Trying to Get People to Stop Watching Tube Sites—But Will It Work?" The Daily Dot, May 15, 2014, accessed June 26, 2019, https://www.dailydot.com/irl/porn-piracy-hashtag-campaign.

45. Auerbach, "Vampire Porn."

46. Siri, "Who owns and operates major porn tube sites? Do these sites have legitimate investors or are they sort of mom and pop shops with possible gang connections or operating illegally? Is there any good investigative journalism on this topic?", Quora, February 24, 2014, accessed June 26, 2019, https://www.quora.com/ Who-owns-and-operates-major-porn-tube-sites-Do-these-sites-have-legitimate -investors-or-are-they-sort-of-mom-and-pop-shops-with-possible-gang -connections-or-operating-illegally-Is-there-any-good-investigative-journalism -on-this-topic/answer/Siri-4.

47. Auerbach, "Vampire Porn."

48. Felix Salmon, "How MindGeek Transformed the Economics of Porn," Splinter, October 10, 2015, accessed February 16, 2019, https://splinternews.com/how -mindgeek-transformed-the-economics-of-porn-1793851713.

49. E. J. Dickson, "When Porn Stars Become Escorts: Lucrative New Trend Could Also Be Risky," Salon, February 24, 2014, accessed June 26, 2019, https://www .salon.com/2014/02/24/when_porn_stars_become_escorts_lucrative_new_trend _could_also_be_risky.

50. Niels Van Doorn, "Keeping It Real: User-Generated Pornography, Gender Reification, and Visual Pleasure," *Convergence* 16, no. 4 (2010): 411–430.

51. Antoine Mazières, Mathieu Trachman, Jean-Philippe Cointet, Baptiste Coulmont, and Christophe Prieur, "Deep Tags: Toward a Quantitative Analysis of Online Pornography," *Porn Studies* 1, no. 1–2 (2014): 80–95.

52. Ogi Ogas and Sai Gaddam, *A Billion Wicked Thoughts: What the Internet Tells Us about Sexual Relationships* (New York: Plume, 2012).

53. Pinsker, "The Hidden Economics of Porn."

54. Pinsker, "The Hidden Economics of Porn."

55. Blake, "UK Porn Is about to Change."

56. Blake, "UK Porn Is about to Change."

57. Blake, "UK Porn Is about to Change."

58. *WIRED*, "Everything We Know about the UK's Path."

59. Violet Blue, "Suicide, Violence, and Going Underground: FOSTA's Body Count," Engadget, April 27, 2018, accessed February 14, 2019, https://www.engadget.com/2018/04/27/suicide-violence-and-going-underground-fosta-sesta.

60. "Blurred Lines: An Exploration of Consumers' Advertising Recognition in the Contexts of Search Engines and Native Advertising." FTC, December 2017, accessed January 30, 2021, https://www.ftc.gov/system/files/documents/reports/blurred-lines-exploration-consumers-advertising-recognition-contexts-search-engines-native/p164504_ftc_staff_report_re_digital_advertising_and_appendices.pdf.

61. "VARN Original Research: Almost 60% of People Still Don't Recognize Google Paid Ads When They See Them," VARN, January 18, 2018, accessed January 20, 2021, https://varn.co.uk/01/18/varn-original-research-almost-60-people-still-dont-recognise-google-paid-ads-see.

62. Brooke Auxier, Lee Rainie, Monica Anderson, Andrew Perrin, Madhu Kumar, and Erica Turner, "Americans and Privacy: Concerned, Confused and Feeling Lack of Control Over Their Personal Information," Pew Research Center, November 15, 2019, accessed January 20, 2021, https://www.pewresearch.org/internet/wp-content/uploads/sites/9/2019/11/Pew-Research-Center_PI_2019.11.15_Privacy_FINAL.pdf.

63. Casey Newton, "Google Tweaks Image Search to Make Porn Harder to Find," CNET, December 12, 2012, accessed June 27, 2018, https://www.cnet.com/news/google-tweaks-image-search-to-make-porn-harder-to-find.

64. Safiya U. Noble, *Algorithms of Oppression: How Search Engines Reinforce Racism* (New York: NYU Press, 2018), 87–88.

65. Jonathan Coopersmith, "Does Your Mother Know What You Really Do? The Changing Nature and Image of Computer-Based Pornography." *History and Technology* 22, no. 1 (2006): 1–25; Gail Dines, *Pornland: How Porn Has Hijacked Our Sexuality* (Boston: Beacon Press); Jennifer A. Johnson, "Mapping the Feminist Political

Economy of the Online Commercial Pornography Industry: A Network Approach," *International Journal of Media and Cultural Politics* 7, no. 2 (2011): 189–208; Katharine Sarikakis and Zeenia Shaukat, "The Global Structures and Cultures of Pornography: The Global Brothel," in *Feminist Interventions in International Communication: Minding the Gap*, eds. Katharine Sarikakis and Leslie Regan Shade (Lanham, MD: Rowman & Littlefield), 106–128; Nicola Simpson, "The Money Shot: The Business of Porn," *Critical Sense* 13, no. 1 (2005): 11–40.

66. Johnson, "Mapping the Feminist Political Economy."

67. Johnson, "Mapping the Feminist Political Economy," 202.

68. Kath Albury, "Porn and Sex Education, Porn as Sex Education." *Porn Studies* 1, no. 1–2 (2014): 172–181.

69. Feona Attwood, "'Other' or 'One of Us'?: The Porn User in Public and Academic Discourse," *Participations: Journal of Audience & Reception Studies* 4, no. 1 (2007).

70. This co-creation can take the form of commenting, building playlists, remixing scenes, modifying the objects, outfits, people, and atmosphere in the room of the viewing, and so on. See Nicola M. Döring, "The Internet's Impact on Sexuality: A Critical Review of 15 Years of Research," *Computers in Human Behavior* 25, no. 5 (2009): 1089–1101.

71. Feona Attwood, Clarissa Smith and Martin Barker, "'I'm Just Curious and Still Exploring Myself': Young People and Pornography," *New Media & Society* 20, no. 10 (October 2018): 3738–3759, 3748–3750.

72. As has repeatedly been the case, there are almost no empirical studies that describe how users navigate pornographic content online nor on how users navigate sex educational content online, though both have been called for and would offer valuable insights. See Nicola M. Döring, "The Internet's Impact on Sexuality" and Kristian Daneback, Sven-Axel Månsson, Michael W. Ross, and Christine M. Markham, "The Internet as a Source of Information about Sexuality," *Sex Education: Sexuality, Society and Learning* 12, no. 5 (2012): 583–598, respectively.

73. Attwood, Smith, and Barker, "'I'm Just Curious and Still Exploring Myself,'" 3749.

74. Donn Bryne and Julie A. Osland, "Sexual Fantasy and Erotica/Pornography: Internal and External Imagery," in *Psychological Perspectives on Human Sexuality*, eds. Lenore T. Szuchman and Frank Muscarella (New York: John Wiley & Sons), 283–308; Patricia Goodson, Deborah McCormick, and Alexandra Evans, "Sex on the Internet: College Students' Emotional Arousal When Viewing Explicit Materials On-line," *Journal of Sex Education and Therapy* 25, no. 4 (December 1, 2000): 252–260.

75. V. Cardonnier, "Cybersex and Addiction: Is Therapy Possible?" *Sexologies* 15, no. 3 (2006): 202–209; Döring, "The Internet's Impact on Sexuality"; Gert-Jan Meerkerk, Regina J. J. M. Van Den Eijnden, and Henk F. L. Garretsen, "Predicting

Compulsive Internet Use: It's All about Sex!" *CyberPsychology & Behavior* 9, no. 1 (2006): 95–103; Kimberly S. Young, "Internet Sex Addiction: Risk Factors, Stages of Development, and Treatment," *American Behavioral Scientist* 52, no. 1 (2008): 21–37.

76. See Gorin Koletić, "Longitudinal Associations between the Use of Sexually Explicit Material and Adolescents' Attitudes and Behaviors: A Narrative Review of Studies," *Journal of Adolescence* 57 (2017): 119–133; Jochen Peter and Patti M. Valkenburg, "Adolescents' Exposure to Sexually Explicit Material on the Internet," *Communication Research* 33, no. 2 (2006): 178–204; Jochen Peter and Patti M. Valkenburg, "The Use of Sexually Explicit Internet Material and Its Antecedents: A Longitudinal Comparison of Adolescents and Adults," *Archives of Sexual Behavior* 40, no. 5 (2011): 1015–1025; Chiara Sabina, Janis Wolak, and David Finkelhor, "The Nature and Dynamics of Internet Pornography Exposure for Youth," *CyberPsychology & Behavior* 11, no. 6 (2008): 691–693; Janis Wolak, Kimberly Mitchell, and David Finkelhor, "Unwanted and Wanted Exposure to Online Pornography in a National Sample of Youth Internet Users," *Pediatrics* 119, no. 2 (2007): 247–257.

77. Jane D. Brown and Kelly L. L'Engle, "X-Rated: Sexual Attitudes and Behaviors Associated With U.S. Early Adolescents' Exposure to Sexually Explicit Media," *Communication Research* 36, no. 1 (February 2009): 129–51; Koletić, "Longitudinal Associations"; Aleksandar Štulhofer, Vesna Buško, and Ivan Landripet, "Pornography, Sexual Socialization, and Satisfaction among Young Men," *Archives of Sexual Behavior* 39, no. 1 (2010): 168–178; Paul J. Wright, "A Longitudinal Analysis of US Adults' Pornography Exposure," *Journal of Media Psychology* 24 (2012): 67–76.

78. Attwood, Smith, and Barker, "'I'm Just Curious and Still Exploring Myself'"; Susanna Paasonen, "Labors of Love: Netporn, Web 2.0 and the Meanings of Amateurism," *New Media & Society* 12, no. 8 (2010): 1297–1312; Clarissa Smith and Feona Attwood, "Anti/Pro/Critical Porn Studies," *Porn Studies* 1, no. 1–2 (2014): 7–23; Linda Williams, "Pornography, Porno, Porn: Thoughts on a Weedy Field," *Porn Studies* 1, no. 1–2 (2014): 24–40.

79. Feona Attwood, ed., *Porn.com: Making Sense of Online Pornography* (New York: Peter Lang, 2010); Attwood, Smith, and Barker, "'I'm Just Curious and Still Exploring Myself'"; Sylvain C. Boies, Gail Knudson, and Julian Young, "The Internet, Sex, and Youths: Implications for Sexual Development," *Sexual Addiction & Compulsivity* 11, no. 4 (October 1, 2004): 343–363; Jane Juffer, *At Home with Pornography: Women, Sexuality, and Everyday Life* (New York: NYU Press, 1998); Rachael Liberman, "'It's a Really Great Tool': Feminist Pornography and the Promotion of Sexual Subjectivity," *Porn Studies* 2, no. 2–3 (2015): 174–191; Smith and Attwood, "Anti/Pro/Critical Porn Studies"; Whitney Strub, *Obscenity Rules: Roth v. United States and the Long Struggle over Sexual Expression* (Lawrence, KS: University Press of Kansas, 2013). N.B., these studies also tend to focus solely on male attitudes and behaviors. See Karen Boyle, "The Pornography Debates: Beyond Cause and Effect," *Women's Studies International Forum* 23, no. 2 (March–April 2000): 187–195; Liberman, "'It's a Really Great Tool.'"

80. Laura Kipnis, *Bound and Gagged: Pornography and the Politics of Fantasy in America* (Durham, NC: Duke University Press), 176.

81. Eileen M. Alexy, Ann W. Burgess, and Robert A. Prentky, "Pornography Use as a Risk Marker for an Aggressive Pattern of Behavior among Sexually Reactive Children and Adolescents," *Journal of the American Psychiatric Nurses Association* 14, no. 6 (2009): 4420–453; Brown and L'Engle, "X-Rated"; Drew A. Kingston, Neil M. Malamuth, Paul Fedoroff, and William L. Marshall, "The Importance of Individual Differences in Pornography Use: Theoretical Perspectives and Implications for Treating Sexual Offenders," *Journal of Sex Research* 46, no. 2–3 (2009): 216–232; Koletić, "Longitudinal Associations"; Neil Malamuth and Mark Huppin, "Pornography and Teenagers: The Importance of Individual Differences," *Adolescent Medicine Clinics* 16, no. 2 (2005): 315–326; Michele L. Ybarra and Kimberly J. Mitchell, "Exposure to Internet Pornography among Children and Adolescents: A National Survey," *Cyberpsychology & Behavior* 8, no. 5 (2005): 473–486; Michele L. Ybarra, Kimberly J. Mitchell, Merle Hamburger, Marie Diener-West, and Philip J. Leaf, "X-Rated Material and Perpetration of Sexually Aggressive Behavior among Children and Adolescents: Is There a Link?," *Aggressive Behavior* 37, no. 1 (2011): 1–18.

82. Jane D. Brown, Sarah Keller, and Susannah Stern, "Sex, Sexuality, Sexting, and Sexed: Adolescents and the Media," *The Prevention Researcher* 16, no. 4 (2009): 12–17; Jochen Peter and Patti M. Valkenburg, "The Influence of Sexually Explicit Internet Material on Sexual Risk Behavior: A Comparison of Adolescents and Adults," *Journal of Health Communication* 16, no. 7 (2011): 750–765; Gina M. Wingood, Ralph J. DiClemente, Kathy Harrington, Suzy Davies, Edward W. Hook, and M. Kim Oh, "Exposure to X-Rated Movies and Adolescents' Sexual and Contraceptive-Related Attitudes and Behaviors," *Pediatrics* 107, no. 5 (2001): 1116–1119.

83. Jochen Peter and Patti M. Valkenburg, "Adolescents' Exposure to a Sexualized Media Environment and Their Notions of Women as Sex Objects," *Sex Roles* 56, no. 5–6 (2007): 381–395; Jochen Peter and Patti M. Valkenburg, "Adolescents' Exposure to Sexually Explicit Internet Material and Notions of Women as Sex Objects: Assessing Causality and Underlying Processes," *Journal of Communication* 59, no. 3 (2009): 407–433; Jochen Peter and Patti M. Valkenburg, "The Influence of Sexually Explicit Internet Material and Peers on Stereotypical Beliefs about Women's Sexual Roles: Similarities and Differences between Adolescents and Adults," *Cyberpsychology, Behavior, and Social Networking* 14, no. 9 (2011): 511–517.

84. Attwood, Smith, and Barker, "'I'm Just Curious and Still Exploring Myself'"; Sylvain C. Boies, "University Students' Uses of and Reactions to Online Sexual Information and Entertainment: Links to Online and Offline Sexual Behavior," *The Canadian Journal of Human Sexuality* 11, no. 2 (2002): 77–89; Döring, "The Internet's Impact on Sexuality"; Sune Innala, "Pornography on the Net: Same Attraction, but New Options," *Sexologies* 16, no. 2 (2007): 112–120; Katrien Jacobs, Marije Janssen, and Matteo Pasquinelli, eds., *C'lickme: A Netporn Studies Reader* (Amsterdam: Institute of Network Cultures, 2007).

85. Döring, "The Internet's Impact on Sexuality," 1094.

86. Attwood, "'Other' or 'One of Us'?"; Mark Dery, "Naked Lunch: Talking Real-core with Sergio Messina," in *C'lickme: A Netporn Studies Reader*, ed. Katrien Jacobs, Marije Janssen, and Matteo Pasquinelli (Amsterdam: Institute of Network Cultures, 2007), 17–31; Döring, "The Internet's Impact on Sexuality"; Katrien Jacobs, "Pornography in Small Places and Other Spaces," *Cultural Studies* 18, no. 1 (2004): 67–83; Liberman, "'It's a Really Great Tool'"; Paasonen, "Labors of Love"; Terrie Schauer, "Women's Porno: The Heterosexual Female Gaze in Porn Sites 'for Women,'" *Sexuality and Culture* 9, no. 2 (2005): 42–64; Nishant Shah, "PlayBlog: Pornography, Performance and Cyberspace," in *C'Lick me: A Netporn Studies Reader*, edS. Katrien Jacobs, Marije Janssen, and Matteo Pasquinelli (Amsterdam: Institute of Network Cultures, 2007), 31–44.

87. Mark Jancovich, "Naked Ambitions: Pornography, Taste and the Problem of the Middlebrow," *Scope: An Online Journal of Film Studies* (June 2001); Paasonen, "Labors of Love"; Susanna Paasonen, *Carnal Resonance: Affect and Online Pornography* (Cambridge, MA: MIT Press, 2011); Georgina Voss, "'Treating It as a Normal Business': Researching the Pornography Industry," *Sexualities* 15, no. 3–4 (2012): 391–410; Williams, "Pornography, Porno, Porn."

88. Joan Mason-Grant, *Pornography Embodied: From Speech to Sexual Practice* (Lanham, Maryland: Rowman & Littlefield, 2004), 86.

89. Jancovich, "Naked Ambitions."

90. Kipnis, *Bound and Gagged*, 167.

91. Attwood, Smith, and Barker, "'I'm Just Curious and Still Exploring Myself'"; Paasonen, "Labors of Love"; Paasonen, *Carnal Resonance*; Smith and Attwood, "Anti/Pro/Critical Porn Studies"; Williams, "Pornography, Porno, Porn."

92. Florian Cramer, "Sodom Blogging: 'Alternative Porn' and Aesthetic Sensibility," *Texte zur Kunst* 16, no. 64 (2006): 133–136; Florian Cramer and Stewart Home, "Pornographic Coding," in *C'Lick me: A Netporn Studies Reader*, ed. Katrien Jacobs, Marije Janssen, and Matteo Pasquinelli (Amsterdam: Institute of Network Cultures, 2007), 159–170; Döring, "The Internet's Impact on Sexuality"; Marleen J. E. Klaassen and Jochen Peter, "Gender (in) Equality in Internet Pornography: A Content Analysis of Popular Pornographic Internet Videos," *Journal of Sex Research* 52, no. 7 (2015): 721–735; Liberman, "'It's a Really Great Tool'"; Jonathan James McCreadie Lillie, "Cyberporn, Sexuality, and the Net Apparatus," *Convergence: The International Journal of Research into New Media Technologies* 10, no. 1 (2004): 43–54; Shoshana Magnet, "Feminist Sexualities, Race and the Internet: An Investigation of Suicidegirls.com," *New Media & Society* 9, no. 4 (2007): 577–602; Paasonen, "Labors of Love"; Paasonen, *Carnal Resonance*; Don Slater, "Trading Sexpics on IRC: Embodiment and Authenticity on the Internet," *Body & society* 4, no. 4 (1998): 91–117; Doorn, "Keeping It Real."

93. Feona Attwood, "No Money Shot? Commerce, Pornography and New Sex Taste Cultures," *Sexualities* 10, no. 4 (2007): 441–456; Kevin Esch and Vicki Mayer, "How Unprofessional: The Profitable Partnership of Amateur Porn and Celebrity Culture," In *Pornification: Sex and Sexuality in Media Culture*, ed. Susanna Paasonen, Kaarina Nikunen, and Laura Saarenmaa (Oxford: Berg, 2007), 99–111; Katrien Jacobs, *Netporn: DIY Web Culture and Sexual Politics* (Lanham, MD: Rowman & Littlefield, 2007); Katrien Jacobs, "The New Media Schooling of the Amateur Pornographer: Negotiating Contracts and Singing Orgasm," *Spectator* 24, no. 1 (2004): 17–29; Kavita Ilona Nayar, "Working It: The Professionalization of Amateurism in Digital Adult Entertainment," *Feminist Media Studies* 17, no. 3 (2017): 473–488.

94. Cramer and Home, "Pornographic Coding," 165.

95. Van Doorn, "Keeping It Real."

96. Kipnis, *Bound and Gagged*, 200.

97. Paasonen, *Carnal Resonance*, 87.

98. Van Doorn, "Keeping It Real."

99. Magnet, "Feminist Sexualities, Race and the Internet."

100. And, as Van Doorn (2010) has shown, this seems to be as true for platforms like YouPorn as it is for Google writ large. On platforms like YouPorn or Pornhub, users tag their content heteronormatively to garner the largest audience, or, perhaps more accurately, they *imagine* and *produce* their content to *match* mainstream heteroporn's genre conventions.

101. Döring, "The Internet's Impact on Sexuality," 1099.

102. Paasonen, *Carnal Resonance*, 8.

103. Paasonen, *Carnal Resonance*, 17–18.

104. Blue, "Congress Just Legalized Sex Censorship." For an ongoing list of changes in terms of service, censorship, and shutdowns related to FOSTA-SESTA, see "Documenting Tech Actions," Survivors against SESTA, accessed February 16, 2019, https://survivorsagainstsesta.org/documentation.

105. Caty Simon, "On Backpage," *Tits and Sass*, April 25, 2018, accessed February 15, 2019, http://titsandsass.com/on-the-death-of-backpage.

106. Emily McCombs, "'This Bill Is Killing Us': 9 Sex Workers On Their Lives in the Wake of FOSTA," *Huffington Post*, May 11, 2018, accessed February 20, 2019, https://www.huffingtonpost.com/entry/sex-workers-sesta-fosta_us_5ad0d7d0e4b0edca2cb964d9.

107. McCombs, "'This Bill Is Killing Us.'"

108. Samantha Cole, "A New Wave of Reckoning Is Sweeping the Porn Industry," Motherboard, June 10, 2020, accessed January 30, 2021, https://www.vice.com/en/article/wxqn55/sexual-abuse-allegations-on-porn-sets-ryan-madison.

109. Glenn Kessler, "Has the Sex-Trafficking Law Eliminated 90 percent of Sex-Trafficking Ads?," *Washington Post*, August 20, 2018, accessed February 20, 2019, https://www.washingtonpost.com/politics/2018/08/20/has-sex-trafficking-law-eliminated-percent-sex-trafficking-ads.

110. McCombs, "'This Bill Is Killing Us.'"

111. Personal communication with Switter representative; Samantha Cole, "Cloudflare Just Banned a Social Media Refuge for Thousands of Sex Workers," Motherboard, April 19, 2018, accessed January 30, 2021, https://www.vice.com/en/article/8xk78x/switter-down-cloudflare-banned-sex-workers-sesta-fosta; Samantha Cole, "Cloudflare: FOSTA Was a 'Very Bad Bill' That's Left the Internet's Infrastructure Hanging," Motherboard, April 19, 2018, accessed January 30, 2021, https://www.vice.com/en/article/9kgvga/cloudflare-switter-down-fosta-sesta.

112. Daniel Villarreal, "SESTA/FOSTA Is Turning the Web into a G-Rated Minefield. Here's How to Destroy It," LGBTQ Nation, March 16, 2019, accessed February 30, 2021, https://www.lgbtqnation.com/2019/03/sesta-fosta-turning-web-g-rated-minefield-dan-savage-pals-know-2-ways-destroy.

113. Villarreal, "SESTA/FOSTA Is Turning the Web into a G-Rated Minefield."

114. Scott Cunningham, Gregory DeAngelo, and John Tripp, "Craigslist's Effect on Violence against Women," presented at the American Economic Association Conference, Chicago, 2017.

115. Violet Blue, "PayPal, Square and Big Banking's War on the Sex Industry," Engadget, December 2, 2015, accessed February 16, 2019, https://www.engadget.com/2015/12/02/paypal-square-and-big-bankings-war-on-the-sex-industry.

116. "Our Story/Mission," *Lovability*, accessed February 20, 2019, https://lovabilityinc.com/pages/our-story-mission.

117. Blue, "PayPal, Square and Big Banking's War on the Sex Industry."

118. Tina Horn, "How the Financial Sector Is Making Life Miserable for Sex Workers," VICE, July 14, 2014, accessed February 20, 2019, https://www.vice.com/en_us/article/4w74jg/how-the-financial-sector-is-making-life-miserable-for-sex-workers-714; "About Us," NY Toy Collective, accessed February 20, 2019, https://newyorktoycollective.com/about-us.

119. Nicholas Kristof, "The Children of Pornhub," *New York Times*, December 4, 2020, accessed January 30, 2021, https://www.nytimes.com/2020/12/04/opinion/sunday/pornhub-rape-trafficking.html.

120. Samantha Cole, "'War against Sex Workers': What Visa and Mastercard Dropping Pornhub Means to Performers," Motherboard, December 11, 2020, accessed January 30, 2021, https://www.vice.com/en/article/n7v33d/sex-workers-what-visa-and-mastercard-dropping-pornhub-means-to-performers.

121. Blue, "PayPal, Square and Big Banking's War on the Sex Industry."

122. Blue, "PayPal, Square and Big Banking's War on the Sex Industry."

123. Horn, "How the Financial Sector Is Making Life Miserable for Sex Workers."

124. Horn, "How the Financial Sector Is Making Life Miserable for Sex Workers."

125. Blue, "PayPal, Square and Big Banking's War on the Sex Industry."

126. "How This Works," MakeLoveNotPorn.tv, accessed February 20, 2019, https://makelovenotporn.tv/pages/about/how_this_works.

127. Blue, "PayPal, Square and Big Banking's War on the Sex Industry."

128. E. J. Dickson, "Amazon Is Deleting Sex Workers' Wish Lists without Warning," The Daily Dot, May 2, 2014, accessed February 14, 2019, https://www.dailydot.com/irl/amazon-sex-worker-wish-lists.

129. Patreon, accessed February 20, 2019, https://www.patreon.com.

130. "About," Patreon, accessed February 20, 2019, https://www.patreon.com/about.

131. Liara Roux, "An Open Letter to Patreon," Openlettertopateron.com, accessed February 20, 2019, http://www.openlettertopatreon.com.

132. Daniel Cooper, "Patreon's Pornapocalypse Is Back," Engadget, June 29, 2018, accessed February 14, 2019, https://www.engadget.com/2018/06/29/patreon-crackdown-sex-worker-accounts.

133. "Terms of Use," Patreon, accessed July 6, 2019, https://www.patreon.com/policy/legal.

134. Daniel Cooper, "The Real Consequences of Patreon's Adult Content Crackdown," Engadget, October 27, 2017, accessed February 20, 2019, https://www.engadget.com/2017/10/27/patreon-adult-content-crowdfunding-uncertainty.

135. Daniel Cooper, "The Real Consequences."

136. Samantha Cole, "Patreon Is Suspending Adult Content Creators because of Its Payment Partners," Motherboard, June 28, 2018, accessed February 14, 2019, https://motherboard.vice.com/en_us/article/vbqwwj/patreon-suspension-of-adult-content-creators.

137. Cooper, "The Real Consequences."

138. Lux Alptraum, "Patreon Ends Payments Discrimination against Adult Content," Motherboard, July 27, 2016, accessed February 20, 2019, https://motherboard.vice.com/en_us/article/gv5dmb/patreon-paypal-adult-content.

139. Roux, "An Open Letter to Patreon."

140. Roux, "An Open Letter to Patreon."

141. Jack Conte, "A Note to Our Adult Content Creators," Patreon HQ, October 25, 2017, accessed February 20, 2019, https://patreonhq.com/a-note-to-our-adult-content-creators-abef831380e3.

142. Roux, "An Open Letter to Patreon."

143. Blue, "PayPal, Square and Big Banking's War on the Sex Industry."

144. Frank Keating, "Justice Puts Banks in a Choke Hold," *Wall Street Journal*, April 25, 2014, accessed February 20, 2019, https://www.wsj.com/articles/frank-keating -justice-puts-banks-in-a-choke-hold-1398381603.

145. Mary Emily O'Hara, "Is the DOJ Forcing Banks to Terminate the Accounts of Porn Stars?" VICE, April 27, 2014, accessed February 20, 2019, https://news.vice .com/en_us/article/pa8xy9/is-the-doj-forcing-banks-to-terminate-the-accounts -of-porn-stars.

146. Ben Cohen, "Campaign by Right-Wing Trolls to Report Sex Workers to the IRS Raises Concerns," *NOW Toronto*, December 5, 2017, accessed February 15, 2019, https://nowtoronto.com/news/sex-work-mens-rights-incel.

147. Mehak Anwar, "What Does 'Thot' Mean and When, If Ever, Is It OK to Use It? How to Reclaim a Derogatory Term," *Bustle*, May 26, 2015, accessed February 21, 2019, https://www.bustle.com/articles/85756-what-does-thot-mean-and -when-if-ever-is-it-ok-to-use-it-or-how.

148. Elizabeth A. Armstrong and Laura T. Hamilton, *Paying for the Party: How College Maintains Inequality* (Cambridge, MA: Harvard University Press, 2013).

149. Amanda Hess, "A *Thot* Is Not a *Slut*: The Popular Insult Is More about Race and Class than Sex," *Slate*, October 16, 2014, accessed February 21, 2019, https:// slate.com/human-interest/2014/10/a-thot-is-not-a-slut-on-popular-slurs-race -class-and-sex.html.

150. Cohen, "Campaign by Right-Wing Trolls."

151. Roosh V, "Roos Hour #28—Thot Audit," November 25, 2018, accessed February 21, 2019, https://youtu.be/P2yvLgWLCS0.

152. Roosh V, "Roos Hour #28."

153. Roosh V, "Roos Hour #28."

154. "How Do You File a Whistleblower Award Claim Under Section 7623 (a) or (b)?," IRS, accessed February 21, 2019, https://www.irs.gov/compliance/how-do -you-file-a-whistleblower-award-claim-under-section-7623-a-or-b.

155. P. Martineau, "A Quiet War Rages over Who Can Make Money Online," *WIRED*, November 30, 2018, accessed February 15, 2019, https://www.wired.com /story/quiet-war-rages-who-can-make-money-online.

156. Martineau, "A Quiet War Rages."

157. Martineau, "A Quiet War Rages."

158. Martineau, "A Quiet War Rages."

159. S. Cole, #ThotAudit Is Compiling Massive Databases of Sex Workers and Reporting Them to PayPal, Motherboard, December 4, 2018, accessed February 15,

2019, https://motherboard.vice.com/en_us/article/gy7wyw/thotaudit-databases
-of-sex-workers-and-reporting-them-to-paypal.

160. Cole, #ThotAudit Is Compiling."

161. Martineau, "A Quiet War Rages."

162. Martineau, "A Quiet War Rages."

163. L. Alptraum, #ThotAudit Is Just the Latest Tactic People Are Using to Harass
Sex Workers Online, The Verge, November 30, 2018, accessed February 15, 2019,
https://www.theverge.com/2018/11/30/18119688/thotaudit-sex-work-irs
-online-harassment.

CONCLUSION

1. Kate Ruane, "The EARN IT Act Is a Disaster for Online Speech and Privacy,
especially for the LGBTQ and Sex Worker Communities," ACLU, June 30, 2020,
accessed January 30, 2021, https://www.aclu.org/news/free-speech/the-earn-it
-act-is-a-disaster-for-online-speech-and-privacy-especially-for-the-lgbtq-and-sex
-worker-communities.

2. "ACLU EARN IT Act Opposition Letter." ACLU, August 14, 2020, accessed
January 30, 2021, https://www.aclu.org/letter/aclu-earn-it-act-opposition-letter.

3. ACLU, "ACLU EARN IT Act Opposition Letter."

4. Riana Pfefferkorn, "The EARN IT Act: How to Ban End-to-End Encryption
without Actually Banning It," Center for Internet and Society, January 30, 2020,
accessed January 30, 2021, http://cyberlaw.stanford.edu/blog/2020/01/earn-it-act
-how-ban-end-end-encryption-without-actually-banning-it.

5. Ruane, "The EARN IT Act Is a Disaster."

6. Ruane, "The EARN IT Act Is a Disaster."

7. Samantha Cole, "Sex Workers to Host Self-Destructing Digital Variety Show
against EARN-IT," Motherboard, July 29, 2020, accessed January 30, 2021, https://
www.vice.com/en/article/jgxbag/sex-workers-earn-it-virtual-protest-e-viction.

8. Marina Warner, Six Myths of Our Time (New York: Vintage, 1995).

9. Henry Giroux, Stealing Innocence: Youth, Corporate Power, and the Politics of Culture
(New York: Palgrave, 2000), 2.

10. Michele Barrett and Mary McIntosh, The Anti-social Family, 2nd ed. (New York:
Verso, 2015), 56.

11. Lisa Nakamura, "Glitch Racism: Networks as Actors within Vernacular Internet Theory," Culture Digitally, December 10, 2013, accessed January 30, 2021,
https://culturedigitally.org/2013/12/glitch-racism-networks-as-actors-within
-vernacular-internet-theory.

12. Erik Larkin, "Google Shareholders Vote against Anti-Censorship Proposal," *PCWorld*, May 10, 2007, accessed February 5, 2020, https://www.pcworld.com/article/131745/article.html.

13. "For Artificial Intelligence to Thrive, It Must Explain Itself," *Economist*, February 15, 2018, accessed February 5, 2020, https://www.economist.com/science-and-technology/2018/02/15/for-artificial-intelligence-to-thrive-it-must-explain-itself.

14. Chris Olah, Alexander Mordvintsev, and Ludwig Schubert, "Feature Visualization: How Neural Networks Build Up Their Understanding of Images," *Distill*, November 7, 2017, accessed February 5, 2020, https://distill.pub/2017/feature-visualization.

15. On sex worker activist groups, see Juno Mac and Molly Smith, *Revolting Prostitutes: The Fight for Sex Workers' Rights* (New York: Verso, 2020), 210–212. On LGBTQ activist groups see, Dean Spade, *Normal Life: Administrative Violence, Critical Trans Politics, & the Limits of Law* (Durham, NC: Duke University Press, 2015).

16. Ching-In Chen, Jai Dulani, and Leah Lakshmi Piepzna-Samarasinha, *The Revolution Starts at Home: Confronting Intimate Violence within Activist Communities* (New York: South End Press); "Toolkit," Creative Interventions, accessed January 30, 2021, http://www.creative-interventions.org/tools/toolkit.

INDEX

Note: Page numbers in *italics* indicate figures.